Lecture Notes in Computer Scienc

T0237791

Commenced Publication in 1973
Founding and Former Series Editors:
Gerhard Goos, Juris Hartmanis, and Jan van Leeuwen

Editorial Board

Stefano Spaccapietra   Paolo Atzeni
François Fages   Mohand-Saïd Hacid
Michael Kifer   John Mylopoulos
Barbara Pernici   Pavel Shvaiko
Juan Trujillo   Ilya Zaihrayeu (Eds.)

Journal on Data Semantics VIII

 Springer

Volume Editors

Stefano Spaccapietra
EPFL, Lausanne, Switzerland, E-mail: stefano.spaccapietra@epfl.ch

Paolo Atzeni
Università Roma Tre, Italy, E-mail: atzeni@dia.uniroma3.it

François Fages
INRIA Rocquencourt, France, E-mail: Francois.Fages@inria.fr

Mohand-Saïd Hacid
Université Lyon 1, France, E-mail: mshacid@bat710.univ-lyon1.fr

Michael Kifer
State University of New York at Stony Brook, USA, E-mail: kifer@cs.sunysb.edu

John Mylopoulos
University of Toronto, Canada/University of Trento, Italy, E-mail: jm@cs.toronto.edu

Barbara Pernici
Politecnico di Milano, Italy, E-mail: barbara.pernici@polimi.it

Pavel Shvaiko
Ilya Zaihrayeu
University of Trento, Italy, E-mail: {pavel,ilya}@dit.unitn.it

Juan Trujillo
University of Alicante, Spain, E-mail: jtrujillo@dlsi.ua.es

CR Subject Classification (1998): H.2, H.3, I.2, H.4, C.2

LNCS Sublibrary: SL 3 – Information Systems and Application, incl. Internet/Web and HCI

ISSN   1861-2032
ISBN-10   3-540-70663-1 Springer Berlin Heidelberg New York
ISBN-13   978-3-540-70663-2 Springer Berlin Heidelberg New York

Springer is a part of Springer Science+Business Media

springer.com

© Springer-Verlag Berlin Heidelberg 2007
Printed in Germany

Typesetting: Camera-ready by author, data conversion by Scientific Publishing Services, Chennai, India
Printed on acid-free paper   SPIN: 11980711   06/3142   5 4 3 2 1 0

The LNCS Journal on Data Semantics

Computerized information handling has changed its focus from centralized data management systems to decentralized data exchange facilities. Modern distribution channels, such as high-speed Internet networks and wireless communication infrastructure, provide reliable technical support for data distribution and data access, materializing the new, popular idea that data may be available to anybody, anywhere, anytime. However, providing huge amounts of data on request often turns into a counterproductive service, making the data useless because of poor relevance or inappropriate level of detail. Semantic knowledge is the essential missing piece that allows the delivery of information that matches user requirements. Semantic agreement, in particular, is essential to meaningful data exchange.

Semantic issues have long been open issues in data and knowledge management. However, the boom in semantically poor technologies, such as the Web and XML, has boosted renewed interest in semantics. Conferences on the Semantic Web, for instance, attract big crowds of participants, while ontologies on their own have become a hot and popular topic in the database and artificial intelligence communities.

Springer's LNCS *Journal on Data Semantics* aims at providing a highly visible dissemination channel for most remarkable work that in one way or another addresses research and development on issues related to the semantics of data. The target domain ranges from theories supporting the formal definition of semantic content to innovative domain-specific application of semantic knowledge. This publication channel should be of the highest interest to researchers and advanced practitioners working on the Semantic Web, interoperability, mobile information services, data warehousing, knowledge representation and reasoning, conceptual database modeling, ontologies, and artificial intelligence.

Topics of relevance to this journal include:

- Semantic interoperability, semantic mediators
- Ontologies
- Ontology, schema and data integration, reconciliation and alignment
- Multiple representations, alternative representations
- Knowledge representation and reasoning
- Conceptualization and representation
- Multi-model and multi-paradigm approaches
- Mappings, transformations, reverse engineering
- Metadata
- Conceptual data modeling
- Integrity description and handling
- Evolution and change
- Web semantics and semi-structured data

- Semantic caching
- Data warehousing and semantic data mining
- Spatial, temporal, multimedia and multimodal semantics
- Semantics in data visualization
- Semantic services for mobile users
- Supporting tools
- Applications of semantic-driven approaches

These topics are to be understood as specifically related to semantic issues. Contributions submitted to the journal and dealing with semantics of data will be considered even if they are not from the topics in the list.

While the physical appearance of the journal issues is like the books from the well-known Springer LNCS series, the mode of operation is that of a journal. Contributions can be freely submitted by authors and are reviewed by the Editorial Board. Contributions may also be invited, and nevertheless carefully reviewed, as in the case for issues that contain extended versions of best papers from major conferences addressing data semantics issues. Special issues, focusing on a specific topic, are coordinated by guest editors once the proposal for a special issue is accepted by the Editorial Board. Finally, it is also possible that a journal issue be devoted to a single text.

The journal published its first volume in 2003 (LNCS 2800). That initial volume, as well as volumes II (LNCS 3360), V (LNCS 3870), this volume, VIII, and the next volume, IX, represent the annual occurrence of a special issue devoted to publication of selected extended versions of best conference papers from the previous year's conferences. Volumes III and VI were special issues on a dedicated topic. Volume III (LNCS 3534), coordinated by guest editor Esteban Zimányi, addressed Semantic-Based Geographical Information Systems, while volume VI (LNCS 4090), coordinated by guest editors Karl Aberer and Philippe Cudre-Mauroux, addressed Emergent Semantics. Volumes IV and VI were "normal" volumes, built from spontaneous submissions on any of the topics of interest to the journal.

The Editorial Board comprises an Editor-in-Chief (with overall responsibility), a Co-editor-in-Chief, and several members. The Editor-in-Chief has a four-year mandate. Members of the board have a three-year mandate. Mandates are renewable, and new members may be elected anytime.

We are happy to welcome you to our readership and authorship, and hope we will share this privileged contact for a long time.

Stefano Spaccapietra
Editor-in-Chief
http://lbdwww.epfl.ch/e/Springer/

JoDS Volume VIII

To foster the dissemination of the best ideas and results, the *Journal on Data Semantics* (JoDS) pursues a policy that includes annually publishing extended versions of the best papers from selected conferences whose scope encompasses or intersects with the scope of the journal.

This initiative is motivated by the difference in goals between conferences and journals. Conferences usually have a faster turnaround and a focused audience, but they have to enforce space limitation and a fixed time frame, with no chances for improving a paper by producing multiple versions. In contrast, journals offer more space, room for debate and refinement, and are usually considered the real archival venue.

Therefore, the publication of an extended version of a conference paper is a much appreciated opportunity for researchers to widely disseminate a significantly improved presentation of their work, where they can develop the appropriate motivations, reasoning, results and comparative analysis. Moreover, by gathering best papers from various conferences, JoDS special issues provide a unique opportunity for researchers to find in a single publication every year the best of ongoing research in the field of data semantics.

For this issue, papers from the following six 2005 international conferences were invited:

- The Seventh International Conference on Data Warehousing and Knowledge Discovery (DaWaK 2005),
- The 3rd International Workshop on Principles and Practice of Semantic Web Reasoning, (PPSWR 2005),
- The 1st International Workshop on Contexts and Ontologies, Theory, Practice and Applications (C&O 2005), joint event with the 25th National Conference on Artificial Intelligence (AAAI 2005),
- The 2nd International Workshop on Peer-to-Peer Knowledge Management (P2PKM 2005), joint event with the 2nd Annual International Conference on Mobile and Ubiquitous systems (Mobiquitous 2005)
- The 13th International Conference on Cooperative Information Systems, (CoopIS 2005) and the International Conference on Ontologies, Databases, and Applications of Semantics (ODBASE 2005), which both took place October 31 to November 4, 2005, Agia Napa, Cyprus.

In addition, this issue includes one paper from the 23rd International Conference on Conceptual Modeling (ER 2004), which was accepted but could not be included in JoDS V because of late delivery of the final version.

Papers from these conferences were invited based on their quality, relevance and significance, and the viability of extending their results. Extended versions prepared by authors were subject to the traditional two-round scholarly review process, and the authors were required to respond to all concerns expressed by the reviewers before papers were accepted.

The paper by Velcin and Ganascia, originating from ER 2004, considers a model dealing with sparse data sets and describes a theoretical framework for inducing knowledge out of them. The general framework relies on a lattice structure, and it is illustrated within two formalisms: the attribute-value formalism and Sowa's conceptual graphs. The induction engine is based on a non-supervised algorithm called default clustering, which uses the concept of stereotype and a new notion of default subsumption, inspired by the default logic theory.

The selection of CoopIS 2005 best papers eventually resulted in the acceptance of three papers. The paper "Semantic Matching: Algorithms and Implementation" by Giunchiglia, Yatskevich and Shvaiko provides a framework that views *match* as an operator that takes two graph-like structures and produces a mapping between the nodes of the graphs that correspond semantically to each other. The authors introduce model-based techniques at the structure level.

The paper "Semantic-Guided Clustering of Heterogeneous XML Schemas" by De Meo, Quattrone, Terracina and Ursino investigates a semantic-based approach for clustering heterogeneous XML schemas. The proposed approach makes use of the semantics of the underlying schemas by capturing the interschema properties among concepts of the schemas. The experimental analysis shows that the approach is scalable.

The paper "A Formal Framework for Adaptive Access Control Models" by Rinderle and Reichert proposes a framework that is suitable for handling evolution of organizational models and related access rules. The paper introduces a set of well-defined operators for defining and capturing changes in organizational models. In addition, the framework allows adaptation of access rules when the model changes.

DaWak 2005 contributed its best paper, "Processing Sequential Patterns in Relational Databases" by Shang and Sattler. The paper proposes an efficient SQL-based algorithm to mine sequential patterns in relational database systems. Authors start by saying that traditionally data mining techniques have been applied on flat files instead of on databases due to the low performance and high cost associated in implementing data mining with SQL on relational databases. Authors claim that it is possible to achieve a reasonable performance by implementing association rule mining and sequential pattern mining with carefully tuned SQL formulations. To this extent, authors depart from inefficient a-priori methods and propose an efficient SQL-based algorithm, called Prospad (PROjection Sequential PAttern Discovery), to mine sequential patterns in relational database systems. Prospad adopts the divide-and-conquer strategy and projects the sequence table into a set of frequent item-related projected tables. Experimental results show that the Prospad algorithm can get higher performance than k-way joins based on a-priori approaches, especially on large and dense datasets, although it has severe limitations in performance compared to in-memory PrefixSpan algorithms.

Two extended articles were selected from PPSWR 2005. The paper "A Tool for Evaluating Ontology Alignment Strategies," by Lambrix and Tan, addresses the important issue of aligning different ont logies, so that multiple sources of information can be exploited altogether. The paper describes a framework for the comparative evaluation of ontology alignment strategies and their combinations, and reports on the performance of an implementation of this framework. The test cases used for the evaluation are composed of five biomedical ontologies. A detailed example shows the use of two matchers in combination.

The paper "SomeRDFS in the Semantic Web," by Adjiman, Goasdoué and Rousset, envisions the Semantic Web as a huge peer data management system, where data on the Web are annotated by ontologies networked together by mappings. The paper describes the SomeRDFS peer data management system architecture, its data model, query language, and query answering algorithm based on query rewriting techniques that are formally justified in the paper.

The selection from C&O 2005 resulted in three extended papers being accepted for JoDS.

The paper "Putting Things in Context: A Topological Approach to Mapping Contexts to Ontologies" by Segev and Gal, provides a framework that defines the relationship between contexts and ontologies by using topological structures. This work has been motivated by the needs of the eGovernment domain. In this approach ontologies are viewed as the result of a manual effort to model a domain, while contexts are automatically generated models. The uncertainty, which usually exists in automatic context extraction, is managed through the definition of distance among contexts and a ranking of ontology concepts with respect to a given context. The approach has been implemented and evaluated on two real-world data sets: Reuters news reports and RSS news headlines.

The paper "Context Dependency Management in Ontology Engineering: A Formal Approach," by De Leenheer, de Moor, and Meersman, introduces a framework that uses lexical knowledge to manage context dependences in ontology engineering tasks. The formalization of the context dependency management is built on top of the DOGMA ontology-engineering framework. The proposed approach is validated by a case study of inter-organizational competency ontology engineering.

The paper "Encoding Classifications into Lightweight Ontologies" by Giunchiglia, Marchese, and Zaihrayeu provides a theory of how to translate standard classifications, such as DMoz, into formal classifications, namely, graph structures where labels are written in a propositional concept language. Formal classifications turn out to be a form of lightweight ontologies. This allows reducing essential tasks on classifications, such as document classification and query answering, to reasoning about subsumption.

While the paper selected from P2PKM is still in the review process at this time, four extended versions of ODBASE 2005 papers were granted acceptance. The paper "Creating Ontologies for Content Representation - The OntoSeed Suite," by Paslaru Bontas Simperl and Schlangen, proposes a natural language-based technique to help ontology engineers decide which concepts to model in any particular domain. Unlike other NLP-based techniques, this approach does not require in-depth linguistic expertise. Instead it relies on the Web for collecting the documents against which to compare domain-specific texts.

"Metadata Management in a Multiversion Data Warehouse," a paper by Wrembel and Bebel, deals with the problem of evolving data warehouses in the presence of changes in the schema of the underlying data sources. The paper proposes a solution, called multiversion data warehouse, which maintains extensive metadata about the external data sources.

The paper by Kensche, Quix, Chatti, and Jarke, "GeRoMe: A Generic Role-Based Metamodel for Model Management," proposes a generic mechanism for describing data models. This approach assigns multiple roles to model elements and permits accurate description of these elements using only a small number of roles and metaclasses. This contrasts favorably with metamodel languages that are based exclusively on metaclasses, since such languages may require an exponentially large number of metaclasses.

The paper on "Security Ontology for Annotating Resources," by Kim, Luo, and Kang, proposes an ontology for describing security requirements of Web services. The goal of such an ontology is to enable Web service discovery that meets a client's security requirements, such as protocols, objectives, and credentials. The proposed ontology is more comprehensive and detailed than other similar ontologies.

Because of size limitations, only eight of the 14 above-described papers appear in this volume. The other six papers will appear in the next volume, JoDS IX, scheduled for Spring 2007.

C&O 2005 Co-chair
Pavel Shvaiko, University of Trento, Italy

CoopIS 2005 PC Co-chairs
Mohand-Saïd Hacid, University Lyon 1, France
John Mylopoulos, University of Trento, Italy and University of Toronto, Canada
Barbara Pernici, Politecnico Milano, Italy

DAWAK 2005 Co-chair
Juan Trujillo, University of Alicante, Spain

ER 2004 Co-chair
Paolo Atzeni

ODBASE 2005 Co-chairs
Michael Kifer, State University of New York at Stony Brook, USA
Stefano Spaccapietra, EPFL, Switzerland

PPSWR 2005 Co-chair
François Fages, INRIA Rocquencourt, France

P2PKM Co-chair
Ilya Zaihrayeu, University of Trento, Italy

Organization

Reviewers

We would like to express our gratitude to the following colleagues who helped in the review process by contributing detailed reviews of the submitted papers and provided invaluable feedback to the authors and editors alike:

Antoni Olive, Universitat Politècnica de Catalunya, Spain
Massimo Paolucci, University of Genova, Italy
Torben Bach Pedersen, Aalborg University, Denmark
Jean-Marc Petit, INSA de Lyon, France
Dimitris Plexousakis, University of Crete, Greece
Axel Polleres, Universidad Rey Juan Carlos, Spain
David Robertson, The University of Edinburgh, UK
Marie-Christine Rousset, IMAG, France
Peter Pater-Schneider, Bell Labs, Murray Hill, USA
Marta Sabou, The Open University, UK
Vasile-Marian Scuturici, INSA de Lyon, France
Manuel Serrano, University of Castilla La Mancha, Spain
Sylvain Soliman, INRIA Rocquencourt, France
Heiner Stuckenschmidt, University of Mannheim, Germany
York Sure, University of Karlsruhe, Germany
Thodoros Topaloglou, University of Toronto, Canada
Farouk Toumani, Université Blaise Pascal, France
Athena Vakali, Aristotle University of Thessaloniki, Greece
Panos Vassiliadis, University of Ioannina, Greece
Holger Wache, Vrije Universiteit Amsterdam, The Netherlands
Howard Williams, Heriot-Watt University, Edinburgh, UK
Xing Xie, Microsoft Research, USA
Esteban Zimányi, Université Libre de Bruxelles, Belgium

JoDS Editorial Board

Co-Editors-in-Chief   Lois Delcambre, Portland State University, USA
                             Stefano Spaccapietra, EPFL, Switzerland

Members of the Board
    Carlo Batini, Università di Milano Bicocca, Italy
    Alex Borgida, Rutgers University, USA
    Shawn Bowers, University of California Davis, USA
    Tiziana Catarci, Università di Roma La Sapienza, Italy
    David W. Embley, Brigham Young University, USA
    Jerome Euzenat, INRIA Alpes, France
    Dieter Fensel, University of Innsbruck, Austria
    Nicola Guarino, National Research Council, Italy
    Jean-Luc Hainaut, FUNDP Namur, Belgium
    Ian Horrocks, University of Manchester, UK
    Arantza Illarramendi, Universidad del País Vasco, Spain
    Larry Kerschberg, George Mason University, USA
    Michael Kifer, State University of New York at Stony Brook, USA
    Tok Wang Ling, National University of Singapore, Singapore

Table of Contents

Default Clustering with Conceptual Structures

J. Velcin and J.-G. Ganascia

LIP6, Université Paris VI
8 rue du Capitaine Scott
75015 Paris
France
{julien.velcin,jean-gabriel.ganascia}@lip6.fr

Abstract. This paper describes a theoretical framework for inducing knowledge from incomplete data sets. The general framework can be used with any formalism based on a lattice structure. It is illustrated within two formalisms: the attribute-value formalism and Sowa's conceptual graphs. The induction engine is based on a non-supervised algorithm called default clustering which uses the concept of stereotype and the new notion of default subsumption, inspired by the default logic theory. A validation using artificial data sets and an application concerning the extraction of stereotypes from newspaper articles are given at the end of the paper.

1 Introduction

This paper presents a model dealing with sparse data sets. Our original goal was to simulate common-sense inductive reasoning. It appears from previous research [1,2,3] that common-sense reasoning is highly related to reasoning from partially described data. The general framework we propose treats such data by following a default reasoning. It can be applied to automatically process heterogeneous data which often fit this property of sparseness. The main considered application deals with newspaper articles translated into a logical formalism. Our goal is to extract characteristic representations called *stereotypes* from these newspapers. The extracted representations can be seen as a way of summarizing the data in a simplified and rough manner.

More precisely, we refer to representations that can be obtained through a task of clustering. Conceptual clustering, a fundamental machine learning task [4], takes a set of object descriptions, or *observations*, as input and creates a classification scheme. Our interest will be more focused on the concepts used to name the classes than on the classes themselves. However, information sparseness is a recurrent problem in clustering. This may be for several reasons: voluntary omissions, human error, broken equipment which causes a loss of data, etc. [5]. The phenomena increases drastically when you consider the information extracted from newspapers because the vocabulary used is often very heterogeneous. Usually, existing algorithms are not adapted when there are many missing values. One solution is to fill the holes, i.e. the unknown values, by analogy with the

S. Spaccapietra et al. (Eds.): Journal on Data Semantics VIII, LNCS 4380, pp. 1–25, 2007.

other data. However, these imputation techniques [6] are separated from the clustering task and mostly adapted to numerical variables.

The proposed model uses a default reasoning schema in order to induce knowledge from sparse and categorical data sets. What this induction model does is to build categories from incomplete data and name them thanks to specific conceptual descriptions. The concept of stereotype was chosen to reflect internal coherence within the clusters. It can be formed thanks to a new relation we have introduced, called *default subsumption*, that has been inspired from the default logic theory [7]. But contrary to this logic, which is used for default deduction, default subsumption is a specific logic for default induction. Furthermore, our model uses an original constraint named *cognitive cohesion* inspired by the notion of family resemblance of L. Wittgenstein [8].

This model of default clustering and its applications relies on the hypothesis that popular inductions are not only biased by lack of facts, but also by the poor description of existing facts [9]. Hence, experiments was made in the field of scientific discovery which confirm that missing values can lead to erroneous representations [1,2] whereas complete data do not. With a high rate of missing values, we state that each piece of information is crucial and must be used to build rich and relevant representations of the data. Stereotype sets seem really appropriate as a base for such representations. These sets provide coherent and cohesive descriptions that go beyond the usual approach used in clustering. All the above is closely linked to the context of sparse data, in which data extracted from textual data sets are often placed. For instance, Press Content Analysis becomes a natural object of such a cognitive model. This subarea of social psychology aims to analyse representations through the manipulation of concepts and relationship among these concepts from newspapers [10,11]. This is the reason why the model of default clustering is well designed to extract stereotypes from such data.

The paper is divided into five parts. Section 1 introduces the problem of missing values within the clustering process. Section 2 gives the abstract and logical framework of default clustering. This framework makes use both of the notion of default subsumption and of the concept of stereotype, which models the way sparse descriptions may be categorized. Section 3 goes on to instantiate this model of default clustering into two formalisms: the attribute-value formalism and the conceptual graph formalism. Section 4 presents the validation of the model using artificial data sets and a real application dealing with social misrepresentations. Section 5 suggests further lines of research.

2   Dealing with Missing Values

2.1   Missing Values and Clustering

Generally, in Data Analysis, missing values are primarily solved just before starting the "hard" analysis itself. Three kinds of strategies are generally used to handle such data [6]:

- ignoring the incomplete observations (the so-called "listwise deletion"),
- estimating the unknown values with other variables (single or multiple imputation, k-nearest-neighbors [12], maximum likelihood approaches [13]),
- using the background knowledge to complete automatically the unknown data with default values (arbitrary values, default rules).

But this pre-processing methods are mainly adapted to numerical data and seem not really flexible in a classification task with very sparse data.

Clustering is a classification task performed in a non-supervised way. It means that the categories are discovered without knowing previously the class to which each object belongs (like with a teacher). The most famous clustering algorithms are k-means (in fact its categorical version: k-modes [14]) and EM [15] (as Expectation-Maximization) that will be briefly described in section 5.3. But contrary to these algorithms that can easily lead to local optima, we have chosen to achieve the clustering using a combinatorial optimization approach, like in [16,17]. Besides, our goal here is not only to cluster examples but also and mainly to describe the clusters easily and in a non-probabilistic way. The problem can thus be stated as finding a set of readable, consistent, cohesive and rich descriptions of the data.

2.2 Overview of Default Logic

During the eighties, there were many attempts to model deductive reasoning where implicit information exists. A lot of formalisms [18,19,7] were developed to encompass the inherent difficulties of such models, especially their non-monotony: close-world assumption, circumscription, default logic, etc. Since our goal here is to model the way people induce empirical knowledge from partially and non homogeneously described facts, we face a very similar problem: in both cases, it is to reason where implicit information exists. Therefore, it is natural to make use of similar formalisms.

In this case, we have chosen default logic formalism, which was developed in the eighties by R. Reiter [7]. This logic for default reasoning is based on the notion of default rule which makes it possible to infer new formulas when the hypotheses are not inconsistent. More generally, a default rule always has the following form: $A : B_1, B_2 \ldots B_n / C$ where A is called the prerequisite, B_i the justifications and C the conclusion. This default rule can be interpreted as follows: if A is known to be true and if it is not inconsistent to assume $B_1, B_2 \ldots B_n$ then conclude C.

For instance, let us consider the default rule below:

$$\frac{politician(X) \land introducedAbroad(X) : \neg diplomat(X)}{traitor(X)}$$

This rule translates a usual way of reasoning for people living in France during the end of the 19th century; it means that one can suspect all politicians who are introduced abroad of being traitors towards their own countries, except for diplomats. In other words, it states that the conclusion traitor(X) can be derived if X is a politician who is known to be introduced abroad and that we cannot prove that he is a diplomat.

It should be noted that information conveyed by default rules refers to implicit connotations. For example, the antinomy between patriots and internationalists and the rule that considers almost all the politicians involved with foreigners to be traitors both correspond to connotations and may facilitate the completion of partial descriptions. The key idea is that people have in mind stereotypes that correspond to strong images stored in their memory which associates features and makes them connote each others.

2.3   Default Clustering

Conceptual clustering is a machine learning task defined by R. Michalski [4] which does not require a teacher and uses an evaluation function to discover classes of similar observations with data. In the same time, these classes are named with appropriate conceptual descriptions. Conceptual clustering was principally studied in a probabilistic context (see D. Fisher's Cobweb algorithm [20]) and seldom used really sparse data sets. For instance, the experiments done by P.H. Gennari do not exceed 30% of missing values [21].

This paper proposes a new technique called *default clustering* which is inspired by the default logic. We use a similar principle but for induction, when missing information exists. The main assumption is the following: if an observation is grouped with other similar observations, you can use these observations to complete unknown information in the original fact if it remains consistent with the current context. Whereas default logic needs implicit knowledge expressed by default rules, default clustering only uses information available in the data set. The next section presents this new framework. It shows how to extract stereotype sets from very sparse data sets: first it extends the classical subsumption, next it discusses the way stereotypes are choosed, and finally it proposes a local search strategy to find the best solution.

3   Logical Framework of Default Clustering

3.1   General Framework

Let there be a description space noted $\mathcal{D}$. A description d of $\mathcal{D}$ is defined as a logical structure (for instance a graph or a vector) describing objects, persons, events, etc. The observations we want to classify are associated to a set of such descriptions. Let us now suppose that this space can be structured into a lattice through the two binary operators $\wedge$ and $\vee$. Here is the precise definition of a lattice:

Definition 1. *An algebra $< \mathcal{D}; \wedge, \vee >$ is called a* lattice *if $\mathcal{D}$ is a nonempty set, $\wedge$ and $\vee$ are binary operations on $\mathcal{D}$, both $\wedge$ and $\vee$ are idempotent, commutative, and associative, and they satisfy the absorption law.*

A partially ordered set (*poset*) can be defined from the lattice structure through the subsumtion relationship:

Definition 2. *Being given two descriptions* $(d, d') \in \mathcal{D}^2$, d *subsume* d' *(noted $d \leq d'$) if and only if* $d \wedge d' = d$.

The expression $d \leq d'$ means that all the observations *covered* by the description d', i.e. the observations that verify the information given by d', are also covered by d. In other words, d is more general than d' and therefore covers a more important number of observations. At the opposite, d' is a more specific description that covers less observations. If $(d, d') \in \mathcal{D}^2$, $d \wedge d'$ is the lower bound of d and d', which corresponds to the greatest minorant common to the descriptions: $\forall d'', d'' \leq d, d'' \leq d' \Rightarrow d'' \leq d \wedge d'$. In the same way, $d \vee d'$ is the upper bound of d and d', that corresponds to the least common majorant: $\forall d'', d \leq d'', d' \leq d'' \Rightarrow d \wedge d' \leq d''$.

Here is defined the notion of completion:

Definition 3. *Being given two descriptions* $(d, d') \in \mathcal{D}^2$, d' *completes* d *if and only if* $d \leq d'$.

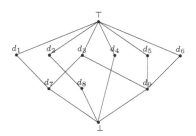

Fig. 1. Illustration of a description lattice

Fig. 1 is an example of a lattice formed from eleven descriptions: $d_1, d_2 \ldots d_9$, $\top, \bot$. $\top$ is the empty-description that subsumes all the possible descriptions, i.e. $\forall d \in \mathcal{D}, \top \leq d$. On the contrary, $\bot$ is the absurd-description that is subsumed by all the other descriptions. In this example, $d_1 \vee d_3 = d_7$, but $d_2 \vee d_4 = \bot$. Otherwise, $d_1 \wedge d_4 = \top$ and $d_7 \wedge d_9 = d_3$. Besides, d_9 completes d_3 which is itself completed by d_7.

Let the descriptions d_1, d_2 and d_3 describe three french meals:

d_1: a meal composed by an onion soup and a steak-potatoes accompanied with red wine;

d_2: a meal composed by a steak-potatoes, bread and red wine.

d_3: a meal composed by a steak-potatoes and bread.

As we can see, $d_3 \not\leq d_1$ because the information about the bread is missing in d_1. However, $d_3 \leq d_2$ because d_3 does not precise the drink and then covers also the meals accompanied with red wine. Furthermore, we can propose the following lower and upper bounds for d_1 and d_2:

$d_1 \wedge d_2$: a meal composed by a steak-potatoes and accompanied with red wine;

$d_1 \vee d_2$: a meal composed by an onion soup, steak-potatoes, bread and red wine.

The above is possible because it is done within the framework of propositional logic framework, which allows the use of a lattice structure. It can be adapted to all formalisms using specialization and generalization operators such as $\vee$ and $\wedge$. The attribute-value formalism (see section 4.1) is just one example of such a description space with the operators $\cup$ and $\cap$. It must be noticed that conceptual graphs or a restricted version of ER structures can also be used if they fit the previous conditions.

3.2 Default Subsumption

Contrary to default logic, the problem here is not to deduce, but to induce knowledge from data sets in which most of the information is unknown. Therefore, we propose the notion of *default subsumption*, which is the equivalent for subsumption of the default rule for deduction.

Let us start with an intuitive idea of this notion before moving to a more formal definition. Let us consider two descriptions d and d' such that d does not subsume d', i.e. $d \not\leq d'$. d subsumes d' *by default* means that d' could be completed in such a way that it would be subsumed by d in the classical way. This completed description d_c brings together the information of d and d'.

More formally:

Definition 4. *For any $(d, d') \in \mathcal{D}^2$, d subsumes d' by default (noted $d \leq_D d'$) if and only if $\exists d_c, d_c \neq \perp$, such that d_c completes d' and $d \leq d_c$.*

Let us note that d_c is a majorant of d and d' in the subsumption lattice. This leads us to the following theorem linked to the lattice theory:

Theorem 1. $\forall (d, d') \in \mathcal{D}^2$, $d \leq_D d' \Leftrightarrow d \vee d' \neq \perp$.

Proof. $d \leq_D d' \Rightarrow \exists d_c \neq \perp /d' \leq d_c$ and $d \leq d_c$ (def. 4). $d \vee d'$ is the lowest majorant common to d and d', so $\forall d_k, d \leq d_k, d' \leq d_k \Rightarrow d \vee d' \leq d_k$. In particular, $d \vee d' \leq d_c \neq \perp$, so $d \vee d' \neq \perp$. Reciprocally, $d \vee d' \neq \perp$ is a majorant of d and d'. If $d_c = d \vee d'$ then $d \leq d_c$ and $d' \leq d_c$. d_c is a description $\neq \perp$ that completes d' and is subsumed by d.

Property 1. The notion of default subsumption is more general than the classical subsumption since, if d subsumes d', i.e. $d \leq d'$, then d subsumes d' by default, i.e. $d \leq_D d'$. The converse is not true.

Proof. Since $d \leq d'$, let us state $d_c = d'$; $d' = d_c \leq d_c$ (thanks to the absorption law of $\wedge$) and $d \leq d_c = d' \Rightarrow d \leq_D d'$ (def. 4).

Property 2. The default subsumption relationship is symmetrical, i.e. $\forall (d, d') \in \mathcal{D}^2$, if $d \leq_D d'$ then $d' \leq_D d$.

Proof. $d \leq_D d' \Rightarrow d \lor d' \neq \bot$ (th. 1); since the operator $\lor$ is commutative, $d' \lor d \neq \bot$; th. 1 $\Rightarrow d' \leq_D d$.

Let us note that the notion of default subsumption may appear strange for people accustomed to classical subsumption because of its symmetry. As a consequence, it does not define an ordering relationship on the description space $\mathcal{D}$. The notation $\leq_D$ may be confusing with respect to this symmetry, but it is relative to the underlying idea of generality.

Fig. 2 gives two examples extracted from fig. 1 where the default subsumption is verified and a third case where it is not.

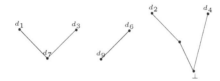

Fig. 2. $d_1 \leq_D d_3$ and $d_9 \leq_D d_6$, but $d_2 \not\leq_D d_4$

Let us consider the previous descriptions d_1 and d_2 of two french meals. It is assumed that d_1 and d_2 are partial descriptions. For instance, we do not know if there is a starter in the meal d_2 or not. Hence, d_2 can be completed into d_c by adding the onion soup, such as:

d_c: a meal composed by an onion soup, a steak-potatoes, bread and red wine.

Since d_1 subsumes d_c, i.e. $d_1 \leq d_c$, d_1 subsumes d_2 by default, i.e. $d_1 \leq_D d_2$. d_1 could be completed in the same way, which leads to conclude $d_2 \leq_D d_1$. Let us note that the number of observations covered by d_c is necessarily less (or equal) than that of d_1 and that of d_2.

3.3   Concept of Stereotype

E. Rosch saw the categorization itself as one of the most important issues in cognitive science [22]. She observed that children learn how to classify first in terms of concrete cases rather than through defining features. She therefore introduced the concept of prototype [22,23] as the ideal member of a category. Membership of a class is therefore defined by the proximity to the prototype and not by the number of shared features.

For example, a robin is closer to the bird prototype than an ostrich is, but they are both closer to it than they are to the prototype of a fish, so we call them both birds. However, it takes longer to decide that an ostrich is a bird than it takes to decide that a robin is a bird because the ostrich is further from the prototype. J. Sowa defines a prototype as a typical instance formed by joining one or more schemata [24]. Instead of describing a specific individual, it describes a typical or "average" individual.

Even if the original idea behind the concept of prototype and our approach have several features in common, we prefer to refer to the older concept of stereotype that was introduced by the publicist W. Lippman [25] and developped later by H. Putnam [26]. For Lippman, stereotypes are perceptive schemas (as structured association of characteristic features) shared by a group about other person or object categories. These simplifying and generalizing images about reality affect human behavior and are very subjective. Below are three main reasons to make such a choice.

First of all, the concept of prototype (whatever the term: centroid, medoid, etc.) is often misused in data mining techniques. It is reduced to either an average observation of the examples or an artificial description built on the most frequent shared features. Nevertheless, both of them are far from the underlying idea in family resemblance. Especially in the context of sparse data, it seems more correct to speak about combination of features found in different example descriptions than about average or mode selection. The second argument is that the concept of stereotype is often defined as an imaginary picture that distorts reality. Our goal is precisely to generate such pictures even if they are caricatural of the observations. Finally, these specific descriptions are more adapted for fast classification (we can even say discrimination) and prediction than prototypes. This is closely linked to Lippman's definition.

In order to avoid ambiguities, we restrict the notion of stereotype to the following:

Definition 5. *A stereotype is a specific description $s \in \mathcal{D}$.*

However, the next subsection does not handle stereotypes alone but stereotype sets to cover a whole description set.

Let us now consider a set E of *facts* (or *examples*) and a function δ that maps each fact $e \in E$ to its description $\delta(e) \in \mathcal{D}$. The objective is to automatically construct a set of stereotypes that cover E, whereas most of the studies are focused on already fixed stereotype usage [27,28]. Keeping this in mind, the space of all the possible stereotype sets is browsed in order to discover the best one, i.e. the set that best covers the examples of E with respect to some similarity measure. In a word, the stereotype set search can be summarized as an optimization problem. Before addressing this problem, let us introduce the relation of relative cover that will be used to fix the criterion to be optimized.

3.4   Stereotype Sets and Relative Cover

Groups of people share implicit knowledge, which makes them able to understand each other without having to express everything explicitly. This sort of knowledge can be expressed in terms of erudite theories (e.g. the "blocking perspiration" theory in [2]) or use a more "naive" formulation. Our hypothesis is that this implicit knowledge can be stored in terms of sets of stereotypes. This means that many people have in mind stereotype sets and that they use them to reason in a stereotyped way by associating new facts to known stereotypes.

To formalize this idea, let us first state a very general measure of similarity M_{sim} defined on $\mathcal{D}$. This measure reflects the degree of similarity between two descriptions d_1 and d_2 of $\mathcal{D}$: the more the score, the closer d_1 and d_2. For instance,

M_{sim} can be based on the number of common shared descriptors in the attribute-value formalism.

Let us now consider a stereotype $s \in \mathcal{D}$ and a fact $e \in E$. We say that the stereotype s is able to cover the fact e if s subsumes $\delta(e)$ by default and if $M(s, \delta(e))$ reflects some similarities. In other words:

Definition 6. *Let s be a stereotype $\in \mathcal{D}$ and e an example $\in E$, s covers e if and only if $s \leq_D \delta(e)$ and $M_{sim}(s, \delta(e)) > 0$.*

This notion can be extended to consider a set of facts:

Definition 7. *Let s be a stereotype $\in \mathcal{D}$ and E' a part of E, s covers E' if and only if $\forall e \in E'$, s covers e.*

Thus, the idea is to find a set of stereotypes that are able together to cover the whole set E:

Definition 8. *Let $\mathcal{D}$ be a description space, a set of stereotypes S is a set of $n + 1$ descriptions $\{s_1, s_2 \ldots s_n, \top\} \in \mathcal{D}^{n+1}$.*

Given a set of facts E and a set of stereotypes S, it is possible to calculate a categorization of E where each example $e \in E$ is associated to a description of S. The categorization is calculated by bringing together the facts that are covered by the same stereotype. The descriptions of the facts $e \in E$ can then be completed thanks to this stereotype. But it is also possible to predict the values of new observed facts that were not initially in E.

More precisely, completion is possible when there exists at least one stereotype $s_i \in S$ such that $s_i \neq \top$ and s_i covers the description $\delta(e)$ of the fact e (belonging to E or not). In other words, thinking by stereotype is possible when the descriptions are so sparse that they seem consistent with existing stereotypes. This capacity to classify and to complete the descriptions is closely linked to the concept of stereotype as introduced by Lippman in [25].

When one and only one stereotype s_i (except $\perp$) covers by default the fact e, the description of e may be completed by the stereotype s_i. However, it happens that facts may be covered by two or more stereotypes. So, the stereotype associated with a fact e is the one that maximizes the measure of similarity M_{sim}, i.e. it is the stereotype s_i which both covers $\delta(e)$ by default and maximizes $M_{sim}(\delta(e), s_i)$. It is called the relative cover of e, thanks to the measure of similarity M_{sim} and to the set of stereotypes $S = \{s_1, s_2 \ldots s_n, \top\}$.

Definition 9. *The relative cover of a fact e, with respect to a set of stereotypes $S = \{s_1, s_2 \ldots s_n, \top\}$, noted $C_S(e)$, is the stereotype s_i if and only if:*

1. $s_i \in S$,
2. $s_i \leq_D \delta(e)$,
3. $M_{sim}(\delta(e), s_i) > 0$,
4. $\forall k \in [1, n], k \neq i, M_{sim}(\delta(e), s_i) \geq M_{sim}(\delta(e), s_k)$.

It means that a fact e is associated to the most-similar and "covering-able" stereotype *relative* to the set S. If there are two competing stereotypes (or more than two) with an equal higher score of similarity, then two strategies can be used: either associate the fact arbitrarily to one or other of these stereotypes, or reject the fact under the empty-stereotype whose description is $\top$. It may also happen that no stereotype covers the fact e, which means that $\delta(e)$ is inconsistent with all s_i. The example is then directly associated to the empty-stereotype and no completion can be calculated. Fig. 3 shows how the example $e \in E$ is covered by s_3 relatively to the set S of stereotypes.

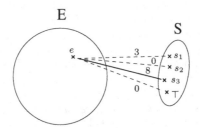

Fig. 3. The example e is covered by s_3 relatively to S

3.5 Extraction of Stereotypes

In this paper, default reasoning is formalized using the notions of both default subsumption and stereotype set. Up to now, these sets were supposed to be given. This section shows how the classification can be organized into such sets in a non-supervised learning task. It can be summarized as follows.

Given:

1. An example set E.
2. A description space $\mathcal{D}$.
3. A description function $\delta \colon E \longrightarrow \mathcal{D}$ which associates a description $\delta(e) \in D$ to each example belonging to the training set E.

The function of a non-supervised learning algorithm is to organize the initial set of facts E into a structure (for instance a hierarchy, a lattice or a pyramid). In the present case, the structure is limited to partitions of the training set, which corresponds to searching for stereotype sets as discussed in the previous sections. These partitions may be generated by $(n + 1)$ stereotypes $S = \{s_1, s_2 \ldots s_n, \top\}$: it is sufficient to associate to each s_i the set E_i of examples e belonging to E and covered by s_i relative to S. The examples that cannot be covered by any stereotype are put into the $E_\top$ cluster and associated to $\top$.

To choose among the numerous possible partitions, which is a combinatorial problem, a non-supervised algorithm requires a function for evaluating stereotype set relevance. Because of the categorical nature of data and the previous definition of relative cover, it appears natural to make use of the similarity measure M_{sim}. This is exactly what we do by introducing the following evaluation function h_E:

Definition 10. *Given an example set E, a stereotype set $S = \{s_1, s_2 \ldots s_n, \top\}$ and the function C_S that associates to each example $e \in E$ its relative cover, i.e. its closest stereotype with respect to M_{sim} and S, the evaluation function h_E is defined as follows:*

$$h_E(S) = \sum_{e \in E} M_{sim}(\delta(e), C_S(e))$$

While other non-supervised learning algorithms, such as k-modes or EM, are straightforward, i.e. each step leads to the next one until convergence, we reduce here the non-supervised learning task to an optimization problem. This approach offers several interesting features: avoiding local optima (especially with categorical and sparse data), providing "good" solutions even if not the best ones, better control of the search. In addition, it is not necessary to specify the number of expected stereotypes that are also discovered during the search process.

There are several methods for exploring such a search space (hill-climbing, simulated annealing, etc.). We have chosen the meta-heuristic called *tabu search* which improves the local search algorithm. Previous work studying the use of tabu search for clustering problems can be found in [29,30].

Let us recall that the local search process can be schematized as follows:

1. An initial solution S_{ini} is given (for instance at random).
2. A neighborhood $V(S_i)$ is calculated from the current solution S_i with the assistance of permitted movements. These movements can be of low influence (enrich one stereotype with a descriptor, remove a descriptor from another) or of high influence (add or retract one stereotype to or from the current stereotype set).
3. The better movement, relative to the evaluation function h_E, is chosen and the new current solution S_{i+1} is computed.
4. The process is iterated a specific number of times and the best up-to-now discovered solution is recorded.

Then, the solution is the stereotype set S_{max} that best maximizes h_E in comparison to all the crossed sets. Fig. 4 shows the process of searching through the space of all the potential solutions.

As in almost all local search techniques, there is a trade-off between exploitation, i.e. choosing the best movement, and exploration, i.e. choosing a non optimal state to reach completely different areas. The tabu search extends the basic local search by manipulating short and long-term memories which are used to

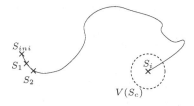

Fig. 4. Local search through the potential solutions

avoid loops and to intelligently explore the search space. For instance, a *tabu list* can be used in order to avoid the solutions that have been already visited. We shall not detail here this meta-heuristic but suggest the reader to consult the book of Glover and Laguna [31].

3.6   Cognitive Cohesion

A constraint inspired by the family resemblance relationship has been added to reflect internal cohesion within the categories. This constraint, called *cognitive cohesion*, checks cohesion within the example set $E_j \subset E$, relative to the corresponding stereotype $s_j \in S$. The idea is that all the features (descriptors in the A/V formalism, concepts with the conceptual graphs) of s are somehow linked by a succession of co-occurences. It means that cognitive cohesion is verified if there exists a path through the example descriptions that links the different elements constituting the stereotype description. A similar approach for clustering can be found in [32].

Let us consider the following descriptions:

d_1: a scientist with a red beard;
d_2: a tall man with a beard;
d_3: a tall red-haired scientist;
d_4: a small black-haired woman.

This example clearly shows a first category bringing the descriptions d_1, d_2 and d_3 together, whereas the description d_4 seemingly has to be placed in a separate group.

This constraint is used both to restrain the search space and to assure a good cohesion within the stereotypes. It removes the solutions that do not correspond to our assumption and are considered irrelevant. This is closely linked to the context of sparse descriptions. It will be explained in much more detail in the section dealing with the attribute-value formalism.

4   Implementation of Default Clustering

Now that the framework of default clustering has been given, this section shows how it can be used with two different formalisms. The first one is the well-known attribute-value formalism, derived from the propositional logic. The second one is the conceptual graph formalism introduced by J.F. Sowa [24].

4.1   Attribute-Value Formalism

Let us consider a set $\mathcal{A}$ of m categorical attributes. Each attribute $A_i, 1 \leq i \leq m$, can take a finite number of mutually exclusive values V_{ij}. The descriptor space $\mathcal{V}$ corresponds to all the tuples built from an attribute associated with a value, which is noted $(A_i = V_{ij})$. Thus, the description space $\mathcal{D}$ is composed of all the possible combinations of descriptors, i.e. $\mathcal{P}(\mathcal{V})$, with the strong constraint that an attribute can take only one value for each description. Here is an example of a description about a French meal:

$$d = \{(Starter = onion - soup), (Dish = steak - potatoes), (Drink = wine)\}$$

Here E constitutes a base of French meals and each example $e \in E$ is mapped to one description of $\mathcal{D}$ thanks to the function δ. The definition 4 of the default subsumption can be rewritten, thanks to the theorem 1, as shown below:

Definition 11. *For any $(d, d') \in \mathcal{D}^2$, d subsumes d' by default (i.e. $d \leq_D d'$) if and only if $d_c = d \cup d' \neq \perp$.*

To illustrate this new definition, here are some descriptions that can be compared with respect to the default subsumption:

$d_1 = \{(Starter = onion - soup), (Drink = red - wine)\}$
$d_2 = \{(Starter = onion - soup), (Dish = steak - potatoes)\}$
$d_3 = \{(Dish = sole)\}$
$d_4 = \{(Starter = onion - soup), (Drink = red - wine), (EndWith = coffee)\}$
$d_1 \leq_D d_2$ and $d_2 \leq_D d_1$ because $\exists d_c$ such that $d_c = d_1 \cup d_2 \neq \perp$:

$$d_c = \{(Starter = onion - soup), (Dish = steak - potatoes), (Drink = red - wine)\}$$

$d_1 \leq_D d_4$ because $d_1 \leq d_4$ (property 1). However, considering the new constraint that red wine cannot be drunk with fish and vice-versa, which could be assumed as an implicit statement in French cuisine, d_1 does not subsume d_3 by default, i.e. $d_1 \nleq_D d_3$.

In order to measure the degree of similarity between two descriptions d and $d' \in \mathcal{D}$, we propose a very basic function that counts the number of common descriptors of $\mathcal{V}$ belonging to d and d'. The unknown values are ignored and the default subsumtion relationship is taken into account.

$$M_{sim}: \mathcal{D} \times \mathcal{D} \longrightarrow \mathbb{N}^+$$
$$(d_i, d_j) \longmapsto M_{sim}(d_i, d_j) = |d_i \cap d_j| \text{ if } d_i \leq_D d_j \text{ and}$$
$$M_{sim}(d_i, d_j) = 0 \text{ if } d_i \nleq_D d_j.$$

Let us now present the constraint of *cognitive cohesion* in the attribute-value formalism. This constraint is verified if and only if, being given two descriptors v_1 and $v_2 \in \mathcal{V}$ of $s \in S$, it is always possible to find a series of examples in E that makes it possible to pass by correlation from v_1 to v_2. More formally:

Definition 12. *Being given a stereotype $s \in \mathcal{D}$ and a set E of examples covered by s, s is said to check the cognitive cohesion constraint if and only if $\forall c_1 \forall c_2 \in s, \exists u_n = e_{i(1)}, e_{i(2)} \ldots e_{i(m)} / e_{i(k)} \in E, c_1 \in e_{i(1)}, c_2 \in e_{i(m)}$ with $\forall j \in [1, m - 1], \exists c \in \mathcal{V} / c \in e_{i(j)}$ and $c \in e_{i(j+1)}$.*

Let us continue with the previous illustration of a french meal (see fig. 5). Five attributes are considered because they are instantiated by the stereotype: *Starter, Main-dish, Drink, Dessert* and *End-with*. For instance, *Starter* can take the values *green-salad, onion-soup, fish-soup,* and *Main-dish* the values *steak-potatoes, sole-rice, chicken-puree.*

	Starter	Main-dish	Drink	Dessert	End-with
s_1 :	green-salad	steak-potatoes	beer	cream-puff	coffee
e_1 :	green-salad	?	?	?	coffee
e_2 :	green-salad	steak-potatoes	?	?	?
e_6 :	?	?	beer	?	?
e_8 :	?	steak-potatoes	beer	cream-puff	?
e_{42} :	green-salad	?	beer	?	?

	Starter	Main-dish	Drink	Dessert	End-with
s_2 :	green-salad	steak-potatoes	beer	cream-puff	coffee
e_0 :	green-salad	steak-potatoes	?	?	?
e_8 :	?	?	?	cream-puff	?
e_9 :	green-salad	steak-potatoes	?	?	?
e_{51} :	?	?	beer	?	coffee
e_{101} :	?	?	beer	?	coffee

Fig. 5. Two example sets with their covering stereotype

The examples covered by the stereotype s_1 verify the constraint. Hence, it is always possible to pass from each descriptor *green-salad*, *steak-potatoes*, *beer*, *cream-puff* or *coffee* to another descriptor belonging to s_1. To take an example of path, you can go from *coffee* to *cream-puff* by using e_1, e_{42} and e_8. This path is illustrated in the figure below:

The examples covered by the stereotype s_2 do not verify the constraint. Hence, it is never possible with s_2 to pass from *green-salad* to *beer*. In the case of s_1, you are always able to find a "correlation path" from one descriptor of the description to another, that is to say examples explaining the relationship between the descriptors in the stereotype.

4.2 Conceptual Graphs Formalism

Let us now consider the conceptual graph formalism applied to the default clustering model, following the notations given by Sowa. But first, here is a reminder of the main assumption of conceptual graphs [24]:

Assumption 1. A *conceptual graph* is a finite, connected, bipartite graph.

- The two kinds of nodes of the bipartite graph are concepts and conceptual relations.
- Every conceptual relation has one or more *arcs*, each of which must be linked to some concepts.

- If a relation has n arcs, it is said to be *n-adic*, and its arcs are labeled $1, 2 \ldots n$. The term *monadic* is synonymous with 1-adic, *dyadic* with 2-adic, and *triadic* with 3-adic.
- A single concept by itself may form a conceptual graph, but every arc of every conceptual relation must be linked to some concept.

Given two conceptual graphs g and g_S, $g_S \leq g$ means that g_S is a specialization of g and g is a generalization of g_S, i.e. g subsumes g_S. This means that g_S is canonically derivable from g, possibly with the join of other conceptual graphs. For the sake of clarity, let us simply consider that the join of graph u and v is the graph w obtained by aggregating the concepts and relations of u and v. For further details, please see [24].

Remark 1. Let us emphasize that the symbol $\leq$ has the opposite meaning in the conceptual graph formalism and in the attribute-value formalism we exposed previously. However, it is the notation followed by Sowa in his book [24]. Thus, $g \leq g'$ means that the conceptual graph g' is more general than the conceptual graph g.

Now, let a stereotype be a specific conceptual graph s. If this stereotype is more general than g_S, i.e. $g_S \leq s$, then it subsumes g *by default*. More formally, definition 4 can be rewritten this way:

Definition 13. *Let e be a fact represented by the conceptual graph $g = \delta(e)$ and s a stereotype. s subsumes g by default (i.e. $s \leq_D g$) if and only if there exists a graph g_S with $g_S \leq g$ and $g_S \leq s$. g_S is therefore a graph formed by the join operator performed on the graphs g and s.*

Fig. 6 presents the fact *The meal of Jules is composed of steak, red wine, and ends with a cup of very hot coffee* which can be subsumed by default by the stereotype *The meal is composed of steak with potatoes and French bread, and ends with a cup of coffee* because the fact can be completed to *The meal of Jules is composed of steak with potatoes and French bread, red wine, and ends with a cup of very hot coffee*. If the stereotype had presented a meal ending with a liqueur, it would not match the fact and so could not subsume it by default.

We want now to link the relation of default subsumption to the notion of compatibility as developed by Sowa. But first, here is the definition of *compatibility* given by Sowa [24]:

Definition 14. *Let conceptual graphs u_1 and u_2 have a common generalization v with projections $\pi_1 : v \rightarrow u_1$ and $\pi_2 : v \rightarrow u_2$. The two projections are said to be compatible if for each concept c in v, the following conditions are true:*

- *$type(\pi_1 c) \cap type(\pi_2 c) > \perp$.*
- *The referents of $\pi_1 c$ and $\pi_2 c$ conform to $type(\pi_1 c) \cap type(\pi_2 c)$.*
- *If $referent(\pi_1 c)$ is the individual marker i, then $referent(\pi_2 c)$ is either i or $*$.*

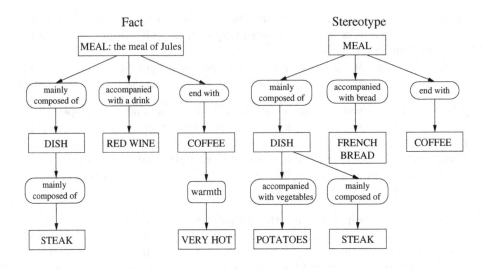

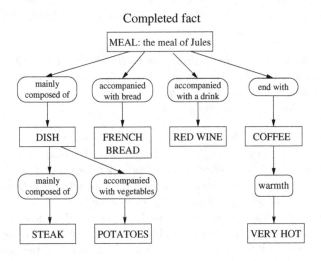

Fig. 6. The stereotype *subsumes by default* the fact description. The description below is the result of the join operator, i.e. the completed fact.

where *type* maps concepts into a set of *type labels* (e.g. *meal* or *wine*) and *referent* is either an *individual marker* (e.g. *the meal of Tom*) or the *generic marker* *.

We state the following theorem in order to link the notions of compatibility and default subsumption:

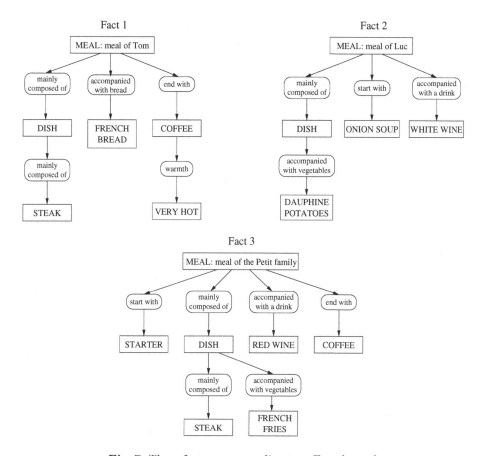

Fig. 7. Three facts corresponding to a French meal

Theorem 2. *Let conceptual graphs u_1 and u_2 have the least common generalization v with projections $\pi_1 : v \to u_1$ and $\pi_2 : v \to u_2$. π_1 and π_2 are compatible if and only if u_1 subsumes u_2 by default.*

Proof. If π_1 and π_2 are compatible then there exists a common specialization w of u_1 and u_2 (cf. theorem 3.5.7 [24]). According to definition 13, u_1 subsumes u_2 by default. Reciprocally, if u_1 subsumes u_2 by default then there exists a common specialization w. Suppose that π_1 and π_2 are not compatible. There therefore exists at least one concept in v with $type(\pi_1 c) \cap type(\pi_2 c) = \perp$, or with the referent of $\pi_1 c$ or $\pi_2 c$ not conform to $type(\pi_1 c) \cap type(\pi_2 c)$, or with $referent(\pi_1 c) = i$ and $referent(\pi_2 c) = j$, $i \neq j$. These three cases are absurd because they contradict the construction of w. Therefore, π_1 and π_2 are compatible.

Fig. 8 represents a stereotype formed from three facts taken from fig. 7 corresponding to French meals. The missing values in these facts can be completed using default reasoning with the corresponding values in the stereotype because

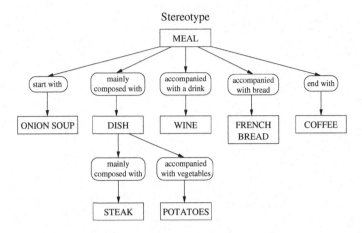

Fig. 8. A stereotype of a French meal

there is no contradiction between them. Thus, we can infer for instance that Tom drinks wine or that the Petit family eat French bread with their meal.

We do not propose a similarity measure associated to conceptual graphs because this problem is combinatorial and much more difficult to handle than with the attribute-value formalism. For further information, see [33], that deals with graph matching and proposes an interesting heuristic to calculate this similarity.

5   Experiments

This section starts by presenting experiments performed on artificial data sets. It goes on to give an original comparison in a real data case with three well-known clusterers. Default clustering was implemented in a Java program called PRESS (*Programme de Reconstruction d'Ensembles de StéréotypeS*). All the experiments for k-modes, EM and Cobweb were performed using the Weka platform [34]. To get a brief description of the three clusterers, see section 5.3.

5.1   Validation on Artificial Data Sets

Artificial data sets are used to validate the robustness of the non-supervised learning algorithm, which builds sets of stereotypes from a learning set E and a description language $\mathcal{D}$. It should be remembered that stereotypes are supposed to be more or less shared by many people living in the same society. Since the use of stereotypes is the way to model implicit reasoning, this could explain why pre-judgements and pre-suppositions are almost identical in a group. Secondly, it is assumed that people reason from sparse descriptions that are completed and organized into stereotype sets in their memory. It follows that people who have shared different experiences and who have read different newspapers, are able to build very similar sets of stereotypes from very different learning sets.

Therefore, our attempt to model construction of stereotype sets using a non-supervised learning algorithm ought to have this stability property. This is what we evaluate here on artificial data.

Let us now consider the attribute-value formalism. Given this description language, we introduce some full consistent descriptions, e.g. $\{s_1, s_2, s_3\}$, which stand for the description of a stereotype set. Let us note as n_s the number of such descriptions. These n_s descriptions may be randomly generated. The only point is that they need to be complete and consistent.

The second step in the generation of the artificial set is to duplicate these descriptions n_d times, for instance 50 times, making $n_s \times n_d$ artificial examples. Then, these $n_s \times n_d$ descriptions are arbitrarily degraded: descriptors belonging to these duplications are chosen randomly to be destroyed. The only parameter is the percentage of degradation, i.e. the ratio of the number of destroyed descriptors on the total number of descriptors. The generated learning set contains $n_s \times n_d$ example descriptions, which all correspond to degradations of the n_s initial descriptions.

The default clustering algorithm is tested on these artificially generated and degraded learning sets. Then, the stability property is evaluated by weighing the stereotype set built by the non-supervised algorithm against the n_s descriptions initially given when generating the artificial learning set.

Our first evaluation consists in comparing of quality –i.e. the percentage of descriptors– and the number of generated stereotypes to the n_s initial descriptions, while the percentage of degradation increases from 0% to 100%. It appears that in up to 85% of degradation, the stereotype sets correspond most of the time to the initial ones (see fig. 9). Although the data were highly degraded, the correct number of stereotypes was discovered through the default clustering process.

The second test counts the classification error rate, i.e. the rate of degraded facts that are not covered by the right stereotype. By "right stereotype" we mean the discovered description that corresponds to the initial fact the degraded facts come from. Fig. 10 shows the results of our program PRESS relative to three classic classification algorithm: k-modes (categorical version of k-means), COBWEB and EM. These experiments clearly show that the results of PRESS

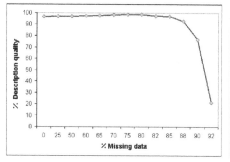 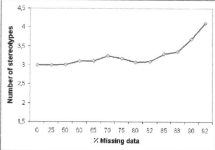

Fig. 9. Quality and number of stereotypes discovered

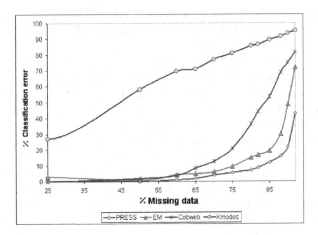

Fig. 10. Classification error of degraded examples

are really good with a very stable learning process: up to 75% of degradation, the error rate is less than 10% and better than the others three.

5.2 Studying Social Misrepresentation

The second part of the experiments deals with real data extracted from a newspaper called "Le Matin" of the end of the 19th century in France. The purpose is to automatically discover stereotype sets from a translation of events related to the political disorder in the first ten days of September 1893. The results of PRESS are compared to those of the three clusterers k-modes, EM and Cobweb. It should be pointed out that our principal interest is focused on the cluster descriptions, which we call *representatives* to avoid any ambiguity, rather than on the clusters themself.

The articles linked to the chosen theme were gathered and represented using a language of 33 attributes (for instance: political party, religion, linked with a foreign country, corrupted by the Freemasonry, etc.). The terms of this language, i.e. attributes and associated values, were extracted manually. Most of the attributes are binary, some accept more than two values and some are ordinals. The number of extracted examples is 63 and the rate of missing data is nearly 87%, which is most unusual. In these experiments, a constraint of *no-redundancy* was added in order to get a perfect separation between the stereotypes because, in this context of very high sparseness, it seems important to extract contrasted descriptions by forbidding redundant descriptors.

5.3 Evaluation of Default Clustering

In order to evaluate PRESS, a comparison was made with three classical clusterers: k-modes, EM and Cobweb.

K-modes [14] is an adaptation of the widespread algorithm k-means for categorical data. The process is here summarized: a set of n initial centres called *centroids* are chosen (randomly most of the time); the objects are then allocated to the nearest centroid; each centroid is recalculated from the set of covered objects; the objects are allocated one more time; the process is iterated until convergence. EM [15] (for Expectation-Maximization) is a method of doing maximum likelihood estimation for incomplete data. It uses probabilistic distributions to describe the clusters and can be considered as a generalization of k-means algorithm. Finally, Cobweb [20] is an hierarchical clusterer that relies on the category utility notion proposed by E. Rosch. The "flat" clustering is obtained by cutting through the resulting tree.

The output of two of these algorithms is a set of probabilistic distributions. To perform the comparison with PRESS, we need to extract a non-probabilistic description of the clusters they built. The same process was extended to the clusters given by k-modes algorithm. Four techniques were considered:

(1) using the most frequent descriptors (mode approach),
(2) the same as (1) but forbidding contradictory features between the examples and their representative,
(3) dividing the descriptors between the different representatives,
(4) the same as (3) but forbidding contradictory features.

Three remarks need to be made. Firstly, the cluster descriptions resulting from k-modes correspond to technique (1). Nevertheless, we tried the other three techniques exhaustively. Secondly, representatives resulting from extraction techniques (3) and (4) entail *by construction* a redundancy rate of 0%. Thirdly, it must be recalled that the number of stereotypes has not to be given but is discovered by PRESS during the clustering process.

The classification error rate and the notion of quality relative to the original descriptions can no longer be used in these new experiments. This is the reason why the comparison was made according to the three following points:

The first approach considers the contradictions between an example and its representative. The *example contradiction* is the percentage of examples containing at least one descriptor in contradiction with its covering representative. In addition, if you consider one of these contradictory examples, *average contradiction* is the percentage of descriptors in contradiction with its representative. This facet of conceptual clustering is very important, especially in the sparse context.

Secondly, we check if the constraint of cognitive cohesion (see 3.6 and 4.1) is verified. The rate of descriptor redundancy is also considered. These two notions are linked to the concept of stereotype and to the sparse data context.

Finally, we consider the degree of similarity between the examples and their covering representatives. This corresponds to the notion of compactness within clusters, but without penalizing the stereotypes with many descriptors. The function h_E seems really adapted to render an account of representative relevance. In fact, we used a version of h_E normalized between 0 and 1, by dividing by the total number of descriptors.

5.4   Results

Fig. 11 gives the results obtained from the articles published in Le Matin. Experiments for the k-modes algorithm were carried out with $N = 2..8$ clusters, but only $N = 6$ results are presented in this comparison. It corresponds to the number of stereotypes that was discovered with PRESS. The rows of the table show the number n of extracted representatives, the two scores concerning contradiction, the result of h_E, the redundancy score and whether or not cognitive cohesion constraint is verified. The columns represent each type of experiment (k-modes associated with techniques from (1) to (4), EM and Cobweb as well, and finally our algorithm PRESS).

Let us begin by considering the scores concerning contradiction. They highlight a principal result of default clustering: using PRESS, the percentage of examples having contradictory features with their representative is always equal to 0%. In contrast, the descriptions built using techniques (1) and (3) (whatever the clusterer used) possess at least one contradictory descriptor with 27% to 57% of the examples belonging to the cluster. Furthermore, around 50% of the descriptors of these examples are in contradiction with the covering description, and that can in no way be considered as a negligible noise. This is the reason why processes (1) and (3) must be avoided, especially in the sparse data context, when building such representatives from k-modes, EM or Cobweb clustering. Hence, we only consider techniques (2) and (4) in the following experiments.

	k-Modes				EM				Cobweb				PRESS
	(1)	(2)	(3)	(4)	(1)	(2)	(3)	(4)	(1)	(2)	(3)	(4)	
n	6	6	6	6	2	2	2	2	2	2	2	2	6
ex. contradiction	27	0	27	0	48	0	48	0	56	0	57	0	0
av. contradiction	42	0	44	0	56	0	56	0	52	0	51	0	0
h_E	.89	.60	.74	.50	.85	.66	.83	.65	.82	.56	.68	.46	.79
redundancy	70	63	0	0	17	7	0	0	72	55	0	0	0
cog. cohesion	×	×	×	×	×	×	×	×	×	×	×	×	✓

Fig. 11. Comparative results on *Le Matin*

Let us now study the results concerning clustering quality. This quality can be expressed thanks to the compactness function h_E, the redundancy rate and cognitive cohesion.

PRESS marked the best score (0.79) for cluster compactness with six stereotypes. That means a very good homogeneity between the stereotypes and the examples covered. It is perfectly consistent since our algorithm tries to maximize this function. The redundant descriptor rate is equal to 0%, according to the constraint of no-redundancy. Furthermore, PRESS is the only algorithm that is able to verify the cognitive cohesion. Using technique (2), EM obtains the second best score (0.66) and redundant descriptor rate remains acceptable (7%). However, the number of expected classes must be given or guessed, using a cross-validation technique, for instance. K-modes and Cobweb come in at third and fourth positions with respectively 0.6 and 0.56 if we consider technique (2), but redundancy is very high with 63% and 55%. The scores fell to 0.5 et 0.46 using technique (4), if the aim is to decrease the redundancy. K-modes and Cobweb also have to use external mechanism to discover the final number of clusters.

It should be noted that the stereotypes extracted using PRESS correspond to the political leanings of the newspaper. For instance, the main stereotype produces a radical, socialist politician, corrupted by the foreign money and the Freemasonry, etc. It corresponds partly to the difficulty in accepting the major changes proposed by the radical party and to the fear caused in France since 1880 by the theories of Karl Marx. These first results are really promising and should lead to advanced experiments.

6   Future Work

The first point that needs to be examined is the process of translation from newspaper articles into logical facts, which is still very subjetive if done by hand. It is for this reason that we are now studying the development of software to assist a user in this translation process. This software will rely on the idea of reflexivity and make him the ability of backtracking possible in order to obtain entire satisfaction.

Secondly, this work should be related to the domain of social representations as introduced by Serge Moscovici in [10]. According to him, social representations are a sort of "common sense" knowledge which aims at inducing behaviors and allows communication between individuals. We think that social representations can be constructed with the help of stereotype sets. The way these representations change can be studied through the media over different periods and social groups in comparison with such sets. Hence, future work could be done on choosing key dates of the Dreyfus affair and automatically extracting stereotypical characters from different newspapers. These results will then be compared and contrasted with the work of sociologists and historians of this period. This represents as yet an unexplored way for enriching historical and social analysis.

7   Conclusion

Flows of information play a key role in today's society. However, the value of information depends on its being interpreted correctly, and implicit knowledge has a considerable influence on this interpretation. This is the case in many of today's heterogeneous data that are far from complete and, consequently, need special techniques to be automatically completed. This is particularly true of the media, including newspapers, radio and television, where the information given is always sparse. It seems that Data Mining techniques, such as conceptual clustering, represent an alternative to deal with this kind of information.

In this context we propose a cognitive model called default clustering based on stereotype sets which summarize facts by "guessing" the missing values. Stereotypes are an alternative to prototypes and are more suitable in the categorization of sparse descriptions. They rely on the notion of default subsumption which relaxes constraints and makes possible the manipulation of such descriptions. Descriptions are then completed according to the closest stereotypes, with respect to the similarity measure M_{sim}. This model can be applied to different formalisms and the two presented in this paper are not exhaustive. Very good results have been found using the attribute-value formalism on artificial data sets. Future experiments will be done in the same formalism, but with real data extracted from the period of the Dreyfus affair, in order to see whether the default clustering model can be used to offer an alternative for Press Content Analysis.

Acknowledgments

The authors would particularly like to thank Rosalind Greenstein for reading and correcting the manuscript.

References

1. Corruble, V.: *Une approche inductive de la découverte en médecine : les cas du scorbut et de la lèpre*, thèse de l'Université Pierre et Marie Curie, rapport interne LAFORIA TH96/18 (1996).
2. Corruble, V., Ganascia, J.-G.: Induction and the discovery of the causes of scurvy : a computational reconstruction, In: *Artificial Intelligence Journal*, vol. 91 (2), pp.205–223, Elsevier Press (1997).
3. Velcin J.: Reconstruction rationnelle des mentalités collectives: deux études sur la xénophobie, DEA report, Internal Report University Paris VI, Paris (2002).
4. Michalski, R.S.: Knowledge acquisition through conceptual clustering: A theoretical framework and algorithm for partitioning data into conjunctive concepts, In: *International Journal of Policy Analysis and Information Systems*, 4 (1980) pp.219–243.
5. Newgard, C.D., Lewis, R.J.: The Imputation of Missing Values in Complex Sampling Databases: An Innovative Approach. In: *Academic Emergency Medicine*, Volume 9, Number 5484. Society for Academic Emergency Medicine (2002).
6. Little, R., Rubin, D.: *Statistical analysis with missing data*, Wiley-Interscience publication (2002).
7. Reiter, R.: A logic for default reasoning. In: *Artificial Intelligence*, number 13 (1980) pp.81–132.
8. Wittgenstein, L.: *Philosophical Investigations*. Blackwell (1953), Oxford, UK.
9. Ganascia, J.-G.: Rational Reconstruction of Wrong Theories, In: *Proceedings of the LMPS-03*, P.V.-V. Hajek,L.;Westerstahl, D., Ed.: Elsevier - North (2004).
10. Moscovici, S.: *La psychanalyse : son image et son public*, PUF (1961), Paris.
11. Fan, D.: *Predictions of public opinion from the mass media: Computer content analysis and mathematical modeling*. New York, NY: Greenwood Press (1988).
12. Huang, C.-C., Lee, H.-M.: A Grey-Based Nearest Neighbor Approach for Missing Attribute Value Prediction, In: *Applied Intelligence*, vol. 20. Kluwer Academic Publishers (2004) pp.239–252.
13. Ghahramani, Z., Jordan, M.-I.: Supervised learning from incomplete data via an EM approach, In: *Advances in Neural Information Processing Systems*, vol. 6. Morgan Kaufmann Publishers (1994), San Francisco.

14. Huang, Z.: A Fast Clustering Algorithm to Cluster Very Large Categorical Data Sets in Data Mining, In: *DMKD* (1997).
15. Dempster, A.P. et al.: Maximum likelihood from incomplete data via the EM algorithm, In: *Royal Statistical Society. Series B (Methodological)*, 39 (1) pp.1–38 (1977).
16. Figueroa, A., Borneman, J., Jiang, T.: *Clustering binary fingerprint vectors with missing values for DNA array data analysis* (2003).
17. Sarkar, M., Leong, T.Y.: Fuzzy K-means clustering with missing values, In: *Proc AMIA Symp.*, PubMed (2001) pp.588–92.
18. McDermott, D., Doyle, J.: Nonmonotonic logic 1. In: *Artificial Intelligence*, number 13 (1980) 41–72.
19. McCarthy, J.: Circumscription: a form of non-monotonic reasoning, In: *Artificial Intelligence*, number 13 (1980) 27–39, 171–172.
20. Fisher, D.H.: Knowledge Acquisition Via Incremental Conceptual Clustering. In: *Machine Learning*, number 2 (1987) pp.139–172.
21. Gennari, J.H.: *An experimental study of concept formation*, Doctoral dissertation (1990), Department of Information & Computer Science, University of California, Irvine.
22. Rosch, E.: Cognitive representations of semantic categories, In: *Journal of Experimental Psychology: General*, number 104 (1975) pp.192–232.
23. Rosch, E.: Principles of categorization, In: *Cognition and Categorization*. NJ: Lawrence Erlbaum, Hillsdale (1978) pp.27–48.
24. Sowa, J.F.: *Conceptual Structures: Information Processing in Mind and Machine*, Addison-Wesley Publishing Company (1984), Massachusetts, The Systems Programming Series.
25. Lippman, W.: *Public Opinion*, Ed. MacMillan (1922), NYC.
26. Putnam, H.: The Meaning of 'Meaning', In: *Mind, Language, and Reality* Cambridge University Press (1975) pp.215–271.
27. Rich, E.: User Modeling via Stereotypes, In: *International Journal of Cognitive Science*, 3 (1979) pp.329–354.
28. Amossy, R., Herschberg Pierrot, A.: *Stéréotypes et clichés : langues, discours, société*. Nathan Université (1997).
29. Al-Sultan, K.: A Tabu Search Approach to the Clustering Problem, In: *Pattern Recognition*, vol. 28 (9). Elsevier Science Ltd (1995) pp.1443–1451.
30. Ng, M.K., Wong, J.C.: Clustering categorical data sets using tabu search techniques, In: *Pattern Recognition*, vol. 35 (12). Elsevier Science Ltd (2002) pp.2783-2790.
31. Glover, F., Laguna, M.: *Tabu Search*, Kluwer Academic Publishers (1997).
32. Guha, S., Rastogi, R., Shim, K.: ROCK: A Robust Clustering Algorithm for Categorical Attributes, In: *Information Systems*, vol. 25, n5 (2000) pp.345–366.
33. Zhong, J., Zhu H., Li J., Yu Y.: Conceptual Graph Matching for Semantic Search, In: *Proceedings of the 10th International Conference on Conceptual Structures: Integration and Interfaces*, Spring-Verlag (2002) 92–106.
34. Garner, S.R.: WEKA: The waikato environment for knowledge analysis, In: *Proc. of the New Zealand Computer Science Research Students Conference* (1995) pp.57–64.

Context Dependency Management in Ontology Engineering: A Formal Approach*

Pieter De Leenheer, Aldo de Moor, and Robert Meersman

Semantics Technology and Applications Research Laboratory (STARLab)
Department of Computer Science
Vrije Universiteit Brussel
Pleinlaan 2, B-1050 BRUSSELS 5, Belgium
{pdeleenh,ademoor,meersman}@vub.ac.be

Abstract. A viable ontology engineering methodology requires supporting domain experts in gradually building and managing increasingly complex versions of ontological elements and their converging and diverging interrelationships. Contexts are necessary to formalise and reason about such a dynamic wealth of knowledge. However, context dependencies introduce many complexities. In this article, we introduce a formal framework for supporting context dependency management processes, based on the DOGMA framework and methodology for scalable ontology engineering. Key notions are a set of context dependency operators, which can be combined to manage complex context dependencies like articulation, application, specialisation, and revision dependencies. In turn, these dependencies can be used in context-driven ontology engineering processes tailored to the specific requirements of collaborative communities. This is illustrated by a real-world case of interorganisational competency ontology engineering.

Keywords: context-driven ontology engineering, context dependency management, ontology evolution, ontology management, lexical disambiguation.

1 Introduction

Though a vast amount of research has been conducted on formalising and applying knowledge representation (KR) models (e.g., [1,2,3,4,5]), there is still a major problem with disambiguation of meaning during the *elicitation* and *application* of an ontology. The problem is principally caused by three facts: (i) no matter how expressive ontologies might be, they are all in fact lexical representations of concepts, relationships, and semantic constraints; (ii) linguistically, there is no bijective mapping between a concept and its lexical representation; and (iii) concepts can have different meaning in different contexts of use.

* We would like to thank our colleagues in Brussels, especially Stijn Christiaens and Ruben Verlinden for the valuable discussions about theory and case. We also would like to thank Tom Mens for the valuable discussions about semantic conflict merging. This research has been partially funded by the EU DIP EU-FP6 507483 project and the EU Leonardo da Vinci Project CODRIVE (BE/04/B/F/PP-144.339).

S. Spaccapietra et al. (Eds.): Journal on Data Semantics VIII, LNCS 4380, pp. 26–56, 2007.

In collaborative applications, multiple stakeholders have multiple views on multiple ontologies. There, humans play an important role in the interpretation and negotiation of meaning during the elicitation and application of ontologies [6]. A viable ontology engineering methodology requires supporting domain experts in gradually building and managing increasingly complex versions of ontological elements and their converging and diverging interrelationships. Contexts are necessary to formalise and reason about the structure, interdependencies, and versioning of these ontologies, thus keeping their complexity manageable.

1.1   Context and Ontologies

Today in AI and linguistics, the word *context* has gained a (confusing) variety of meanings, which have led to diverse interpretations and purposes of context [7,8]. Moreover, context is found in various AI application fields such as database integration [9], knowledge translation [10], reasoning [11,12,13], and lexical disambiguation [7,14,15,16]. Furthermore, notions of context were adopted for scalable management of and reasoning on very large bases of formal artefacts using *micro-theories*, in particular for knowledge in Cyc [17,18] and data models [19]. Here, we only review the key notions which we find useful for the purpose of this article. For a comprehensive survey of context in computer science we refer to [20].

On the Semantic Web [21], the primary role of context is to factor the differences, consequently remove ambiguity, between data sources when aggregating data from them. The Semantic Web is large-scaled and highly distributed in nature, hence, instead of adopting complex context mechanisms that introduce nested contexts and the ability to transcend contexts, rather stronger constraints on the computational complexity and ease of use of the context mechanism are placed [22].

Bouquet et al. [23] introduce an extension to the Web ontology language OWL, viz. Context OWL (C-OWL) for representing so-called contextual ontologies. They argue that not all knowledge should be integrated by an ontology, e.g., knowledge that is mutually inconsistent. In that case the ontology is *contextualised*, and for this reason considered a context. This means its contents are kept local, and are put in relation with the content of other contexts via explicit mappings. Introducing context in OWL required a revision to the OWL syntax and semantics. Giunchiglia [11] was especially motivated by the problem of reasoning on a subset of the global knowledge base. The notion of context is used for this "localisation".

More recently is the so-called Pragmatic Web vision [24,25]. This vision claims that it is not necessary (or even possible) to reach for context-independent ontological knowledge, as most ontologies used in practice assume a certain context and perspective of some community. Taking this in consideration, it is natural that ontologies co-evolve with their communities of use, and that human interpretation of context in the use and disambiguation of an ontology often plays an important role. More concretely, the aim is to augment human collaboration effectively by appropriate technologies, such as systems for negotiation during elicitation and application of ontologies for collaborative applications. In this view, the Pragmatic Web complements the Semantic Web by improving the quality and legitimacy of collaborative, goal-oriented discourses in communities.

Based on these viewpoints, we next define our notion of context-driven ontology engineering.

1.2 Context-Driven Ontology Engineering

We define context-driven ontology engineering as a set of ontology engineering (OE) processes for which managing contexts (and their dependencies) effectively and efficiently is crucial for their success. The context of an entity is the set of circumstances surrounding it. Based on our literature study, we distinguish four key characteristics of context: (i) contexts package related knowledge: in that case a context defines part of the knowledge of a particular domain; (ii) context provides pointers for lexical disambiguation; (iii) lifting rules provide an alignment between assertions in disconnected knowledge bases; and (iv) statements about contexts are themselves in contexts; in other words, contexts can be embedded or linked [16]. In the next paragraphs we outline some important types of context-driven OE processes that address these issues. These are *macro-level* processes in that they provide the goals of the ontology engineering process.

Lexical disambiguation. At the start of the *elicitation* of an ontology (cfr. Fig. 1), its basic knowledge elements (such as concepts and relationships) are extracted from various resources such as a text corpus or an existing schema, or formulated by human domain experts. Many ontology approaches focus on the conceptual modelling task, hence the distinction between lexical level (term for a concept) and conceptual level (the concept itself) is often weak or ignored. In order to represent concepts and relationships lexically, they usually are given a uniquely identifying term (or label). However, the context of the resource the ontology element was extracted from is not unimportant, as the meaning of a concept behind a lexical term is influenced by this *elicitation context*. Phenomena such as synonyms and homonym are typical examples of this, and can result in frustrating misunderstanding and ambiguity when unifying information from multiple sources. An analysis of multiple contexts is generally needed to disambiguate successfully [16,26].

Multiple contextualisations. Similarly for the *application* of an ontology: the interpretation of the knowledge elements (which are referred to by terms) of the ontology is ambiguous if the context of application, such as the purpose of the user, is not considered. Different domain experts might want to "contextualise" elements of an ontology differently for the purpose of their organisation, by e.g., selection, specialisation or refinement, leading to multiple diverging ontologies that are context-dependent on (read: contextualisations of) the same (part of an) ontology.

Ontology integration. An important class of OE processes concerns *ontology integration*. This process has been studied extensively in the literature (for a state-of-the-art survey, cf. [27,28]). Although different groups vary in their exact definition, ontology integration is considered to consist of four key processes (adopting the terminology from [28]):

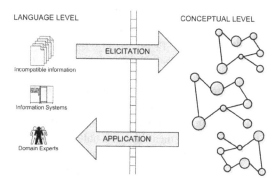

Fig. 1. Ontologies are elicited by extracting knowledge from various sources and are also applied in different contexts

1,2 **mapping and alignment:** given a collection of multiple contextualisations, these often need to be put in context of each other, by means of mapping or aligning (overlapping) knowledge elements pairwise;

3 **schema articulation:** a collection of individual knowledge elements may need to be contextualised, by means of a consensual articulation schema of these (overlapping) elements;

4 **merging:** a collection of individual knowledge elements may need to be contextualised by means of a consensual merging of these (overlapping) elements[1].

Ontology versioning. Parts of an ontology might be revised, expanded, or contracted, resulting in branching of that ontology through time [29,30]. This might possibly trigger a cascade of revisions to all ontologies that are context-dependent on the knowledge elements in the revised part.

1.3 Context Dependency Management

All ontology engineering methodologies use some combination of the above identified context-driven OE macro-processes. However, in their operational implementation of these processes, which we call context-driven OE *micro-processes*, methodologies differ widely. E.g., consider the plethora of Semantic Web and Conceptual Structures research on this matter. Our intention is not to add to these processes themselves, but to identify and *position* them, indicating how they can be used in the bigger picture of real-world ontology engineering processes, such as interorganisational ontology engineering [31]. The question is how to apply and (re)combine them to increase the quality of such processes.

As already mentioned, contexts are important building blocks in our decomposition and linking of ontology engineering processes. *Context dependencies* constrain the

---

[1] An ontology merging process requires an established articulation schema, which is the result of a successful articulation process. However, in this article we do not work out such relations between contextualisations.

possible relations between the entity and its context. Many different types of context dependencies exist, within and between ontological elements of various levels of granularity, ranging from individual concepts of definitions to full ontologies. One of the best studied dependencies are specialisation dependencies [31]. For instance, an organisational definition of a particular task (the entity) can have a specialisation dependency with a task template (its context). The constraint in this case is that each organisational definition must be a specialisation of the template.

In this article, we give an non-exhaustive analysis of context dependency types and meaning conflicts between diverging meanings as a natural consequence of interorganisational ontology engineering. We illustrate these dependencies by formally describing and decomposing the context-driven macro-processes (lexical disambiguation, contextualisation, alignment, and versioning) in terms of a non-exhaustive set of micro-process primitives for selecting, linking, and changing knowledge elements.

When managed consistently, tracing context dependencies by means of micro-process primitives, provides a better understanding of the whereabouts of knowledge elements in ontologies, and consequently makes negotiation and application less vulnerable to ambiguity, hence more practical. Therefore, we outline a context dependency management framework combining these macro-processes and micro-process primitives.

1.4 Towards a Formal Framework

To formalise the context dependency management framework we circumscribed in previous subsection, we adopt and extend the DOGMA[2] ontology engineering approach. This approach has some distinguishing characteristics such as its groundings in the linguistic representations of knowledge, and the explicit separation of conceptualisation and axiomatisation. The DOGMA approach is supported by DOGMA Server, an ontology library system [32], that already features context-driven disambiguation of lexical labels into concept definitions [16]. Provided this basis, it is convenient to extend the DOGMA framework with a layer for managing multiple context dependency types and operators, viz. a context dependency management framework.

For the formalisation of this layer, we reuse existing domain-independent frameworks for managing diverging and converging formal artefacts, and the different types of conflicts between knowledge elements that emerge from this.

As mentioned, we focus on the positioning, not on the implementation of context-driven OE processes. Moreover, we stress the importance of human understanding and interaction during the disambiguation and conflict resolution process. Worthwhile mentioning is that some of the surveyed conflict management techniques tackle this problem rather differently from classical ontology integration techniques. However, if positioned properly, they can contribute to the ontology engineering state-of-the art.

This article is structured as follows: in Sect. 2, we introduce the DOGMA OE framework, along with its extension to support context-driven term disambiguation. Next, in Sect. 3, we formalise a context dependency management framework and suggest possible approaches. Then, in Sect. 4, we illustrate our framework by considering

---

[2] Acronym for Developing Ontology-Grounded Methods and Applications; a research initiative of VUB STARLab.

inter-organisational context dependency management in a real-world case study. Finally we end the article with a discussion in Sect. 5, and a conclusion in Sect. 6.

2 DOGMA Ontology Engineering Framework

DOGMA is an ontology approach and framework that is not restricted to a particular representation language. An important characteristic that makes it different from traditional ontology approaches is that it separates the specification of the *conceptualisation* (i.e. lexical representation of concepts and their inter-relationships) from its *axiomatisation* (i.e. semantic constraints). The goal of this separation, referred to as the *double articulation* principle [33], is to enhance the potential for re-use and design scalability.

This principle corresponds to an orthodox *model-theoretic* approach to ontology representation and development [33]. Consequently, the DOGMA framework consists of two layers: the *Lexon Base* (conceptualisation) and the *Commitment Layer* (axiomatisation).

2.1 Lexon Base

The Lexon Base is an uninterpreted, extensive and reusable pool of elementary building blocks for constructing an ontology. These building blocks (called lexons[3]) are linguistic in nature, and intuitively represent *plausible binary fact-types* (e.g., Person drives/is_driven_by Car). The Lexon Base is stored in an on-line DOGMA server. For guiding the ontology engineer through this very large database, *contexts* impose a meaningful grouping of these *lexons* within the Lexon Base.

The context identifier of a lexon refers to the source it was extracted from. Sources could be terminological[4] or human domain experts. We refer to Gómez-Pérez and Manzano-Macho [35] for a comprehensive survey on text mining methods and tools for creating ontologies. For mining DOGMA lexons in particular, we refer to Reinberger and Spyns [36]. A lexon is defined as:

Definition 1 (lexon). *A lexon is an ordered 5-tuple of the form $\langle \gamma, t_1, r_1, r_2, t_2 \rangle$ where $\gamma \in \Gamma$, $t_1 \in T$, $t_2 \in T$, $r_1 \in R$ and $r_2 \in R$. Γ is a set of identifiers, T and R are sets of strings; t_1 is called the head term of the lexon and t_2 is called the tail term of the lexon; r_1 is the role of the lexon, r_2 is the co-role; γ is the context in which the lexon holds.*

Given a lexon $l = \langle \gamma, t_1, r_1, r_2, t_2 \rangle$, we define accessors as: $\gamma(l) = \gamma$, $t_1(l) = t_1$, $r_1(l) = r_1$, $r_2(l) = r_2$, $t_2(l) = t_2$, and $\forall t_i \in T \cup R : t_i \in l \Leftrightarrow t_i = t_1(l) \vee t_i = r_1(l) \vee t_i = r_2(l) \vee t_i = t_2(l)$.

Role and co-role indicate that a lexon can be read in two directions. A lexon $\langle \gamma, t_1, r_1, r_2, t_2 \rangle$ is a fact type that might hold in a domain, expressing that within the context γ, an object of type t_1 might plausibly play the role r_1 in relation to an object of type t_2. On the other hand, the same lexon states that within the same context γ, an object of type t_2 might play the co-role r_2 in (the same) relation to an object of type t_1.

---

[3] Lexons are DOGMA knowledge elements.

[4] "A context refers to text, information in the text, to the thing the information is about, or the possible uses of the text, the information in it or the thing itself" [34, pp. 178].

Some role/co-role label pairs of lexons in the Lexon Base intuitively express an *onto-logical relationship* (such as taxonomy, meronymy), e.g. $\langle \gamma, manager, is\,a, subsumes, person \rangle$. However, as already mentioned above: the Lexon Base is uninterpreted, so the interpretation of a role/co-role label pair as being a part-of or specialisation rela-tion, is delegated to the Commitment Layer, where the semantic axiomatisation takes place. A lexon could be approximately considered as a combination of an RDF/OWL triple and its inverse. Lexons and commitments are visualised in a NIAM[5]-like schema (cfr. Fig. 2).

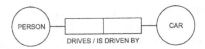

Fig. 2. Illustration of a lexon that is described in a hypothetical context γ

2.2 Commitment Layer

Committing to the Lexon Base in the context of an application means selecting a mean-ingful set Σ of lexons from the Lexon Base that approximates well the intended[6] con-ceptualisation, followed by the addition of a set of constraints, or rules, to this subset. We shall label these semantic constraints. The result (i.e., Σ plus a set of constraints), called an *ontological commitment*, is a logical theory of which the models are first-order interpretations that correspond to the intended meaning of the application (-domain). An ontological commitment constitutes an axiomatisation in terms of a network of lexons logically connected and provides a partial view of the Lexon Base. An important differ-ence with the underlying Lexon Base is that commitments are internally unambiguous and semantically consistent[7]. Once elicited, ontological commitments (i.e. ontologies) are used by various applications such as information integration and mediation of het-erogeneous sources. Though ontologies can differ in structure and semantics, they all are built on a shared Lexon Base.

A commitment is specified in a designated language, called Ω-RIDL [39]. It de-scribes two aspects: (i) semantic constraints in terms of *paths*, covering all classical database constraints (cfr. ORM), and (ii) which role/co-role label pairs are interpreted as which ontological relationship. Consequently, this impacts the semantics of the com-mitment. Commitments are also categorised and stored in a *commitment library* in the DOGMA server. Hence once applied in a commitment, a lexon declares either:

i taxonomical relationship (*genus*): e.g., $\langle \gamma, manager, is\,a, subsumes, person \rangle$;
ii non-taxonomical relationship (*differentia*):
   e.g., $\langle \gamma, manager, directs, directed\,by, company \rangle$.

---

[5] NIAM [37] is the predecessor of ORM [38].

[6] With respect to the application domain.

[7] Although it is outside the scope of this article, we find it valuable to note that in the research community it is debated that consistency is not necessarily a requirement for an ontology to be useful.

Note: a taxonomical relationship is *transitive*. This means that if an arbitrary pair $\langle \gamma, a, is\,a, subsumes, b \rangle, \langle \gamma, b, is\,a, subsumes, c \rangle \in \Sigma$, then we can assert (implicitly) $\langle \gamma, a, is\,a, subsumes, c \rangle \in \Sigma$. Furthermore, if $\langle \gamma, a, is\,a, subsumes, b \rangle, \langle \gamma, b, r_1, r_2, c \rangle \in \Sigma$ (for some arbitrary r_1, r_2), then (implicitly) $\langle \gamma, a, r_1, r_2, c \rangle \in \Sigma$.

A path differs from a lexon because it is directed, but it is trivially constructed from (a concatenation of) lexons. In the following two examples we illustrate two constraints.

Example 1. Suppose we have selected a subset Σ from the Lexon Base in order to conceptualise some domain of interest. Consider following lexons $l_i \in \Sigma$:

$l_1 :=$ ⟨ EUVATDirective, company, publishes, published by, webpage⟩;
$l_2 :=$ ⟨ EUVATDirective, company, is referred by, refers to, name⟩;
$l_3 :=$ ⟨ EUVATDirective, company, is located in, locates, country⟩.

Suppose we want to express that a company might publish *at most one* webpage. This is done by imposing the uniqueness constraint $UNIQ$ on the path p_1=[EUVATDirective, webpage, publishes, published by, company]: $UNIQ(p_1)$.

Example 2. In order to express that a company is identified by the combination of the *name it is referred by,* and the *country it is located in* we state another uniqueness constraint $UNIQ(p_2, p_3)$ in terms of two paths: p_2 =[EUVATDirective, name, refers to, is referred by, company] and p_3 =[EUVATDirective, country, locates, is located in, company]. Another type of constraint we will illustrate is the mandatory constraint $MAND$. Suppose we want to express that a country locates *at least one* company, we state $MAND(p_3)$.

In our next definition of ontology we only consider, as proof of concept, the two constraint types $MAND$ and $UNIQ$ from Ex. 1 and 2, and the taxonomical and meronymical ontological relationships, resp. *isa* and *part_of*. We do this by defining a restricted ontological commitment as follows:

Definition 2 (ontology). *A (isa,partof,UNIQ,MAND)-restricted ontology or ontological commitment, is a tuple $\langle \Sigma, \mathcal{A} \rangle$, where Σ is a strict subset of the Lexon Base, and $\mathcal{A} = \{isa, partof, UNIQ, MAND\}$ is a particular subset or class of constraints or rules. Where $isa, partof \in R \times R$ are role/co-role label pairs that are interpreted as respectively taxonomical and meronymical ontological relationships. Furthermore, each constraint $(UNIQ, MAND)$ is expressed as a collection of sets of paths in Σ.*

Example 3. Reconsider the ontology from Ex. 1 and 2, viz. $O = \langle \Sigma, \mathcal{A} \rangle$ where p_1, p_2, p_3 are paths constructed from lexons $l_1, l_2, l_3 \in \Sigma$. Furthermore, $UNIQ, MAND \in \mathcal{A}$, where $UNIQ = \{\{p_1\}, \{p_2, p_3\}\}$ and $MAND = \{\{p_3\}\}$.

2.3 Contexts

A lexon is a lexical representation of a conceptual relationship between two concepts, however, there is no bijective mapping between a lexical representation and a concept. Consider for example phenomenons such as synonyms and homonyms that can result in frustrating misunderstanding and ambiguity (see Def. 5). As we have seen, the meaning of a lexical term can vary depending on the context it was elicited from.

In DOGMA, a context is used to group lexons that are related[8] to each other in the conceptualisation of a domain. A context in DOGMA has one fundamental property: it is also a mapping function used to disambiguate terms by making them language-neutral. Based on Meersman [15], we can give the following definition for a context:

Definition 3 (context). *A context $\gamma \in \Gamma$ is a mapping $\gamma : T \cup R \rightarrow C$ from the set of terms and roles to the set of concept identifiers C in the domain. In a context, every term or role is intuitively mapped to at most one concept identifier. A context γ is also a reference to one or more documents and/or parts of a document. This reference is defined by the mapping $cd : \Gamma \rightarrow \mathcal{D}$.*

The intuition that a context provides here is: a context is an abstract identifier that refers to implicit and tacit assumptions in a domain, and that maps a term to its intended meaning (i.e. concept identifier) within these assumptions. Notice that a context in our approach is not explicit formal knowledge. In practice, we define a context by referring to a source (e.g., a set of documents, laws and regulations, informal description of best practice, etc.), which, by *human understanding*, is assumed to "contain" the necessary assumptions [40]. The formal account for context is manifested through the interpretation of lexons in commitments, and the context dependencies between them, which we will introduce later in Sect. 3.

A tuple $\langle \gamma, t \rangle$ ideally maps to only one concept identifier. However, during the initial stage of elicitation, when lack of agreement is not often occurs, it could map to a set of concepts that approximately frames the intended one. We elaborate more on this problem in Sect. 2.5.

With a concept we mean the thing itself to which we refer by means of a term (or role) in the Lexon Base. If we want to describe the set of concepts of our domain formally, we can do this, according to Meersman [15], by introducing the partial function $ct : \Gamma \times T \cup R \rightarrow C$ which associates a concept with a tuple consisting of a context and a term (or role). This partial function, which describes a form of *meaning articulation*, is defined as follows:

Definition 4 (meaning articulation). *Given the partial function $ct : \Gamma \times T \cup R \rightarrow C$, then*

$$ct(\gamma, t) = c \Leftrightarrow \gamma(t) = c.$$

An association $ct(\gamma, t) = c$ is called the "meaning articulation" or articulation[9] of a term t (in a particular context γ) into a concept identifier c. ct is called a meaning articulation mapping.

Our definition above includes the most general case where roles are treated like terms, hence we provide the possibility to define meaning articulations for roles as well. In some cases such as task or process ontologies (e.g., the task templates we will consider in Sect.4), it might be useful to clearly disambiguate roles, and even define cross-contextual bridges between roles. However, we must note that in practice it is usually

---

[8] Not necessarily in a logical way but more in an informal way. E.g., lexons are related because they were elicited from the same source, i.e. the elicitation context.

[9] We adopt the term articulation from Mitra et al. ([41]) (see discussion).

less straightforward or even infeasible to disambiguate roles as properly as terms. Example 4 illustrates the latter definition:

Example 4. Consider a term "capital". If this term was elicited from a typewriter manual, it has a different meaning than when elicited from a book on marketing. Therefore, we have resp. two contexts: $\gamma_1 = $ *typewriter manual*, and $\gamma_2 = $ *marketing book*. To express that "capital" is associated with different meanings, we write $ct(\gamma_1, capital) = c_1$, and $ct(\gamma_2, capital) = c_2$.

Until now, the endpoint of the meaning articulation is a meaningless concept identifier $c_1, c_2 \in C$. However, in the next section we will introduce the Concept Definition Server. Each concept identifier itself will point to a particular concept definition. The terms (on the *language level*) that are articulated (using ct) are then mapped to a particular *explication* of a meaning, i.e. a concept definition of a term residing in the Concept Definition Server (on the *conceptual level*), instead of to a meaningless concept identifier. Before we continue, we present some useful terminology about synonyms and homonyms (polysemy), as defined by De Bo and Spyns [42]:

Definition 5 (synonyms and polysemous terms)

- *Two terms $t_1 \in T$ and $t_2 \in T$ are synonyms within a context γ if and only if $(\gamma(t_1) = c \Leftrightarrow \gamma(t_2) = c)$.*
- *A term $t \in T$ is called polysemous if and only if $\exists \gamma_1, \gamma_2 \in \Gamma : \gamma_1(t) \neq \gamma_2(t)$.*

These definitions also hold for roles $r \in R$.

2.4 Concept Definition Server

The idea for a Concept Definition Server (CDS) was first mentioned in [42], and is based on the structure of WordNet [43]. CDS is a database in which one can query with a term, and get a set of different meanings or *concept definitions* (called *senses* in Wordnet) for that term. A concept definition is unambiguously explicated by a gloss (i.e. a natural language (NL) description) and a set of synonymous terms. Consequently we identify each concept definition in the CDS with a concept identifier $c \in C$. The following definition specifies the CDS:

Definition 6 (concept definition server). *We define a Concept Definition Server Υ as a triple $\langle T_\Upsilon, \mathcal{D}_\Upsilon, concept \rangle$ where:*

- *T_Υ is a non-empty finite set of strings (terms) [10];*
- *$\mathcal{D}_\Upsilon$ is a non-empty finite document corpus;*
- *concept : $C \longmapsto \mathcal{D}_\Upsilon \times \wp(T_\Upsilon)$ is an injective mapping between concept identifiers $c \in C$ and concept definitions.*

---

[10] Additionally, we could require $T \cup R \subseteq T_\Upsilon$ (T and R from the Lexon Base). Doing so, we require each term and role in the Lexon Base to be a term in the synset of at least one concept definition.

Further, we define conceptdef(t)

$$= \{concept(c) \mid concept(c) = \langle g, sy \rangle \wedge t \in sy\},$$

where gloss $g \in \mathcal{D}_\mathcal{T}$ and synset $sy \subseteq \mathcal{T}_\mathcal{T}$.

Going from the language level to the conceptual level corresponds to articulating lexons into meta-lexons:

Definition 7 (meta-lexon). *Given a lexon $l := \langle \gamma, t_1, r_1, r_2, t_2 \rangle$, and an instance of an articulation mapping $ct : \Gamma \times T \cup R \rightarrow C$. A meta-lexon $m_{l,ct} := \langle ct(\gamma, t_1), ct(\gamma, r_1), ct(\gamma, r_2), ct(\gamma, t_2) \rangle$ (on the conceptual level) is the result of "articulating" lexon l via ct.*

In Fig. 3 the articulation is illustrated by a *meaning ladder* going from the (lower) language level to the (higher) conceptual level and vice-versa. We refer to Fig. 1, where we introduced the levels and the ladder in the application–elicitation setting.

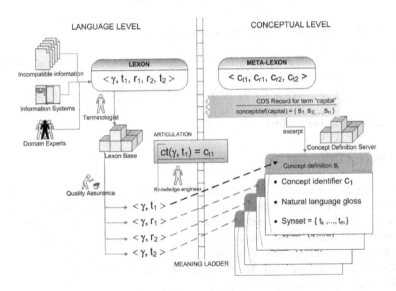

Fig. 3. Illustration of the two levels in DOGMA ontology: on the left – the lexical level, lexons are elicited from various contexts. On the right, there is the conceptual level consisting of a concept definition server. The meaning ladder in between illustrates the articulation of lexical terms into concept definitions.

Given a total articulation mapping ct, applying the articulation to the whole Lexon Base Ω would return a Meta-lexon Base $M_{\Omega,ct} = \{m_{l,ct} \mid l \in \Omega\}$.

Note: One might argue to define commitments in terms of the Meta-lexon Base, and get rid of the Lexon Base. This would translate in redefining paths in terms of meta-lexons. Doing so, however, results in a loss of the language level. The inverse articulation mapping of a meta-lexon could return more than one lexon. On the other hand by defining commitment on the Lexon Base, one can always translate to commitments on the Meta-lexon Base.

We end this section with an illustrative example:

Example 5. As an illustration of the defined concepts, consider Fig. 4. The term "capital" in two different contexts can be articulated to different concept definitions in the CDS. The terms are part of some lexons residing in the Lexon Base. The knowledge engineer first queries the CDS Υ for the various concept definitions of the term: $conceptdef(capital) = S_{capital} \subseteq \mathcal{D}_\Upsilon \times \wp(T_\Upsilon)$. Next, he articulates each term to the concept identifier of the appropriate concept definition:

- Term "capital" was extracted from a typewriter manual, and is articulated to concept identifier c_1 that corresponds to concept definition (or meaning) $s_1 \in S_{capital}$ (as illustrated on the right of Fig. 4). A gloss and set of synonyms (synset) is specified for s_1:

$$concept\big(ct(typewriter\ manual, capital)\big) = s_1.$$

- Term "capital" was extracted from a marketing book, due to the different context it was extracted from, it is articulated to another concept identifier c_2 that is associated with a concept definition $s_2 \in S$:

$$concept\big(ct(marketing\ book, capital)\big) = s_2.$$

On the other hand, suppose we have elicited a term "exercise" from the typewriter manual, and a term "example" from the marketing book. The engineers decide independently to articulate the resp. terms to the same concept definition with concept identifier c_3 with gloss: "a task performed or problem solved in order to develop skill or understanding":

$$c_3 = ct(typewriter\ manual, exercise)$$
$$= ct(marketing\ book, example).$$

This articulation defines a semantic bridge between two terms in two different ontological contexts.

2.5   Articulation and Application of Concepts in Practice

The DOGMA approach above assumes the ideal case where a tuple $\langle \gamma, t \rangle$ maps to exactly one concept identifier (hence concept definition) c. Once, after some iterations, this lexical disambiguation has been achieved, c is further ontologically organised and defined in terms of the binary relationships it has with other concepts, viz. meta-lexons.

The Meta-lexon Base consists of all *plausible* "uses" of a concept. Consequently, an application defines and constrains the genus and differentiae of each concept in its domain, particularly by selecting (read: committing to) a meaningful subset Σ of lexons (hence implicitly meta-lexons) that approximately fits the intended model of its concepts. Finally, a set of rules is added to constrain the possible interpretations, and hence increase the understandability and usability of the ontological commitment.

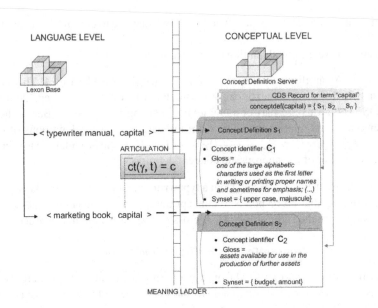

Fig. 4. Illustration of two terms (within their resp. contexts), being articulated (via the mapping *ct*) to their appropriate concept definition

Consequently, the Commitment Layer contains the (possibly empty) collections of all *committed* uses of all concepts.

The use of a concept is defined by, the axiomatised relationships it has with other concepts. Inspired by Putnam's schematic clusters [44, pp. 33–69], we now define a query to retrieve from the Commitment Layer, the collection of all uses, given a concept:

Definition 8 (schematic cluster). *Given a concept $c \in C$, the schematic cluster $\mathcal{SC}_c$ of c w.r.t. to a set of commitments $\mathcal{O}$ is defined as the collection of non-empty lexon sets $\pi(O_i)$ with $O_i = \langle \Sigma_i, \mathcal{A}_i \rangle \in \mathcal{O}$, where $\pi(O_i)$ is defined as $\{l \in \Sigma_i | ct(\gamma(l), t_1(l)) = c \vee ct(\gamma(l), t_2(l)) = c\}$.*

Concept definitions (stored in the CDS) present the essential meaning of a concept, while commitments represent the domain-specific applications of a particular concept. A similar distinction exists between respectively Aristotle and Wittgenstein: Aristotelian "type" definitions are obligatory conditions that state typical properties, while Wittgenstein considers the meaning of a concept to be the set of all its uses [45, pp. 128], the latter is analogue to Putnam's schematic clusters above.

Brachman [46] also believes that a careful distinction must be made between essential and *incidental* properties of a concept. Only essential properties should be defined in the ontology as they are recognized as members of the type in every possible world. From a DOGMA point of view, non-essential properties can always reside in the Metalexon Base, but whether they are committed to, is incidental to the application scenario. If a property is de facto always committed to, it actually becomes essential.

Based on Brachman's ideas, Bachimont [26] claims that organising the domain concepts in a taxonomy is a key component for building ontological commitments. In this process, he emphasizes the importance of a clear *normalisation* (or lexical disambiguation) of the meaning of concepts. Once terms are normalised properly, they can be *formalised* (hence selected and committed to) and *operationalised*. For the normalisation, a differential ontology is built which turns lexical labels into *notions*, based on differential semantics [47]. Practically, this means that notions are orthogonally described in terms of similarities and differences with their parents, children, and siblings. In the resulting taxonomy of notions, the meaning of a node is given by the gathering of all similarities and differences attached to the notions found on the way from the root notion (the more general) to this node.

Summarising, the disambiguation of terms extracted from verbal descriptions is clearly a methodological process of expressing the differences and similarities with other concept definitions using notions of context. In this process it is important to distinguish between necessary and incidental properties. In practice, in a typical ontology elicitation scenario where multiple stakeholders yield tacit and imperfect definitions, ontological definitions will continuously be subject to changing relevance and focus, and the distinction between essential or incidental will evolve as well in some cases, even within the same application domain. Agreeing on one unique concept definition to disambiguate a term, is an incremental process that should result in a right balance where essential properites are comprised in the concept definition, and incidental properties are put rather in commitments depending on the relevance for the respective stakeholders. This enforces our argument to extend our traditional ontology library system, in order to support these kind of OE processes in the management of context dependencies and conflicts between knowledge elements from different ontologies.

3 Context Dependency Management

The management of context dependencies is important for successful disambiguation in OE. Ding and Fensel [32] identify management as one of the three indispensable pillars for an ontology library system. They define management in terms of three features, viz. ontology identification, storage and versioning. We must note that in the collaborative application we envision, we cannot rely on pessimistic versioning control, where all ontologists work on the same library, and parallel contextualisation is prevented by locking. However, if we want ontologists to be able to work completely separately for some time on a personal copy of the ontology (optimistic versioning), we have to deal with the conflicts between parallel contextualisations.

3.1 Formal Framework

We identify the following features in our context dependency management framework:

1. a library of *ontologies*;
2. a sound and complete set of context dependency *operators* on ontologies;
3. a collection of *context dependency types*;
4. a library of *contextualisations*, i.e context dependency relations within between ontologies in the library.

A library of ontologies. The Commitment Layer is a library of ontological commitments. DOGMA Server stores these in a RDBMS, and provides an API for unified access to all structures.

A set of context dependency operators. An additional element of the framework is a sound and complete set of *context dependency operators*. The set should subsume every possible type of ontology access and manipulation (completeness issue), and in particular, the manipulation operators should only generate valid ontologies (soundness issue) [48]. In this article we only give a non-exhaustive set of operators. However, concerning the soundness issue, we make sure these operators are conditional, which means that their applicability depends on pre- and post-conditions.

The resemblance and differences between ontologies and data schema are widely discussed in literature such as [15,33,49]. In the schema and ontology evolution literature, much work focuses on on devising taxonomies of elementary change operators that are sound and complete. Significant examples of data schema evolution include *transformation rules* (in terms of pre- and post-conditions) to effect change operators on data schemas and change propagation to the data [48], frameworks for managing multiple *versions of data schemas* coherently [50,51] and models for different levels of granularity in change operators, viz. *compound change operators* [11] [52]. Furthermore, changes in one facet of an ontology might trigger a cascade of changes in other facets [53]. These triggers could be defined by the semantics of the dependencies.

Main results in ontology evolution include [54,55,29,56], which base their work predominantly in the previous mentioned schema evolution techniques, next to addressing particular needs for evolution of ontologies.

We provide a non-exhaustive list of operators for supporting OE and characterising context dependencies. For now, we ignore axiom operators. We define the pre- and postconditions in terms of the ontology before the operation, denoted by $L = \langle \Sigma_L, \mathcal{A}_L \rangle$, and the ontology after the operation, denoted by $R = \langle \Sigma_R, \mathcal{A}_R \rangle$. Also $isa = \{r_{isa1}, r_{isa2}\} \in \mathcal{A}_{\{L,R\}}$ [12].

1. $artConcept(\langle \gamma, t \rangle, c)$: articulate a term t in a particular context γ into a concept $c \in C$, provided $ct(\gamma, t)$ is not defined.
   $\forall t \in T; \forall \gamma \in \Gamma; \forall c \in C :$
   - $PreCond = \{\langle \gamma, t \rangle \in \Sigma_L; ct(\gamma, t) \, \texttt{undefined}\}$
   - $PostCond = \{\langle \gamma, t \rangle \in \Sigma_R; ct(\gamma, t) = c\}$

2. $defineGenus(\langle \gamma, t \rangle, \langle \gamma, g \rangle)$: set $ct(\gamma, g)$ as genus of a concept $ct(\gamma, t)$.
   $\forall t, g \in T; \forall \gamma \in \Gamma :$
   - $PreCond = \{\langle \gamma, t \rangle \in \Sigma_L, \langle \gamma, g \rangle \in \Sigma_L, \langle \gamma, g, r_{isa1}, r_{isa2}, t \rangle \notin \Sigma_L\}$
   - $PostCond = \{\langle \gamma, t, r_{isa1}, r_{isa2}, g \rangle \in \Sigma_R\}$

3. $defineDiff(\langle \gamma, t \rangle, \bigcup_i d_i)$: add a set of differentiae $\bigcup_i d_i$, where $d_i = \langle \gamma, t, r_1^{d_i}, r_2^{d_i}, t_2^{d_i} \rangle$, to an already defined concept $ct(\gamma, t)$.
   $\forall t, t_2^{d_i} \in T; \forall r_1^{d_i}, r_2^{d_i} \in R; \forall \gamma \in \Gamma :$

---

[11] e.g., moving an attribute x from a class A to a class B, means (more than) successively deleting x in A and adding x in B.

[12] cf. Definition 2.

- $PreCond = \{\langle\gamma,t\rangle \in \Sigma_L; \forall_i \langle\gamma,t_2^{d_i}\rangle \in \Sigma_L; \forall_i d_i \notin \Sigma_L\}$
- $PostCond = \{\langle\gamma,t\rangle \in \Sigma_R; \forall_i \langle\gamma,t_2^{d_i}\rangle \in \Sigma_R; \forall_i d_i \in \Sigma_R\}$

4. $specialiseDiff(\langle\gamma,t\rangle,\langle\gamma,s\rangle,d)$: replace any occurence of $\langle\gamma,t\rangle$ with one of its children $\langle\gamma,s\rangle$ in an existing differentia $d = \langle\gamma,t,r_1,r_2,t_2\rangle$.
   $\forall t,s,t_2 \in T; \forall r_1,r_2 \in R; \forall \gamma \in \Gamma$:
   - $PreCond = \{\langle\gamma,t,r_1,r_2,t_2\rangle,\langle\gamma,s,r_{isa1},r_{isa2},t\rangle \in \Sigma_L; \langle\gamma,s,r_1,r_2,t_2\rangle \notin \Sigma_L\}$
   - $PostCond = \{\langle\gamma,s,r_1,r_2,t_2\rangle,\langle\gamma,s,r_{isa1},r_{isa2},t\rangle \in \Sigma_R; \langle\gamma,t,r_1,r_2,t_2\rangle \notin \Sigma_R\}$

5. $generaliseDiff(\langle\gamma,t\rangle,\langle\gamma,p\rangle,d)$: replace any occurrence of $\langle\gamma,t\rangle$ with a parent $\langle\gamma,p\rangle$ in an existing differentia $d = \langle\gamma,t,r_1,r_2,t_2\rangle$.
   $\forall t,p,t_2 \in T; \forall r_1,r_2 \in R; \forall \gamma \in \Gamma$:
   - $PreCond = \{\langle\gamma,t,r_1,r_2,t_2\rangle,\langle\gamma,t,r_{isa1},r_{isa2},p\rangle \in \Sigma_L; \langle\gamma,p,r_1,r_2,t_2\rangle \notin \Sigma_L\}$
   - $PostCond = \{\langle\gamma,p,r_1,r_2,t_2\rangle,\langle\gamma,t,r_{isa1},r_{isa2},p\rangle \in \Sigma_R; \langle\gamma,t,r_1,r_2,t_2\rangle \notin \Sigma_R\}$

6. $pullUp(\langle\gamma,t\rangle,\langle\gamma,s\rangle)$: pull up an already defined concept (including its children) higher in the taxonomy as a child of $\langle\gamma,s\rangle$.
   $\forall t,t_1,s \in T; \forall \gamma \in \Gamma$:
   - $PreCond = \{\langle\gamma,t,r_{isa1},r_{isa2},t_1\rangle \in \Sigma_L; \langle\gamma,t,r_{isa1},r_{isa2},s\rangle \notin \Sigma_L\}$
   - $PostCond = \{\langle\gamma,t,r_{isa1},r_{isa2},t_1\rangle \notin \Sigma_R; \langle\gamma,t,r_{isa1},r_{isa2},s\rangle \in \Sigma_R\}$

7. $pullDown(\langle\gamma,t\rangle,\langle\gamma,s\rangle)$: pull down an already defined concept (including its children) lower in the taxonomy as a child of $\langle\gamma,s\rangle$.
   $\forall t,t_1,s \in T; \forall \gamma \in \Gamma$:
   - $PreCond = \{\langle\gamma,t,r_{isa1},r_{isa2},t_1\rangle \in \Sigma_L; \langle\gamma,t,r_{isa1},r_{isa2},s\rangle \notin \Sigma_L\}$
   - $PostCond = \{\langle\gamma,t,r_{isa1},r_{isa2},t_1\rangle \notin \Sigma_R; \langle\gamma,t,r_{isa1},r_{isa2},s\rangle \in \Sigma_R\}$

The latter two in fact produce resolution points as there are alternative strategies to resolve the inheritance of differentiae when pulling up or down a concept. As this discussion is outside the scope of this article we take the most straightforward resolution and omit further elaboration on this.

A set of context dependency types. How a new ontology was obtained from the original is determined by a sequence of applied operators. By constraining the possible combinations of operators, we can characterise various types of dependency between the new and the old. We refer to these dependency types by inferring a class of dependency types.

An ontology that is context-dependent on another ontology is called a contextualisation. The contextualisation of ontological definitions might be constrained in different ways. One particular example in the sense of conceptual graph theory [45] would be a specialisation dependency for which the dependency constraint is equivalent to the conditions for CG-specialisation [45, pp. 97]. A specialisation dependency corresponds to a monotone specialisation.

We can identify and express different context dependency types between sub-contexts within one ontology (*intra-ontological*) and between different ontologies (*inter-ontological*): (i) articulation; (ii) application; (iii) specialisation; and (iv) revision. As suggested by discussions, there are many more context dependency types. However, we will only formalise the above four in this article, and characterise them in terms of applicable operators.

Articulation dependency. Usually, lexical labels are used to represent concepts and relations, though there is no bijective mapping between them. Phenomena such as synonyms and homonyms exemplify this, and can result in frustrating misunderstanding and ambiguity when unifying information from multiple sources. The meaning of a concept behind a lexical term is *dependent* on the *context of elicitation*. This ambiguity might be partly resolved by taxonomically categorizing it by setting its genus, however this should be complemented by explicating the *articulation* of a lexical term in a particular context into the intended concept. Hence this dependency type, denoted by ART, is characterised by *artConcept* and *defineGenus*.

Application dependency. Once a term has been articulated into the intended concept and its genus has been set, it is used or applied in multiple ways. Within a particular context of application, a concept is defined in terms of differentiae and axioms, resulting in an ontological definition. An application dependency corresponds to a monotone refinement, consequently this dependency type, denoted by APP, is characterised by *defineDiff*.

Specialisation dependency. The specialisation of ontological definitions is typically constrained to refining differentiae, including specialising concepts. Hence this dependency type, denoted by SPE, is characterised by *specialiseDiff*.

Revision dependency. When considering versioning, evolution steps are stored for later reference, therefore we devise a revision dependency. A revision might be *non-monotone*, i.e. it might correspond to well-formed sequence of expansions and contractions of definitions, or even reclassification in taxonomies. Hence this dependency type's particular characteristics depend on the operators used. Notice that a revision possibly triggers a cascade of revisions to all ontologies that are context-dependent on the knowledge elements in the revised part. This dependency is denoted by REV.

Example 6. As an illustration of defining a context dependency type in terms of constraints on possible operators, the necessary and sufficient condition to assert that O_2 is application-dependent of concept c in O_1, is that O_2 is a monotone refinement of a subset of O_1 in terms of a sequence of exclusively *defineDiff* operations. In that case O_2 is a "concept-application" contextualisation of O_1. We denote this as $O_1 \dashrightarrow_{APP} O_2$.

A library of contextualisations. Context dependency types are instantiated in terms of a source and a target ontology from the library. These instantiations are referred to as contextualisations.

In this subsection, we defined a context dependency framework that is mainly defined by a set of context dependency operators and types. Next, we look at related approaches that might support our framework in the management of these context dependencies, and above all resolution of related meaning conflicts.

3.2 Approaches for Context Dependency Management

In this subsection we suggest some existing approaches for the management of diverging and converging formal artefacts, and the related conflicts, for supporting collaboration. Mens [57] gives an excellent survey of such techniques in the context of software merging. Among these we particularly focus on domain-independent formalisms, so they can be reused for our purposes, viz. the management of context dependencies and emerging conflicts between knowledge elements in ontologies. He considers four types of conflicts that can occur in formal artefacts: textual, syntactic, structural and semantic conflicts.

As mentioned in the introduction, we focus on the positioning, not on the implementation of context-driven OE processes. Moreover, we stress the importance of human interaction during the conflict resolution process. Worthwhile mentioning is that some of the surveyed conflict management techniques provide such facilities for resolving conflicts, which are rather different than classical ontology integration techniques [28]. However, if positioned properly, they can contribute to the ontology engineering state-of-the-art.

Collaborative application frameworks. These frameworks support multiple distributed users working on temporal replicas of a shared artefact, and assistance in the following merging process. Timewarp [58] uses divergent and convergent timelines to support collaboration, and provides facilities for conflict detection resolution comparable to analysis in Ex. 7. The framework is extended with multi-level or inter-leaved timelines, and support for capturing causal relationships in timelines via a nested transaction mechanism. In GINA [59], merging of command histories is achieved by selectively using a redo mechanism to apply one developer's changes to the other's version. The user is assisted by the system when merging diverged replicas. Approaches in this area concentrate especially on the user interface aspects. Therefore, they are in fact complementary to the formal foundations that conceptual graph rewriting provides.

Conditional graph rewriting. Mens [60] defined a domain-independent formalism for detecting and resolving merge conflicts during parallel evolutions of formal artefacts in general, and software in particular. Therefore he adopts principles of graph rewriting (GR) theory [61]. The advantage of GR is that it provides a domain-independent and stable formal foundation for both *descriptive* as *operational* aspects.

In this formalism, we can describe a possibly infinite collection of graphs in a finite way: by stating a set of initial graphs and a set of graph rewriting rules. Through repeated application of these rules, starting from one of the initial graphs, new graphs can be generated. An asset here is that the ontology engineer does not have to explicitly specify this sequence of rules: he only needs to specify how the new ontology should look like. Another advantage of formalising ontology transformations in a conditional GR system is that we can provide a precise and unambiguous definition of context dependency notions, and make it visually attractive.

Next to the descriptive aspect, the graph rewriting rules simplify the composition of context dependency operators, hence its semantics. Furthermore GR, reduces the complexity of the manipulation and analysis during the OE processes we identified above.

E.g., it provides theoretical insights into the parallel and sequential independence of ontology transformations, the latter which are described in terms of sequences of operators. This means, translated to context-driven OE, support for the detection of possible meaning conflicts between multiple parallel contextualisations of the same original ontology (see Ex. 7).

Example 7. Consider an ontology O, which is contextualised by two ontologists concurrently. The first ontologist adds a differentia to an already existing concept $\langle \gamma, t \rangle$ using $defineDiff(\langle \gamma, t \rangle, \langle \gamma, t, r_1, r_2, t_2 \rangle)$. The second ontologist concurrently defines a genus for $\langle \gamma, t \rangle$, viz. $\langle \gamma, g \rangle$, using $defineGenus(\langle \gamma, t \rangle, \langle \gamma, g \rangle)$. Now consider $\langle \gamma, g, r_1, r_2, t_2 \rangle \in \Sigma_O$. For both operations the pre-conditions w.r.t. to the O are satisfied. However, when merging both contextualisations a conflict would have merged as each operation introduces an element that is forbidden to exist in the pre-condition of the other.

The caveat for reusing Mens' formalism is the definition of a typegraph, a labelled typed (nested) graph representation of the meta-schema for the kind of formal artefact that is to be manipulated. The fact-oriented character of DOGMA ontologies and meta-schema, makes GR particularly suitable for our purposes.

4   Inter-organisational Context Dependency Management

In this section we illustrate context-driven ontology elicitation in a realistic case study of the European CODRIVE[13] project.

4.1   Competencies and Employment

Competencies describe the skills and knowledge individuals should have in order to be fit for particular jobs. Especially in the domain of vocational education, having a central shared and commonly used competency model is becoming crucial in order to achieve the necessary level of interoperability and exchange of information, and in order to integrate and align the existing information systems of competency stakeholders like schools or public employment agencies. None of these organisations however, have successfully implemented a company-wide "competency initiative", let alone a strategy for inter-organisational exchange of competency related information.

The CODRIVE project aims at contributing to a competency-driven vocational education by using state-of-the-art ontology methodology and infrastructure in order to develop a conceptual, shared and formal KR of competence domains. Domain partners include educational institutes and public employment organisations from various European countries. The resulting shared "Vocational Competency Ontology" will be used by all partners to build interoperable competency models.

The example concerns collaborative OE between two participating stakeholders EI and PE, each containing organisations being resp. *educational institute* and *public employment agency*. Core shared and individual organisational ontologies have already

---

[13] CODRIVE is an EU Leonardo da Vinci Project (BE/04/B/F/PP-144.339).

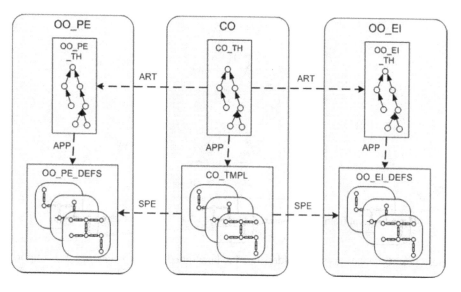

Fig. 5. The scenario illustrates a snapshot of contexts and context dependencies emerging from different OE processes by multiple stakeholders in inter-organisational ontology engineering: (i) term articulation (ART); (ii) template creation (APP); and (iii) template specialisation (SPE)

been defined for both EI and PE. Fig. 5 illustrates the initial versions, say $V0$, of the different contexts[14]:

– CO is the common ontology, containing two sub-contexts, viz. CO_TMPL and CO_TH. The latter is CO's type hierarchy (detailed in Fig. 6). It has among its concepts $Task$, with as subtypes $Educational\,Task$ and $Job\,Task$. The concepts are in fact terms, but within the context CO they refer to at most one concept definition. CO_TMPL is a set of templates that define applications of concepts in CO_TH in terms of differentiae, consequently CO_TMPL is application-dependent on CO_TH.
– OO_EI and OO_PE are the individual organisational ontologies for resp. educational institutes and public employment agencies. Organisational ontologies also contain two sub-contexts: e.g., OO_EI_TH is EI's type hierarchy whose concepts are articulation-dependent on CO_TH. OO_EI_DEFS contains EI's ontological definitions refining the templates in CO_TMPL, hence OO_EI_DEFS is application-dependent on CO_TMPL.

The different contextualisations above, illustrate the *grounding* of the individual organisational definitions in the common ontology CO.

In the following subsections we consider a scenario where we show that in order to effectively and efficiently define shared relevant ontological meanings, context dependencies are indispensable. In building the shared ontology, the individual organisational

---

[14] In this case study, each context corresponds to exactly one ontology and vice-versa. However, an ontology engineer might select lexons from various contexts for modelling his ontology.

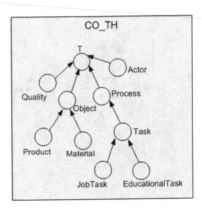

Fig. 6. Excerpt from a sub-context CO_TH in CO. $\top$ denotes the root concept.

ontologies of the various stakeholders need to be aligned *insofar necessary*. It is important to realise that costly alignment efforts only should be made when necessary for the shared collaboration purpose.

The scenario illustrates the following processes by different stakeholders, necessary in inter-organisational ontology engineering: (i) term disambiguation in OO_EI and OO_PE; (ii) template creation in CO; (iii) template specialisation OO_EI; and finally (iv) template revision, triggering a cascade of revisions to context-dependent subcontexts. These processes are triggered by business rules tailored to the specific requirements of a collaborative community. Even with a few simple operators, already many context dependencies are introduced.

4.2   Term Disambiguation in OO_EI

EI is a national bakery institute, responsible for defining curriculum standards for bakery courses. As such, much of its organisational terminology should be grounded in the common ontology CO. It now wants to add a new term "panning" to its OO_EI ontology. It defines this informally as the act of "depositing moulded dough pieces into baking pans with their seam facing down".

First the ontology maintainer defines the term's genus ($defineGenus$) and articulation ($artConcept$) in a sub-context OO_EI_TH of OO_EI. OO_EI_TH is supposed to be articulation-dependent on CO_TH, so EI is allowed to define and articulate the new term in its ontology. However, in this EI case, the precondition is that the genus is predefined in CO_TH (Fig. 6). This is inferred from the production $defineGenus$ defined in Sect. 3 strengthened by the following business rule[15]:

R1: The CODRIVE ontology server (COS) asks EI to classify the shared concept to which the term belongs.

Hence, The EI representative classifies $Panning$ as an $Educational Task$ in taxonomy OO_EI_TH.

---

[15] The concepts underlined in the rules below are modelled but not shown.

Next, EI decides to articulate $Panning$ as follows:

$$concept\big(ct(OO\_EI\_TH, panning)\big) = \langle g, sy \rangle$$

where gloss g corresponds to "depositing moulded dough pieces into baking pans with their seam facing down". The synset sy is ignored here. The above operations are applications of resp. $defineGenus$ and $artConcept$ which results in following articulation-contextualisation:

$$CO\_TH \dashrightarrow_{ART} OO\_EI\_TH.$$

4.3 Template Creation in CO

One of the business rules in the CoDrive ontology server demands:

R2: IF a <u>New Task</u> is an <u>Educational Task</u>, and the <u>Individual Ontology Owner</u> is an <u>Educational Institute</u> THEN a <u>Full Semantic Analysis</u> of the <u>New Task</u> needs to be added to the <u>Individual Ontology</u> of the <u>Individual Ontology Owner</u>;

another meta-rule fires as an immediate consequence:

R3: IF a <u>Full Semantic Analysis</u> needs to be made of a <u>Concept</u> in an <u>Individual Ontology</u> or <u>Shared Ontology</u> THEN the <u>Concept Template</u> needs to be filled out in that <u>Ontology</u>. Furthermore, for each <u>Term</u> and <u>Role</u> of these definitions, a <u>Meaning Articulation</u> needs to be defined.

The template was created in a separate process by the common ontology maintainer. Creating a template corresponds to applying a sequence of $defineDiff$ operations in order to define differentiae of a given concept. This results in an application dependency (APP arrows in Fig. 5):

$$CO\_TH \dashrightarrow_{APP} CO\_TMPL. \tag{1}$$

Hence, it resides in a sub-context of CO, viz. CO_TMPL. The template is shown in Fig. 7. In this case the template states it is necessary to know who is the performer of the task (e.g. $Student$), what inputs and materials are necessary for the task (e.g. $Baking\_Pan, Dough$), what is the result of the task ($Greased\,Pan$), and so on.

4.4 Template Specialisation in OO_EI

A template is an ontological definition that needs to be specialised using the specialisation dependency (SPE arrows in Fig. 5).

In OO_EI_DEFS (a sub-context of OO_EI), the new task $Panning$ is specialised, which boils down to specialising (and in a way disambiguating) the differentiae in the template (illustrated by Fig. 7). Each new term or role to be used in the specialisation must first be defined and articulated in OO_EI_TH. Similar to before, this produces new operations that extend our articulation contextualisation:

$$CO\_TH \dashrightarrow_{ART} OO\_EI\_TH. \tag{2}$$

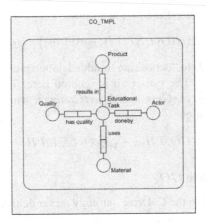

Fig. 7. Template for *Educational Task*, defined in CO_TMPL, sub-context of CO

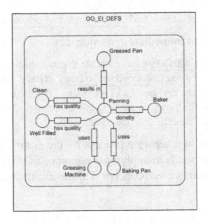

Fig. 8. A specialisation-contextualisation $CO\_TMPL \dashrightarrow_{SPE} OO\_EI\_DEFS$

The specialisation of the template is done by iteratively applying the *specialise Diff* production which results in following specialisation-contextualisation:

$$CO\_TMPL \dashrightarrow_{SPE} OO\_EI\_DEFS. \qquad (3)$$

4.5 Term Disambiguation in OO_PE

Concurrently with **R3**, following business rule is triggered:

R4: IF an <u>Educational Task</u> is added to an <u>Individual Ontology</u> THEN a corresponding <u>Job Task</u> needs to be defined in all instances of <u>Individual Ontology</u> of all <u>Public Employment Agencies</u>

The rationale for this rule is that public employment agencies need to be aware of changes to the curricula of educational institutes, so that they are better able to match job seekers with industry demands. However, unlike the definitions of educational tasks, the job task definitions in public employment agency ontologies only require a short informal description of the concept itself, not an extended template definition:

R5: IF a `JobTask` is added to an `IndividualOntology` THEN a `Gloss` needs to be defined for that `Concept`.

Of course, public employment agencies also could have the need for template definitions, but those would refer to the job matching processes in which the tasks play a role (*why* is panning needed), not to *how* the tasks themselves are to be performed.

Hence, **R4** requires the PE representative to classify *Panning* as an *JobTask* in OO_PE_TH.

Next, he decides to articulate *Panning* as follows:

$$concept\big(ct(OO\_PE\_TH, panning)\big) = \langle g, sy \rangle$$

where gloss g corresponds to "an essential skill in baking". The synset sy is ignored here.

Again, the above operations are applications of resp. $defineGenus$ and $artConcept$ which results in following articulation-contextualisation:

$$CO\_TH \dashrightarrow_{ART} OO\_PE\_TH.$$

4.6   Template Revision in CO_TMPL

Figure 5 shows the version 0 snapshot of a library of ontologies and their context dependencies, the latter denoted by arrows in different directions. When considering the revision dependency type, we must introduce a timeline that is orthogonal to all arrows so far. A revision to a knowledge element in some ontology should result in a new version of that ontology. As a consequence, a cascade of revision requests is triggered to all ontologies that are context-dependent on the revised element. This in order to keep the context dependencies intact, and hence anticipate on conflicts. In the following example, we will show that, as an additional problem, in most cases there are multiple alternative ways to resolve the conflict. Our framework identifies conflicts, hence ambiguity, and delegates these decision options to the human ontologist.

Suppose that the template we created (cf. Fig. 7) is expanded with a new differentia. First a new concept *Lecture Room* is defined and then articulated in CO_TH:

$$defineGenus(\langle CO, LectureRoom \rangle, \langle CO, Object \rangle)$$

$$artConcept(\langle CO, LectureRoom \rangle, c)$$

for some $c \in C$. This results in the following revision-contextualisation:

$$CO\_TH \dashrightarrow_{REV} CO\_TH\_V1.$$

Note the version-id that is appended, which brings CO_TH_V1 to a time snapshot different from all other ontologies so far. Next, we define a new differentia in CO_TMPL using the new concept in CO_TH_V1:

$$defineDiff(\langle CO, EducationalTask \rangle,$$
$$\langle CO, EducationalTask, has, of, Lecture\ Room \rangle).$$

This results in another revision-contextualisation:

$$CO\_TMPL \dashrightarrow_{REV} CO\_TMPL\_V1,$$

constrained by following application dependency:

$$CO\_TH\_V1 \dashrightarrow_{APP} CO\_TMPL\_V1.$$

This application dependency itself can be considered as an extension of the previously created dependency in (1).

The latter revision, forces us to evolve all ontologies that are context-dependent on CO_TMPL. As an illustration, take the specialisation-contextualisation

$$CO\_TMPL \dashrightarrow_{SPE} OO\_EI\_DEFS$$

in Fig. 8. Because the template has been expanded, this template-specialisation has now become underspecified: first, it tells nothing about some *Lecture Room* room in which *Panning* is being instructed; and secondly, it doesn't specify in which particular type of *Lecture Room* that *Panning* is being instructed.

Hence, rule **R3** is triggered again. This rule required that templates should be fully specified. The process that follows is analogue to the template specialisation that we described earlier, so we skip the details. In short, in order to specialise the newly intro-duced differentia in the template, *LectureRoom* is specialised by introducing a new subconcept *PreparationRoom* in OO_EI_TH. This results in following revision-contextualisations:

$$OO\_EI\_TH \dashrightarrow_{REV} OO\_EI\_TH\_V1,$$

$$OO\_EI\_DEFS \dashrightarrow_{REV} OO\_EI\_DEFS\_V1,$$

again constrained by following articulation and specialisation dependencies respectively:

$$CO\_TH\_V1 \dashrightarrow_{ART} OO\_EI\_TH\_V1,$$

$$CO\_TMPL\_V1 \dashrightarrow_{SPE} OO\_EI\_DEFS\_V1,$$

being extensions of previously created dependencies in (2) and (3) respectively.

5   Discussion

The previous scenario, although using only a few simple operators, already demon-strated the complex dependencies emerging in a typical case of context-driven ontology engineering. When introducing additional context dependency operators, complexity only grows. Furthermore, we have only considered relatively straightforward expansion operators. Contraction even makes context dependency management more difficult. Es-pecially then there is special need for conflict pair analysis (cf. Ex. 7), which we did not touch upon in the scenario.

Some further observations:

1. Context-driven ontology elicitation and disambiguation avoids wasting valuable modelling time and enormous cost. This is illustrated by the density of lexon elicitation in the EI_DEFS ontology compared to the sparsely populated PE_DEFS for term "panning". The density reflects the minimal level of modelling details needed. For other terms this might be vice-versa.
2. Context dependencies can be defined between sub-contexts within one ontology and between different ontologies. Their types are characterised by applicable operators. This is illustrated by the arrows between the various nested boxes.
3. The context dependency arrows define a lattice. Management and access is facilitated by properly navigating through its branches. This suggests the need for an appropriate query language.
4. Some contextualisations require the pre-existence of other types of contextualisation. Reconsider the specialisation of CO_TMPL which required a number of applications of articulations first.

It is clear that proper management of these dependency complexities is essential for context-driven ontology engineering to be successful. In this article, we have presented the foundation of an extensible context dependency management framework. It currently contains a number of important context dependency types and operators. In future research, we will produce a more detailed typology.

Next some more reflections on related work and future research.

5.1 Lexical Disambiguation

Shamsfard et al. [62] provide a comprehensive survey of methods and tools for (semi) automatic ontology elicitation. However, in this article our focus is not on automation. Work which is strongly related with what we need is e.g., Mitra et al. [41], who indirectly adopt some of those features we concluded with in our synthesis earlier. They illustrate a semi-automatic tool for creating a mapping between two ontologies (in fact contexts). Their motivation is that two different terms can have the same meaning and the same term can have different meanings, which exactly defines the lexical disambiguation problem. This mapping is manifested by an *articulation ontology*, which is automatically generated from a set of *articulation rules* (i.e. semantic relationships) between concepts in each context resp. Finally, we refer to the MikroKosmos project [63], which is concentrated in the domain of ontology-based disambiguation for natural-language processing in a multi-cultural context.

In our framework, the CDS provides a basic means for relevant alignment of heterogeneous ontologies. The concept definitions (gloss, synset) in the CDS support the meaning articulation of language level terms. As was illustrated in Ex. 5, the articulation of terms from different contexts to a shared CDS, results in cross-context equivalence relations, i.e. synonyms.

The meta-rules we made in step 3 and 5, were not formalised explicitly in this article. However, we could devise a syntax, e.g.:

$$ct(EI, panning) \preceq ct(SHARED, educational\,task)$$
$$ct(PE, panning) \preceq ct(SHARED, job\,task)$$

The rules above extend the cross-context equivalence: they allow us to specify an alignment between a term in one context to a possibly more general term in another context. In the future we will extend this feature and provide a formal semantics of meta-rules. This can be very powerful in context-driven ontology elicitation and application such as meta-reasoning on context and ontology alignment processes, and meaning negotiation processes between stakeholders. Currently we are exploring reasoning for commitment analysis and conceptual graph tools for ontology elicitation and analysis.

Initially, the lexon base and CDS are empty, but the CDS can be easily populated by importing similar information from publically available electronic lexical databases, such as WordNet [43] or Cyc [64]. The Lexon Base is populated during the first step of an ontology elicitation process by various (not necessarily human) agents. See Reinberger & Spyns [36] for unsupervised text mining of lexons. The second step in the elicitation process is to articulate the terms in the "learned" lexons.

5.2   Context Dependency Management

For supporting context-driven OE, we consider two points of view to manage (storage, identification, versioning [32]) the disambiguation of meaning – ontologies in particular – in our framework:

1. The context-dependency-driven way is to store only the initial ontologies and the restricted derivation sequences. Access to the contextualisations is done by navigating through the lattice composed by the context dependencies. Once arrived, the contextualisation is generated automatically by completing the pushout of the derivation sequence, the latter being gradually built from the path followed in the lattics.
2. The meta-data-driven way would be to store all the ontologies, but none of the context dependencies between them. Access to these contextualisations is by identifying them with domain-specific meta-data tags (cf. Cyc [65]). This might include authorship and space-time allocation. Other dimensions are correlations with other contexts, in our case, context dependencies. We have to investigate whether it is possible, given any pair of ontologies, to induce this information.

The context dependency types and operators we introduced in this article are not exhaustive. Currently, we have only defined expanding and specialising operators, which did not turn out to be very conflictive. However, to support complete revision capability, we must add contracting and more generalising operators of which we could expect following troublesome scenarios:

- Revisions will trigger cascades of revisions to existing context dependencies, usually implying alternative resolutions in which the human has to make choices.
- A revision resulting from a sequence of concept generalisations and specialisations could force the concept to be unnaturally reclassified in a different branch in the taxonomy.
- Introducing operators for axioms, implying new "axiomatisation" dependency types, could return unexpected behaviour. In this article we did not consider the semantic constraints completely. The only visible constraint is the interpretation of ontological relationships. We aim to extend our framework with typical ORM [38]

constraints such as uniqueness, mandatory, and exclusion. We can expect conflicts between axiom restriction and relaxation operators.

Existing work might help is in the future extension to a broader set of context dependencies and operators. E.g., in [66], algorithms are described for detecting unsatisfiability of ORM schema. There, conflict patterns provide insights for the specification of application conditions for productions on axioms. Furthermore, by founding our framework in terms of graph rewriting (Sect. 3.2), we aim to extend the use of conflict pair analysis we introduced in Ex. 7. Successful application of this exist in software evolution [60] and collaborative applications [59,58], but could have a whole new application domain in context-driven ontology engineering.

6   Conclusion

Contexts play a very important role in real-world, gradual ontology elicitation and application efforts. In context-driven ontology engineering processes, such as ontology disambiguation, integration, and versioning, managing contexts effectively and efficiently is crucial for their success. However, contexts and especially their dependencies are still little understood.

In this article, we introduced a formal framework for supporting context dependency management processes, based on the DOGMA framework and methodology for scalable ontology engineering. Key notions are a set of context dependency operators, that can be combined to manage complex context dependencies like articulation, application, specialisation, and revision dependencies. In turn, these dependencies can be used in context-driven ontology engineering processes tailored to the specific requirements of collaborative communities. This was illustrated by a case of interorganisational competency ontology engineering.

With the foundation of the framework firmly established, research can shift to developing more extensive descriptions of context dependency operators and types, and their systematic integration in community workflows through business rules. By including these context modules in the existing DOGMA methodologies and tools in the near future, experiments can be done to see which combinations of dependency management processes are required in practice. It is our conviction that this will demonstrate the true power of systematic context dependency management. Instead of being frustrated by out-of-control change processes, proper context dependency management support will allow human experts to focus on the much more interesting meaning interpretation and negotiation processes. This, in turn should make ontologies much more useful in practice.

References

1. Gruber, T.: Cyc: a translation approach to portable ontologies. Knowledge Acquisition **5(2)** (1993) 199–220
2. Guarino, N.: Formal ontology and information systems. In: Proc. of the 1st Int'l Conf. on Formal Ontologies in Information Systems (FOIS98) (Trento, Italy), IOS Press (1998) 3–15

3. Meersman, R.: The use of lexicons and other computer-linguistic tools in semantics, design and cooperation of database systems. In: Proc.of the Conf. on Cooperative Database Systems (CODAS99), Springer Verlag (1999) 1–14

4. Ushold, M., Gruninger, M.: Ontologies: Principles, methods and applications. The Knowledge Engineering Review **11(2)** (1996) 93–136

5. Farquhar, A., Fikes, R., Rice, J.: The ontolingua server: a tool for collaborative ontology construction. Int'l Journal of Human-computer Studies **46(6)** (1997) 707–727

6. de Moor, A.: Ontology-guided meaning negotiation in communities of practice. In Mambrey, P., Gräther, W., eds.: Proc. of the Workshop on the Design for Large-Scale Digital Communities at the 2nd International Conference on Communities and Technologies (C&T 2005) (Milano, Italy). (2005)

7. McCarthy, J.: Notes on formalizing context. In: Proc. of the 15th Int-l Joint Conf. Artificial Intelligence (IJCAI93) (Chambéry, France), Morgan Kaufmann (1993) 555–560

8. Sowa, J.: Peircean foundations for a theory of context. In: Conceptual Structures: Fulfilling Peirce's Dream, Springer-Verlag (1997) 41–64

9. Farquhar, A., Dappert, A., Fikes, R., Pratt, W.: Integrating information sources using context logic. In Knoblock, C., Levy, A., eds.: Information Gathering from Heterogeneous, Distributed Environments, Stanford University, Stanford, California (1995)

10. Buvač, S., Fikes, R.: A declarative formalization of knowledge translation. In: Proc. of 4th Int'l Conf. on Information and Knowledge Management (ACM CIKM 95). (1995)

11. Giunchiglia, F.: Contextual reasoning. special issue on I Linguaggi e le Macchine **XVI** (1993) 345–364

12. Nayak, P.: Representing multiple theories. In: Proc. of the 12th Nat'l Conf. on Artificial Intelligence (AAAI 94)(Seattle, Washington), AAAI Press (1994)

13. McCarthy, J., Buvač, S.: Formalizing context (expanded notes). Technical Report STAN-CS-TN-94-13, Stanford University (1994)

14. Buvač, S.: Resolving lexical ambiguity using a formal theory of context. In Van Deemter, K., Peters, S., eds.: Semantic Ambiguity and Underspecification, CSLI Publications (1996)

15. Meersman, R.: Reusing certain database design principles, methods and techniques for ontology theory, construction and methodology. Technical report, VUB STAR Lab, Brussel (2001)

16. De Leenheer, P., de Moor, A.: Context-driven disambiguation in ontology elicitation. In Shvaiko, P., Euzenat, J., eds.: Context and Ontologies: Theory, Practice, and Applications. Proc. of the 1st Context and Ontologies Workshop, AAAI/IAAI 2005, Pittsburgh, USA, July 9, 2005. (2005) 17–24

17. Guha, R., D., L.: Cyc: a midterm report. AI Magazine **11(3)** (1990) 32–59

18. Guha, R.: Contexts: a formalization and some applications. Technical Report STAN-CS-91-1399, Stanford Computer Science Department, Stanford, California (1991)

19. Theodorakis, M.: Contextualization: an Abstraction Mechanism for Information Modeling. PhD thesis, University of Crete, Greece (1999)

20. Guha, R., McCarthy, J.: Varieties of contexts. In: CONTEXT 2003. (2003) 164–177

21. Berners-Lee, T.: Weaving the Web. Harper (1999)

22. Guha, R., McCool, R., Fikes, R.: Contexts for the semantic web. In McIlraith, S.A., Plexousakis, D., van Harmelen, F., eds.: Proceedings of the International Semantic Web Conference. Volume 3298 of Lecture Notes in Computer Science., Springer Verlag (2004)

23. Bouquet, P., Giunchiglia, F., van Harmelen, F., Serafini, L., Stuckenschmidt, H.: C-owl: Contextualizing ontologies. In: Proc. of the 2nd Int'l Semantic Web Conference (ISWC 2003) (Sanibel Island, Florida)", LNCS 2870, Springer Verlag (2003) 164–179

24. Singh, M.: The pragmatic web: Preliminary thoughts. In: Proc. of the NSF-OntoWeb Workshop on Database and Information Systems Research for Semantic Web and Enterprises. (2002) 82–90

25. Schoop, M., de Moor, A., Dietz, J.: The pragmatic web: A manifesto. Communications of the ACM 49(5) (2006)
26. Bachimont, B., Troncy, R., Isaac, A.: Semantic commitment for designing ontologies: a proposal. In Gómez-Pérez, A., Richard Benjamins, V., eds.: Proc. of the 13th Int'l Conf. on Knowledge Engineering and Knowledge Management. Ontologies and the Semantic Web (EKAW 2002) (Siguenza, Spain), Springer Verlag (2002) 114–121
27. Euzenat, J., Le Bach, T., Barrasa, J., et al.: State of the art on ontology alignment. Knowledge web deliverable KWEB/2004/d2.2.3/v1.2 (2004)
28. Kalfoglou, Y., Schorlemmer, M.: Ontology mapping: The state of the art. In: Proc. of the Dagstuhl Seminar on Semantic Interoperability and Integration (Dagstuhl, Germany). (2005)
29. Klein, M., Fensel, D., Kiryakov, A., Ognyanov, D.: Ontology versioning and change detection on the web. In: Proc. of the 13th European Conf. on Knowledge Engineering and Knowledge Management (EKAW02) (Siguenza, Spain). (2002) 197–212
30. De Leenheer, P., Kopecky, J., Sharf, E., de Moor, A.: A versioning tool for ontologies (2006) EU IP DIP (FP6-507483) Deliverable D2.4.
31. de Moor, A., De Leenheer, P., Meersman, R.: DOGMA-MESS: A meaning evolution support system for interorganizational ontology engineering. In: In Proc. of the 14th Int'l Conference on Conceptual Structures (ICCS 2006) (Aalborg, Denmark). LNAI 4068, Springer Verlag (2006) 189–203
32. Ding, Y., Fensel, D.: Ontology library systems: the key to succesful ontology re-use. In: Proc. of the 1st Semantic Web Symposium (SWWS01) (Stanford, California). (2001)
33. Spyns, P., Meersman, R., Jarrar, M.: Data modelling versus ontology engineering. SIGMOD Record 31(4) (2002) 12–17
34. Sowa, J.: Knowledge Representation - Logical, Philosophical and Computational Foundations. Brooks/Cole Publishing Co. (2000)
35. Gómez-Pérez, A., Manzano-Macho, D.: A survey of ontology learning methods and techniques. OntoWeb Deliverable D1.5 (2003)
36. Reinberger, M.L., Spyns, P.: Unsupervised text mining for the learning of DOGMA-inspired ontologies. In: Buitelaar P., Handschuh S., and Magnini B.,(eds.), Ontology Learning and Population, IOS Press (2005) in press
37. Verheijen, G., Van Bekkum, J.: NIAM, an information analysis method. In: Proc. of the IFIP TC-8 Conference on Comparative Review of Information System Methodologies (CRIS 82), North-Holland (1982)
38. Halpin, T.: Information Modeling and Relational Databases (From Conceptual Analysis to Logical Design). Morgan Kauffman (2001)
39. Verheyden, P., De Bo, J., Meersman, R.: Semantically unlocking database content through ontology-based mediation. In: Proc. of the 2nd Workshop on Semantic Web and Databases, VLDB Workshops (SWDB 2004) (Toronto, Canada), Springer-Verlag (2004) 109–126
40. Jarrar, M., Demey, J., Meersman, R.: On reusing conceptual data modeling for ontology engineering. Journal on Data Semantics 1(1) (2003) 185–207
41. Mitra, P., Wiederhold, G., Kersten, M.: A graph-oriented model for articulation of ontology interdependencies. In: EDBT '00: Proceedings of the 7th International Conference on Extending Database Technology, London, UK, Springer-Verlag (2000) 86–100
42. De Bo, J., Spyns, P., Meersman, R.: Assisting ontology integration with existing thesauri. In: Proc. of On the Move to Meaningful Internet Systems (OTM2004) (Ayia Napa, Cyprus), Springer Verlag (2004) 801–818
43. Fellbaum, C., ed.: Wordnet, an Electronic Lexical Database. MIT Press (1998)
44. Putnam, H.: Mind, Language, and Reality. Cambridge University Press, Cambridge (1962)
45. Sowa, J.: Conceptual Structures: Information Processing in Mind and Machine. Addison-Wesley (1984)

46. Brachman, R., McGuiness, D., Patel-Schneider, P., Resnik, L., Borgida, A.: Living with classic: When and how to use a KL-ONE-like language. In Sowa, J., ed.: Principles of Semantic Networks, Morgan Kaufmann (1991) 401–456

47. Rastier, F., Cavazza, M., Abeillé, A.: Sémantique pour L'analyse. Masson, Paris (1994)

48. Banerjee, J., Kim, W.: Semantics and implementation of schema evolution in object-oriented databases. In: ACM SIGMOD Conf., SIGMOD Record. (1987) 311–322

49. Noy, N., Klein, M.: Ontology evolution: Not the same as schema evolution. Knowledge and Information Systems **6**(4) (2004) 428–440

50. Kim, W., Chou, H.: Versions of schema for object-oriented databases. In: Proc. of the 14th Int'l Conf. on Very Large Data Bases (VLDB88) (L.A., CA.), Morgan Kaufmann (1988) 148–159

51. Roddick, J.: A survey of schema versioning issues for database systems. Information and Software Technology **37**(7) (1995) 383–393

52. Lerner, B.: A model for compound type changes encountered in schema evolution. ACM Transactions on Database Systems (TODS) **25**(1) (2000) 83–127

53. De Leenheer, P.: Revising and managing multiple ontology versions in a possible worlds setting. In: Proc. of On the Move to Meaningful Internet Systems Workshops (OTM2004) (Ayia Napa, Cyprus), LNCS 3292, Springer Verlag (2004) 798–818

54. Oliver, D., Shahar, Y., Musen, M., Shortliffe, E.: Representation of change in controlled medical terminologies. AI in Medicine **15**(1) (1999) 53–76

55. Heflin, J.: Towards the Semantic Web: Knowledge Representation in a Dynamic, Distributed Environment. PhD thesis, University of Maryland, Collega Park, MD, USA (2001)

56. Stojanovic, L., Maedche, A., Motik, B., Stojanovic, N.: User-driven ontology evolution management. In: Proc. of the 13th European Conf. on Knowledge Engineering and Knowledge Management (EKAW02) (Siguenza, Spain). (2002) 285–300

57. Mens, T.: A state-of-the-art survey on software merging. IEEE Transactions on Software Engineering **28**(5) (2002) 449–462

58. Edwards, W., Igarashi, T., LaMarca, A., Mynatt, E.: A temporal model for multi-level undo and redo. In Press, A., ed.: Proc. of the 13th annual ACM symposium on User interface software and technology (San Diego, CA). (2000) 31–40

59. Berlage, T., Genau, A.: A framework for shared applications with a replicated architecture. In Press, A., ed.: Proc. of the 6th annual ACM symposium on User interface software and technology (Atlanta, GA). (1993) 249–257

60. Mens, T.: Conditional graph rewriting as a domain-independent formalism for software evolution. In: Proc. of the Int'l Conf. on Applications of Graph Transformations with Industrial Relevance (Agtive 1999). Volume 1779., Springer-Verlag (2000) 127–143

61. Löwe, M.: Algebraic approach to single-pushout graph transformations. Theoretical Computer Science **109** (1993) 181–224

62. Shamsfard, M., Barforoush, A.: The state of the art in ontology learning: a framework for comparison. the Knowledge Engineering Review **18**(4) (2003) 293–316

63. Beale, S., Nirenburg, S., Mahesh, K.: Semantic analysis in the MikroKosmos machine translation project. In: In Proc. of the 2nd Symposium on Natural Language Processing (Bangkok, Thailand). (1995) 297–307

64. (OpenCyc) http://www.opencyc.org.

65. Lenat, D.: The dimensions of context-space. Cycorp technical report (1998)

66. Jarrar, M., Heymans, S.: Unsatisfiability reasoning in orm conceptual schemes. In: Proc. of Int'l Conf. on Semantics of a Networked World (Munich, Germany), Springer Verlag (2006) Lecture Notes in Artificial Intelligence, in press.

Encoding Classifications into Lightweight Ontologies*

Fausto Giunchiglia, Maurizio Marchese, and Ilya Zaihrayeu

Department of Information and Communication Technology
University of Trento, Italy
{fausto, marchese, ilya}@dit.unitn.it

Abstract. Classifications have been used for centuries with the goal of cataloguing and searching large sets of objects. In the early days it was mainly books; lately it has also become Web pages, pictures and any kind of digital resources. Classifications describe their contents using natural language labels, an approach which has proved very effective in manual classification. However natural language labels show their limitations when one tries to automate the process, as they make it very hard to reason about classifications and their contents. In this paper we introduce the novel notion of *Formal Classification*, as a graph structure where labels are written in a propositional concept language. Formal Classifications turn out to be some form of lightweight ontologies. This, in turn, allows us to reason about them, to associate to each node a normal form formula which univocally describes its contents, and to reduce document classification and query answering to reasoning about subsumption.

1 Introduction

In today's information society, as the amount of information grows larger, it becomes essential to develop efficient ways to summarize and navigate information from large, multivariate data sets. The field of classification supports these tasks, as it investigates how sets of "objects" can be summarized into a small number of classes, and it also provides methods to assist the search of such "objects" [11]. In the past centuries, classification has been the domain of librarians and archivists. Lately a lot of interest has focused also on the management of the information present in the web: see for instance the WWW Virtual Library project[1], or the web directories of search engines like Google, or Yahoo!.

Standard classification methodologies amount to manually organizing topics into hierarchies. Hierarchical library classification systems (such as the Dewey

---

* This paper is an integrated and extended version of two papers: the first with title "Towards a Theory of Formal Classification" was presented at the 2005 International Workshop on Context and Ontologies; the second with title "Encoding Classifications into Lightweight Ontologies" was presented at the 2006 European Semantic Web Conference.

[1] The WWW Virtual Library project, see http://vlib.org/

S. Spaccapietra et al. (Eds.): Journal on Data Semantics VIII, LNCS 4380, pp. 57–81, 2007.

Decimal Classification System (DDC) [3] or the Library of Congress classification system (LCC)[2]) are attempts to develop static, hierarchical classification structures into which all of human knowledge can be classified.

More recently, many search engines like Google, Yahoo as well as many eCommerce vendors, like Amazon, offer classification hierarchies (*i.e.*, web directories) to search for relevant items. Such web directories are sometimes referred to as *lightweight ontologies* [29]. However, as such, they lack at least one important property that ontologies must have: ontologies must be represented in a *formal language*, which can then be used for *automating reasoning* [21]. None of the existing human crafted classifications possesses this property. Because classification hierarchies are written in natural language, it is very hard to automate the classification task, and, as a consequence, standard classification approaches amount to *manually* classifying objects into classes. Examples include DMoz, a human edited web directory, which *"powers the core directory services for the most popular portals and search engines on the Web, including AOL Search, Netscape Search, Google, Lycos, DirectHit, and HotBot, and hundreds of others"* [28].

Although all the above mentioned classifications are based on well-founded classification methodologies, they have a number of limitations:

- the semantics of a given category is implicitly codified in a natural language label, which may be ambiguous and may therefore be interpreted differently by different classifiers;
- a link, connecting two nodes, may also be ambiguous in the sense that it may be considered to specify the meaning of the child node, of the parent node, or of both. For instance, a link connecting the parent node *"programming"* with its child node *"Java"* may, or may not mean that (a) the parent node means "computer programming" (and not, for example, "events scheduling"); (b) that the child node means "Java, the programming language" (and not "Java, the island"); or (c) that the parent node's meaning excludes the meaning of the child node, *i.e.*, it is "programming and *not* Java";
- as a consequence of the previous two items, the classification task also becomes ambiguous in the sense that different classifiers may classify the same objects differently, based on their *subjective* opinion. This observation has an impact in particular on the fact that both current tasks of classification and search by means of browsing do not scale to large amounts of information.

In the present paper we propose an approach to converting classifications into Formal Classifications, or lightweight ontologies, thus eliminating the three ambiguities discussed above. This in turn allows us to automate, through propositional reasoning, the essential tasks of document classification and query answering. Concretely, we propose a three step approach:

- first, we convert a classification into a new structure, which we call *Formal Classification* (*FC*), where all the labels are expressed in a propositional Description Logic (DL) language (*i.e.*, a DL language without roles) [1];

---

[2] The Library of Congress Classification system, see http://www.loc.gov/catdir/cpso/lcco/lcco.html/

– second, we convert a FC into a *Normalized Formal Classification (NFC)*. In NFCs each node's label is a propositional DL formula, which univocally codifies the meaning of the node in the classification, taking into account both the label of the node and its position within the classification;
– third, we encode document classification and query answering in NFCs as a propositional satisfiability (SAT) problem, and solve it using a sound and complete SAT engine.

NFCs are *full-fledged* lightweight ontologies, and have many nice properties. Among them:

– NFC node labels univocally codify the set of documents which can be classified in these nodes;
– NFCs are *taxonomies* in the sense that, from the root down to the leaves, labels of child nodes are subsumed by the labels of their parent nodes;
– as nodes' labels codify the position of the nodes in the hierarchy, document classification and query answering can be done simply by analyzing the set of labels. There is no need to inspect the edge structure of the NFC.

The remainder of the paper is organized as follows. In Section 2 we introduce classifications and discuss how they are currently used in real use cases. In Section 3 we motivate a formal approach to dealing with classifications. In Section 4 we introduce the notion of FC as a way to disambiguate labels in classifications. In Section 5 we discuss how we disambiguate links in classifications by introducing the notion of NFC. In Section 6 and Section 7 we show how the two main operations performed on classifications, namely classification and search, can be fully automated in NFCs by means of propositional reasoning. In Section 8 we discuss related work. Section 9 summarizes the results and concludes the paper.

2 Classifications

Classifications are hierarchical structures used to organize large amounts of objects [17]. These objects can be of many different types, depending on the characteristics and uses of the classification itself. In a library, they are mainly books or journals; in a file system, they can be any kind of file (*e.g.*, text files, images, applications); in the directories of Web portals, the objects are pointers to Web pages; in market places, catalogs organize either product data or service titles. Classifications are useful for both object classification and retrieval. Users browse the hierarchies and catalogue or access the objects associated with different concepts, which are described by natural languages labels. Noteworthy, many widely used classifications impose a simple structure of a rooted tree. Examples of tree-like classifications are DMoz, DDC, Amazon, directories of Google and Yahoo, file system directories, and many others[3].

---

[3] While making this statement we excluded from consideration secondary classification links normally used for improving navigability and which make the classification a DAG. An example of such links is the "related" links of DMoz.

We define the notion of Classification as follows:

Definition 1 (Classification). *A Classification is a rooted tree $C = \langle N, E, L \rangle$ where N is a finite set of nodes, E is a set of edges on N, and L is is a finite set of labels expressed in natural language, such that for any node $n_i \in N$, there is one and only one label $l_i \in L$.*

Classifications, as tree-like structures with natural language node labels, are used in a variety of domains such as standardization (*e.g.*, eCl@ss [4]), controlled thesauri (*e.g.*, MeSH [27]), and many others. Depending on their target application, classifications and their elements are given a specific interpretation and can therefore be treated differently. In this paper, we see classifications as objects whose primary purpose is the classification of and search for documents. We therefore define the *classification semantics* as strongly related to documents, and we define it at three levels:

- **Label:** labels, as such, describe real world entities or individual objects, and the meaning of a label in a classification is the set of documents which are *about* the entities or individual objects described by the label. Note, that a label can denote a document, *e.g.*, a book; and, in this case, the classification semantics of this label is the set of documents which are about the book, *e.g.*, book reviews. Note that the label semantics is fully captured by the label itself and nothing else;
- **Node:** nodes represent complex concepts formed as a combined faceted view of the real world entities and/or individual objects described by the nodes' labels and by the labels of all their ascendant nodes. The meaning of a node in a classification is the set of documents which are about the complex concept represented by the node. The classification semantics of a given node is defined by the labels of the nodes on the path from the root to the node;
- **Classification:** the classification semantics of nodes defines the basis for how they are used for the classification of documents in a specific classification algorithm. The set of documents which are populated in a node defines the semantics of this node at the classification level. In the most general case, the classification semantics is defined by the nodes' labels, by the structure of the classification, and by the employed classification algorithm.

In the rest of this section we briefly describe and discuss two different Classifications: a relatively old librarian classification hierarchy, the Dewey Decimal Classification system (DDC), and an example from a modern web catalogue, namely the DMoz human-edited web directory.

Example 1 (DDC). Since the 19th century, librarians have used DDC to organize vast amounts of books. DDC divides knowledge into ten different broad subject areas, called classes, numbered 000 - 999. Materials which are too general to belong to a specific group (encyclopedias, newspapers, magazines, etc.) are placed in the 000's. The ten main classes are divided up into smaller classes by several sets of subclasses. Smaller divisions (to subdivide the topic even further)

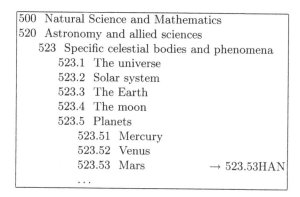

Fig. 1. A part of the DDC system with an example of book classification

are created by expanding each subclass and adding decimals if necessary. A small part of the DDC system is shown on Figure 1.

In DDC, the notation (*i.e.*, the system of symbols used to represent the classes in a classification system) provides a universal language to identify the class and related classes.

Before a book is placed on the shelves it is:

- classified according to the discipline matter it covers (given the Dewey number);
- some letters (usually three) are added to this number (usually they represent the author's last name);
- the number is used to identify the book and to indicate where the book will be shelved in the library. Books can be assigned a Dewey number corresponding to both leaf and non-leaf nodes of the classification hierarchy.

Since parts of DDC are arranged by discipline, not subject, a subject may appear in more than one class. For example, the subject "clothing" has aspects that fall under several disciplines. The psychological influence of clothing belongs to 155.95 as part of the discipline of psychology; customs associated with clothing belong to 391 as part of the discipline of customs; and clothing in the sense of fashion design belongs to 746.92 as part of the discipline of the arts. However, the final Dewey number associated to a book has to be unique and, therefore, the classifier needs to impose a classification choice among all the possible alternatives.

As an example, let's consider the Dewey number for the following book: Michael Hanlon, "*Pictures of Planet Mars*". A possible classification is Dewey number: 523.53 HAN and the classification choice for the book is shown in Figure 1.

The main properties of DDC are:

- the classification algorithm relies on the *get-specific* rule[4]: when you add a new object, get as specific as possible: dig deep into the classification schema,

----

[4] Look at http://docs.yahoo.com/info/suggest/appropriate.html to see how Yahoo! implements this rule.

looking for the appropriate sub-category; it is a bad practice to submit an
object to a top level category, if one more specific exists. At present, the
enforcement of such rule is left to the experience of the classifier;

- each object is placed in exactly one place in the hierarchy. As a result of
this restriction, a classifier often has to choose arbitrarily among several
reasonable categories to assign the classification code for a new document
(see the above example for "clothing"). Despite the use of documents called
"subject authorities", which attempt to impose some control on terminology
and classification criteria, there is no guarantee that two classifiers make
the same decision. Thus, a user, searching for information, has to guess the
classifier's choice in order to decide where to look for, and will typically have
to look in a number of places;

- each non-root node in the hierarchy has only one parent node. This enforces
a tree structure on the hierarchy.   ☐

Example 2 (DMoz). The Open Directory Project (ODP), also known as DMoz
(for Directory.Mozilla.org, the domain name of ODP), is a multilingual open
content directory of World Wide Web links owned by America Online that is
constructed and maintained by a community of volunteer editors. ODP uses a
hierarchical ontology scheme for organizing site listings. Data is made available
through an RDF-like dump that is published on a dedicated download server.
Listings on a similar topic are grouped into categories, which can then include
smaller categories. As of March 10, 2006, the RDF held 5,272,517 listings and
over 590,000 multilingual categories. DMoz powers the core directory services
for the most popular portals and search engines on the Web, including AOL
Search, Netscape Search, Google, Lycos, DirectHit, and HotBot, and hundreds
of others [28].

In DMoz, as in DDC, objects (here mainly web links) are classified by a human
classifier following the get-specific rule. In this classification hierarchy, an object
can be often reached from different paths of the hierarchy, thus providing an
efficient way for finding items of interest following different perspectives. This
normally means that the object is classified in two (or more) nodes or that the
object is classified in one node and there are "related" links from other nodes to
the node where the object is classified.

In the following we present an example of classification for a software programming document in the DMoz web directory. The document title is "*Java
Enterprise in a Nutshell, Second Edition*". In the DMoz web directory, reduced
for sake of presentation, the example title can be found through two different
search paths (see Figure 2), namely:

`Top/Business/Publishing and Printing/Books/Computers/`

`Top/Computers/Programming Languages/Java/`   ☐

From the two specific examples we can see that Web catalogues are more flexible
than classifications like Dewey. In fact, their aim is not to position a resource
in a unique position, but rather to position it in such a way, that the user,

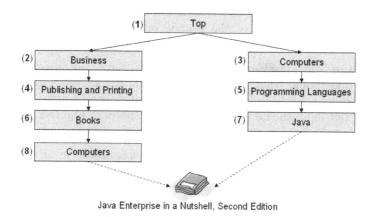

Fig. 2. A part of the DMoz web directory

who navigates the catalogue, will be facilitated in finding appropriate or similar resources related to a given topic.

3   Why Formal Classifications?

There are many methodologies for how to classify objects into classification hierarchies. These methodologies range from the many rigorous rules "polished" by librarians during hundreds of years; to less strict, but still powerful rules of classification in a modern web directory[5]. What is relevant here, is that in all these different cases, a human classifier needs to follow a common pattern, which we summarize in four main steps. These steps are also followed when one searches for an object by means of classification browsing. The only difference is in that now the categories are inspected for where to find an object, and not where to put it. We discuss the four steps below, and we elucidate them on the example of the part of the DMoz web directory presented in Example 2.

1. Disambiguating labels. The challenge here is to disambiguate natural language words and labels. For example, the classifier has to understand that in the label of node n_7 (see Figure 2) the word *"Java"* has at least three senses, which are: an island in Indonesia; a coffee beverage; and an object-oriented programming language. Moreover, words in a label are combined to build complex concepts. Consider, for example, the labels at node n_4, *publishing and printing*, and n_5, *programming languages*. The combination of natural language atomic elements is used by the classifier to aggregate (like in *publishing and printing*) or disambiguate (like in *programming languages*) atomic concepts;

2. Disambiguating links. At this step the classifier has to interpret links between nodes. Namely, the classifier needs to consider the fact that each non-root

---
[5] See, for instance, the DMoz classification rules at http://dmoz.org/guidelines/

node is "viewed" in the *context* of its parent node; and then specify the meanings of the nodes' labels. For instance, the meaning of the label of node n_8, *computers*, is bounded by the meaning of node n_6, *business books' publishing*;

3. Understanding classification alternatives. Given an object, the classifier has to understand what classification alternatives for this object are. For instance, the book "Java Enterprise in a Nutshell, Second Edition" might potentially be put in all the nodes of the hierarchy shown in Figure 2. The reason for this is that the book is related to both business and technology branches;

4. Making classification choices. Given the set of classification alternatives, the classifier has to decide, based on a predefined system of rules, where to put the given object. The system of rules may differ from classification to classification, but the get-specific rule is commonly followed. Note, that there may be more than one category for the classification. For instance, if the get-specific rule was used, then one would classify the above mentioned book into nodes n_7 and n_8, as they most specifically characterize the book.

Humans have proven to be very effective at performing steps 1 and 2, as described above. However, there are still some challenges to be addressed. The main challenge in step 1 is dealing with the ambiguities introduced by multiple possibilities in meaning. One source of this is in that labels contain many conjunctions "and"'s and "or"'s, whereas they actually mean inclusive disjunction, *i.e.*, either the first conjunct, or the second, or both. For instance, the phrase "publishing and printing" means either publishing, or printing, or both. Apart from the conjunctions, multiple possibilities are introduced also by punctuation marks denoting enumeration (*e.g.*, the comma), and by words' senses (recall the various senses of the word "Java"). It has been shown, that cognitive reasoning with the presence of multiple possibilities (distinctions) is an error-prone task for humans [14]. For instance, even if DMoz labels are short phrases, consisting, on average, of 1.81 tokens, they contain 0.23 conjunctions per label; and average polysemy for nouns and adjectives is 3.72 per word[6]. Conjunctions, punctuation, and words' senses count together to 3.79 possibilities in meaning per label.

The challenge of step 2 is that the classifier may need to follow a long path of nodes in order to figure out a node's meaning. It has two consequences: first, the classifier needs to deal with the growing complexity in ambiguity introduced by each new label in the path; and, second, the classifier has to consider each new label in the context of the labels of the ancestor nodes, and, thus, partly resolve the ambiguity. Note, that, for instance, the average length of a path from the root to a leaf node in DMoz is 7.09.

Steps 3 and 4 is where the real problems for humans begin. Even with classifications of average size, it is not easy to find all the classification alternatives. Consider, for instance, how many times you did not find an email in your own

---

[6] A summary of the statistical analysis we performed on DMoz is reported in Table 1. In our analysis we excluded branches leading to non-English labels, such as Top/World/ or Top/Kids and Teens/International/

Table 1. DMoz statistics

Statistics category	Value
Total English labels	477,786
Tokens per label, avg.	1.81
Total links classified in English labels	3,047,643
Duplicate links, % from the total	10.70%
Nouns and adjectives polysemy, avg.	3.72
"and"'s and *"or"*'s per label, avg.	0.23
Total disjunctions per label, avg.	3.79
Root-to-leaf path length, avg.	7.09
Branching factor, avg.	4.00

mail directory. With large classifications this task becomes practically impossible. For instance, think about possible classification alternatives in DMoz, which has 477,786 English categories. Thus, at step 3, a human classifier may not be able to enumerate all the possible classification alternatives for an object.

Step 4 requires abundant expertise and profound methodological skills on the side of the classifier. However, even an expert makes subjective decisions, what leads, when a classification is populated by several classifiers, to nonuniform, duplicate, and error-prone classification. If the get-specific rule is used, then the classifier has to parse the classification tree in a top-down fashion, considering at each parent node, which of its child nodes is appropriate for the classification or for further consideration. The higher the average branching factor in the classification tree, the higher the probability of that two different classifiers will find appropriate two different sibling nodes at some level in the tree. This is because the difference in meaning of the two nodes may be vague or, vice versa, because the two nodes have distinct meanings and they represent different facets of the object being classified. In this latter case the classifiers may simply follow different perspectives (facets) when classifying the object (recall the example with "clothing" from Example 1). Note, that even if DMoz encourages the classification of a Web page in a single category, among 3,047,643 links (classified in English labels), about 10.70% are classified in more than one node[7]. And, about 91.36% of these are classified in two different nodes. This is not surprising given that DMoz is populated by more than 70,000 classifiers, and that it has average branching factor of 4.00.

Given all the above described complexity, humans still outperform machines in natural language understanding tasks [25], which are the core of steps 1 and 2. Still, the availability of electronic repositories that encode world knowledge (*e.g.*, [16,19]), and powerful natural language processing tools (*e.g.*, [22,16]) allows the machines to perform these steps reasonably well. Moreover, machines can be much more efficient and effective at steps 3 and 4, if the problem is encoded in a formal language, which is what we propose to do in our approach.

---

[7] We identified duplicate links by exact equivalence of their URLs.

4   Disambiguating Labels

To support an automatic classifier in step 1 of the classification task (as described in the previous section), we propose to convert classifications into a new structure, which we call *Formal Classification* (FC), more amenable to automated processing.

Definition 2 (Formal Classification). *A Formal Classification is a rooted tree* $FC = \langle N, E, L^F \rangle$ *where* N *is a finite set of nodes,* E *is a set of edges on* N, *and* L^F *is a finite set of labels expressed in Propositional Description Logic language* L^C, *such that for any node* $n_i \in N$, *there is one and only one label* $l_i^F \in L^F$.

FCs and classifications are related in the sense that a FC is a *formalized* copy of a classification. In other words, a FC has the same structure as the classification, but it encodes the classification's labels in a formal language (*i.e.*, L^C), capable of encapsulating, at the best possible level of approximation, their classification semantics. In the following we will call L^C, the *concept language*. We use a *Propositional* Description Logic language for several reasons:

- since natural language labels are meant to describe real world entities, and *not* actions, performed on or by entities, or relations between entities, the natural language labels are mainly constituted of noun phrases; and, therefore, there are very few words which are verbs. This makes it very suitable to use a Description Logic (DL) language as the formal language, as DLs are a precise notation for representing noun phrases [1];
- The set-theoretic semantics of DL allows us to translate syntactic relations between words in a label into the logical operators of DL, preserving, at the best possible level of approximation, the classification semantics of the label. Below in this section we provide concrete examples and argumentation of the translation process and its principles;
- a formula in L^C can be converted into an equivalent formula in a propositional logic language with the boolean semantics. Thus, a problem expressed in L^C can be converted into a *propositional satisfiability problem*[8].

Converting classifications into FCs automates step 1, as described in Section 3. In our approach we build on the work of Magnini et. al. [17]. We translate a natural language label into an expression in L^C by means of mapping different parts of speech (POSs), their mutual syntactic relation, and punctuation to the classification semantics of labels. We proceed in three steps, as discussed below:

1. Build atomic concepts. Senses of common nouns and adjectives become atomic concepts of L^C, whose interpretation is the set of documents about the entities, which are denoted by the nouns, or which possess the qualities denoted

---

[8] For translation rules from a Propositional Description Logic to a Propositional Logic, see [6].

by the adjectives. We enumerate word senses using WordNet [19], and we write x#i to denote an atomic concept corresponding to the ith sense of the word x in WordNet. For instance, `programming#2` is an atomic concept, whose interpretation is the set of documents which are about computer programming; and the atomic concept `red#1` denotes the set of documents which are about red entities, *e.g.*, red cats or red cars. Proper nouns become atomic concepts of L^C, whose interpretation is the set of documents about the individual objects, denoted by the proper nouns. They may be long expressions, denoting names of people, movies, music bands, and so on. Some examples are the movie *"Gone with the Wind"*, and the music band *"The Rolling Stones"*. Apart from proper nouns, multi-words are recognized, and each their distinct sense becomes an atomic concept in the concept language[9]. Words which are not found in WordNet are assigned distinct atomic concepts, which are uniquely identified by the string representation of the words (case ignored). Put it differently, words which are not found in WordNet and whose string representations are equal, are assigned the same atomic concept. As the output of this step, each word (multi-word, or proper noun) is associated with one or more atomic concepts, whereas many of them are associated with the corresponding senses from WordNet.

2. Word sense disambiguation. At this step we discard irrelevant word senses and corresponding atomic concepts. In part, we follow the approach proposed in [17]. Namely, if there is a relation found in WordNet between any two senses of two words in a label, then these senses are retained and other unrelated senses are discarded. The relation looked for in WordNet is synonymy, hypernymy (*i.e.*, the "kind-of" relation, *e.g.*, *car* is a kind of *vehicle*), or holonymy (*i.e.*, the "part-of" relation, *e.g.*, *room* is a part of a *building*). If no relation found, then we check if a relation exists between two WordNet senses by comparing their glosses as proposed in [9]. In this respect we go beyond what is suggested in [17].

3. Build complex concepts. Complex concepts are built from atomic concepts as follows: first, we build words' formulas as the logical disjunction ($\sqcup$) of atomic concepts corresponding to their senses (remaining after step 2), and we write x* to denote the disjunction of the (remaining) senses of word x. For instance, the noun *"Programming"* becomes the concept (`programming#1` $\sqcup$ `programming#2`), whose interpretation is the set of documents which are about event scheduling and/or about computer programming. Second, labels are chunked, *i.e.*, divided into sequences of syntactically correlated parts of words. We then translate syntactic relations to the logical connectives of L^C following a precise pattern. Let us consider a few examples.

A set of adjectives followed by a noun group is translated into the logical conjunction ($\sqcap$) of the formulas corresponding to the adjectives and to the nouns.

---

[9] Because of their negligibly small presence, we do not consider verbs. We neither consider articles, numerals, pronouns and adverbs. However, their share in the labels of real classifications is reasonably small. When such words are found, they are just omitted from the label.

The interpretation of the resulting concept is the set of documents which are about the real world entities denoted by all the nouns, and which possess qualities, denoted by all the adjectives. For instance, the phrase *"long cold winter blizzard"* is translated into the concept `long* ⊓ cold* ⊓ winter* ⊓ blizzard*`.

Prepositions are also translated into the conjunction. The intuition is that prepositions denote some commonality between the two objects they relate; and, in terms of the classification semantics, this "commonality" can be approximated to the set of documents which are about both objects. For instance, the following phrases: *"books of magic"*, *"science in society"*, and *"software for engineering"*, they all denote what the two words, connected by the prepositions, have in common.

Coordinating conjunctions "and" and "or" are translated into the logical disjunction. For instance, *"flights or trains"* and *"animals and plants"* become `flight* ⊔ train*` and `animal* ⊔ plant*` respectively. Punctuation marks such as the period (.), the coma (,) and the semicolon (;) are also translated into the logical disjunction. For instance, the phrase *"metro, bus, and trolley"* is converted into the concept `metro* ⊔ bus* ⊔ trolley*`.

Words and phrases denoting exclusions, such as "excluding", "except", "but not", are translated into the logical negation ($\neg$). For instance, label *"runners excluding sprinters"* becomes the concept `runner* ⊓ ¬sprinter*`. However, since they are meant to describe what "there is" in the world, and not what "there isn't", labels contain very few such phrases.

The use of logical connectives, as described above but with the exception of prepositions, allows it to *explicitly* encode the classification semantics of labels. In other words, the interpretation of the resulting formulas explicitly represents the set of documents which are about the corresponding natural language labels. The translation of prepositions is an approximation, as they may encode meaning, which only partly can be captured by means of the logical conjunction. For example, *"life in war"* and *"life after war"* will collapse into the same logical formula, whereas the classification semantics of the two labels is different.

Example 3 (Disambiguating labels in a web directory). Let us consider how the label of node n_2 in the part of the Amazon book directory shown in Figure 3 can be disambiguated. The label consists of three tokens: "business", "and", and "investing", whereas the first and the last tokens are recognized as nouns, and the second token is recognized as a coordinating conjunction. The noun "business" has nine, and the noun "investing" has one sense in WordNet. Therefore, after step 1 we have two words with associated atomic concepts as shown below:

business (`business#1, business#2, ..., business#9`), and
investing (`investing#1`)

At step 2, the senses of the two words are compared, and it is found that `investing#1` (defined as "the act of investing; laying out money or capital in an enterprise with the expectation of profit") is a second level hyponym of `business#2` (defined as "the activity of providing goods and services involving

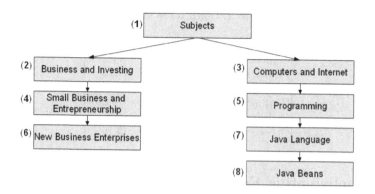

Fig. 3. Amazon Book Directory

financial and commercial and industrial aspects"). Therefore, the second sense (and the atomic concept associated with it) of the word "business" is retained and all the others are discarded.

At step 3 we build a complex concept by considering the fact that the coordinating conjunction "and" is translated into the logical disjunction. We have therefore:

$$l_2^F = \texttt{business\#2} \sqcup \texttt{investing\#1} \qquad \qquad \Box$$

In order to estimate how much of the information encoded into the labels of a real classification can be captured using our approach, we have conducted a grammatical analysis of the DMoz classification. For doing this, we have used the OpenNLP Tools tokenization and POS-tagging library [22], which reports to achieve more than 96% accuracy on unseen data[10]. In Table 2 we show the POS statistics of the DMoz tokens. Note, that about 77.59% of the tokens (nouns and adjectives) become concepts, and about 14.69% (conjunctions and prepositions) become logical connectives of L^C. WordNet coverage for common nouns and adjectives found in DMoz labels is quite high, and constitutes 93.12% and 95.01% respectively. Detailed analysis of conjunctions and prepositions shows that about 85.26% of them are conjunctions "and", and about 0.10% are conjunctions "or". In our analysis we found no words or phrases which would result into the logical negation. Only about 4.56% of tokens are verbs and adverbs in all their forms.

Note, that the propositional nature of L^C allows us to *explicitly* encode about 90.13% of the label data in DMoz (*i.e.*, nouns, adjectives, conjunctions "and" and "or"). Still, this is a rough understated estimation, as we did not take into account multi-word common and proper nouns. In fact, a manual analysis of the longest labels, as well as of the ones with verbs, shows that the majority of these labels represents proper names of movies, games, institutions, music bands, etc.

---

[10] The tool may not function at its expected performance on special data as short labels because it has been trained on well-formed natural language sentences.

Table 2. DMoz token statistics

POS	Share
Common nouns	71.22%
Proper nouns	0.18%
Adjectives	6.19%
Conjunctions and prepositions	14.69%
Verbs, adverbs	4.56%
Other POSs	3.16%

5   Disambiguating Edges

As discussed in Section 2, the classification semantics of nodes codifies the fact that child nodes are always considered in the context of their parent nodes. This means that the meaning of a non-root node is the set of documents, which are about its label, and which are *also* about its parent node. We encode the classification semantics of nodes into their property which we call *concept at a node* [6]. We write C_i to refer to the concept at node n_i, and we define this notion as:

$$C_i = \begin{cases} l_i^F & \text{if } n_i \text{ is the root of } FC \\ l_i^F \sqcap C_j & \text{if } n_i \text{ is not the root of } FC, \text{ where } n_j \text{ is the parent of } n_i \end{cases} \quad (1)$$

There may be two meaningful relations between the concept at a parent node, and the label of its child node, as represented in Figure 4:

– in case (a) the label of the child node is about the parent node, but it is also about something else. In this case the parent node *specializes* the meaning of the child node by bounding the interpretation of the child node's label with the interpretation of the concept at the parent node. For instance, think about a classification where the root node is labeled "Italy" and its sole child node is labeled "Pictures" (see Figure 4a). A human can understand that the meaning of the child node is "pictures of Italy" and not "pictures of Germany", for example. In the corresponding FC this knowledge is encoded into the concept at node $C_2 = \texttt{italy} * \sqcap \texttt{picture}*$;

– in case (b) the child node represents a *specification* of the parent node, and their relation can be, for instance, the "is-a" or the "part-of" relation. Note, that in this case, differently from case (a), the parent node does not influence the meaning of the child node. Suppose that in the previous example the child node's label is "Liguria" (see Figure 4b). A human can understand that the meaning of this node is the same as of its label. In the corresponding FC this knowledge is encoded into the concept at node $C_2 = \texttt{italy} * \sqcap \texttt{liguria}*$, which can be simplified to $C_2 = \texttt{liguria\#1}$, taking into account the fact that both words "Italy" and "Liguria" have only one sense in WordNet, and given that the corresponding axiom ($\texttt{liguria\#1} \sqsubseteq \texttt{italy\#1}$) is memorized in some background knowledge base.

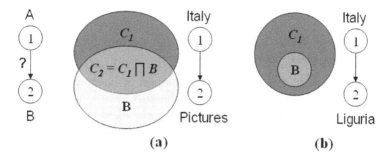

Fig. 4. Edge semantics in FCs

Note, that applying Equation 1 recursively, we can compute the concept at any non-root node n_i as the conjunction of the labels of all the nodes on the path from the root of the FC, n_1, to n_i. This corresponds to how the notion of concept at a node is defined in [7], namely:

$$C_i = l_1^F \sqcap l_2^F \sqcap \ldots \sqcap l_i^F \qquad (2)$$

The concept at a node encodes, but only to a certain extent, the path from the root to the node. In fact, there may be more than one way to reconstruct a path from a concept. Atomic concepts in a concept at a node may be "distributed" differently among different number of nodes, which, in turn, may have a different order in the path. The number of nodes may range from one, when the concept at the node is equivalent to the node's label, to the number of clauses in the CNF equivalent of the concept. However, all the possible paths converge to the same semantically equivalent concept. Consider, for instance, node n_8 in the classification shown in Figure 2. The two paths below will converge to the same concept for the node[11]:

    top/Publishing and Printing/Business Books/Computers/

    top/Business/Publishing and Printing/Computer Books/

We use the notion of concept at a node to define another structure which we call *Normalized Formal Classification* (NFC).

Definition 3 (Normalized Formal Classification). *A Normalized Formal Classification is a rooted tree $NFC = \langle N, E, L^N \rangle$ where N is a finite set of nodes, E is a set of edges on N, and L^N is is a finite set of labels expressed in L^C, such that for any node $n_i \in N$, there is one and only one label $l_i^N \in L^N$ and $l_i^N \equiv C_i$.*

Note, that the main characteristic of NFCs, that distinguishes them from FCs, is the fact that labels of child nodes are always more specific than the labels of their parent nodes. Interestingly, if a taxonomic classification, *i.e.*, a classification

---

[11] For sake of presentation we give these examples in natural language.

with only "is-a" and "part-of" links, is converted into a FC, then the latter is also a NFC.

Apart from this, NFCs have a number of important properties relevant to classifications, discussed below:

- the interpretation of nodes' labels is the set of documents which *can* be classified in these nodes. We underline the "can" since, as we discuss in the next section, documents which *are* actually classified in the nodes are often a subset of the interpretation of the labels in NFCs;
- two nodes, representing in a classification the same real world entities, will have semantically equivalent labels in the NFC. This fact can be exploited for automatic location and/or prevention of adding of such "duplicate" nodes. As an example, consider the different paths that lead to the same concept as described earlier in this section;
- NFCs are full-fledged *lightweight ontologies*, suitable for the automation of the core classification tasks, such as document classification and query answering.

The consideration of the path from the root to any given node allows us not only to compute the concept at that node which leads to the properties discussed above, but also to further disambiguate the senses of the words in its label taking into account the context of the path and, accordingly, to delete corresponding atomic concepts from its label in the NFC. In this task we apply exactly the same technique as the one discussed in Section 4 for sense disambiguation in labels with the only difference in that now all the remaining words' senses in *all* the labels on the path to the root are compared.

Example 4 (Disambiguating edges in a web directory). Recall the example of the part of the DMoz directory shown in Figure 2 and let us see how the concept at node n_7 can be computed. Remember the three senses of the word "java" (which is the label of n_7) discussed earlier in the paper, and consider the parent node's label, "programming languages", which is recognized as a multi-word with only one sense whose gloss is "a language designed for programming computers". Comparing this gloss with the gloss of the third sense of the word "java" (defined as "a simple platform-independent object-oriented programming language...") results that the similarity of the two glosses exceeds a certain threshold and, therefore, a relation is found between these two senses. We therefore compute the concept at node n_7 as:

$$l_7^N = (\texttt{computer\#1} \sqcup \texttt{computer\#2}) \sqcap \texttt{programming\_language\#1} \sqcap \texttt{java\#3} \quad \square$$

6   Document Classification

Before some document d can be classified, it has to be assigned an expression in L^C, which we call the *document concept*, written C^d. The assignment of concepts to documents is done in two steps: first, a set of n keywords is retrieved from the document using text mining techniques (see, for example, [23]); the keywords are then converted into a concept by means of the conjunction of the formulas representing the keywords, translated to L^C as discussed in Section 4.

The interpretation of the document concept of any document includes the document itself (*i.e.*, $d \in (C^d)^{\mathcal{I}}$) as well as other documents which have equivalent or more specific document concepts. In Figure 5 we show an example of how a document and the interpretation of its concept can be interrelated. There, the interpretation of the concept of document d_1, C^{d_1}, includes d_1 itself, d_2, whose concept is equivalent to C^{d_1}, and d_3, whose concept C^{d_3} is more specific than C^{d_1}.

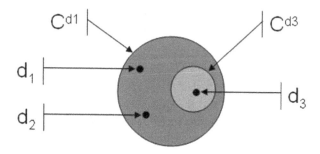

Fig. 5. Document concept

We say that node n_i is a *classification alternative* for the classification of some document d with concept C^d, if $C^d \sqsubseteq l_i^N$. In fact, if this relation holds, and given that $d \in (C^d)^{\mathcal{I}}$, it follows that $d \in (l_i^N)^{\mathcal{I}}$, *i.e.*, document d belongs to the set of documents which can be classified in n_i. For any given document d and a NFC, we compute the set of classification alternatives for d in the NFC as follows:

$$A(C^d) = \{n_i | C^d \sqsubseteq l_i^N\} \qquad (3)$$

By computing Equation 3, we can automate step 3 described in Section 3. The automation of step 4, *i.e.*, making classification choices, depends on what classification algorithm is used. Below we show how it can be automated for some set A of classification alternatives if the get-specific rule (see Section 3) is used:

$$C(A) = \{n_i \in A | \nexists n_j \in A \ (i \neq j), \ such \ that \ l_j^N \sqsubseteq l_i^N\} \qquad (4)$$

The set $C(A)$ includes all the nodes in the NFC, whose labels are more general than the document concept, and more specific among all such labels. As labels of child nodes in NFCs are always more specific than the labels of their parent nodes, $C(A)$ consists of nodes which lie as low in the CNF tree as possible, and which are still classification alternatives for the given document. Note, that the get-specific rule applies not only to nodes located on the same path from the root, but also to nodes located in different branches. For instance, a document about computer graphics will *not* be classified in the node `top/computers/` if the more specific node `top/arts/computers/` exists.

Formula 4 implies that the set of documents classified in some node n_i may (and, in most cases will) be a subset of the interpretation of its label l_i^N. In fact, the set of documents which are *actually* classified in n_i excludes those, which belong to the interpretation of labels, which are more specific than l_i^N. We encode this set in the concept l_i^C which univocally identifies the set of documents classified in node n_i, and, therefore, defines the classification level semantics of n_i in the NFC. We compute l_i^C as follows:

$$l_i^C = l_i^N \sqcap \neg \bigsqcup (l_j^N | j \neq i, l_j^N \sqsubseteq l_i^N) \tag{5}$$

Noteworthy, the concepts which represent the classification semantics at the three levels discussed in Section 2 are related by the subsumption relation as shown below:

$$l_i^C \sqsubseteq l_i^N \sqsubseteq l_i^F \tag{6}$$

Computing Equations 3, 4 and 5 requires verifying whether the subsumption relation holds between two formulas in L^C. In a more general case, if we need to check whether a certain relation rel (which can be $\sqsubseteq, \sqsupseteq, \equiv$, or $\bot$) holds between two concepts A and B, given some knowledge base $\mathcal{KB}$, which represents our a priori knowledge, we construct a propositional formula according to the pattern shown in Equation 7, and check it for validity:

$$\mathcal{KB} \rightarrow rel(A, B) \tag{7}$$

The intuition is that $\mathcal{KB}$ encodes what we know about concepts A and B, and $rel(A, B)$ holds only if it follows from what we know. In our approach $\mathcal{KB}$ is built as the conjunction of a set of axioms which encode the relations that hold between *atomic* concepts in A and B. Relation $rel(A, B)$ is the formula encoding the relation between concepts A and B translated to the propositional logic according to the rules proposed in [6]. As discussed in Section 4, atomic concepts in L^C are mapped to the corresponding natural language words' senses. These senses may be lexically related through the synonymy, antonymy, hypernymy, or holonymy relations. These relations can be translated into axioms, which *explicitly* capture the classification semantics of the relation that holds between the two senses. Thus, for instance, the set of documents which are about *cars* is a subset of the set of documents which are about a hypernym of the word "car", *vehicle*. The idea, therefore, is to find the lexical relations using WordNet and to translate synonymy into the logical equivalence, antonymy into the disjointness, hypernymy and holonymy into the subsumption relation in L^C.

Example 5 (Document classification). As en example, recall the classification in Figure 2, and suppose that we need to classify the book: *"Java Enterprise in a Nutshell, Second Edition"*, whose concept is java#3 ⊓ enterprise#2 ⊓ book#1. It can be shown, by means of propositional reasoning, that the set of classification alternatives includes all the nodes of the corresponding NFC. For sake of presentation we provide concrete formulas only for nodes n_7 and n_8, whose labels are:

$$l_7^N = \texttt{computer} * \sqcap \texttt{programming} * \sqcap \texttt{language} * \sqcap \texttt{java}*, \text{ and}$$

$$l_8^N = \texttt{business} * \sqcap(\texttt{publishing} * \sqcup \texttt{printing}*) \sqcap \texttt{publishing} *$$
$$\sqcap \texttt{books} * \sqcap \texttt{computer}*.$$

We can extract the following knowledge from WordNet: the programming language Java is a kind of programming languages, and it is a more specific concept than computer is; books are related to publishing; and enterprise is a more specific concept than business is. We encode this knowledge in the following set of axioms:

$$a_1 = (\texttt{java\#3} \sqsubseteq \texttt{pr\_language\#1}); \quad a_3 = (\texttt{book\#1} \sqsubseteq \texttt{publishing\#1});$$
$$a_2 = (\texttt{java\#3} \sqsubseteq \texttt{computer\#1}); \quad a_4 = (\texttt{enterprise\#1} \sqsubseteq \texttt{business\#2}).$$

Next, we translate the axioms and the labels into the propositional logic language, and we verify if the condition in Formula 3 holds for the two labels by constructing two formulas, following the pattern of Equation 7, as shown below:

$$(a_2 \wedge a_3 \wedge a_4) \rightarrow (C^d \rightarrow l_8^N); \quad (a_1 \wedge a_2) \rightarrow (C^d \rightarrow l_7^N).$$

We then run a SAT solver on the above formulas, which shows that they are tautologies. It means that both nodes n_7 and n_8 are classification alternatives for the classification of the book. Among all the classification alternatives, only these two nodes satisfy the get-specific rule, and, therefore, they are the final classification choices for the given book. The latter can be shown by computing Equation 4 by means of propositional reasoning. □

Note, that the edges of the NFC are *not* considered in document classification. In fact, the edges of the NFC become redundant, as their information is implicitly encoded in the labels. Note that given a set of labels, there may be several ways to reconstruct the set of edges of a NFC. However, from the classification point of view, all these NFCs are equivalent, as they classify documents *identically*. In other words, nodes with equivalent labels are populated with the same set of documents.

7 Query Answering

When the user searches for a document, she defines a set of keywords or a phrase, which is then converted into an expression in L^C using the same techniques as discussed in Section 4. We call this expression, a *query concept*, written C^q. We define the answer A^q to a query q as the set of documents, whose concepts are more specific than the query concept C^q:

$$A^q = \{d | C^d \sqsubseteq C^q\} \tag{8}$$

Searching directly on all the documents may become prohibitory expensive as classifications may contain thousands and millions of documents. NFCs allow us to identify the maximal set of nodes which contain *only* answers to a query, which we call, the *sound classification answer* to a query (written N_s^q). We compute N_s^q as follows:

$$N_s^q = \{n_i | l_i^N \sqsubseteq C^q\} \tag{9}$$

In fact, as $C^d \sqsubseteq l_i^N$ for any document d classified in any node $n_i \in N_s^q$ (see Formulas 3 and 4), and $l_i^N \sqsubseteq C^q$ (as from Formula 9 above), then $C^d \sqsubseteq C^q$. Thus, all the documents classified in the set of nodes N_s^q belong to the answer A^q (see Formula 8).

We extend N_s^q by adding nodes, which constitute the classification set of a document d, whose concept is $C^d \equiv C^q$. We call this set, the *query classification set*, written Cl^q; and we compute it following Formula 4. In fact, nodes in Cl^q may contain documents satisfying Formula 8, for instance, documents whose concepts are equivalent to C^q.

Thus, for any query q, the user can compute a sound query answer A_s^q by taking the union of two sets of documents: the set of documents which are classified in the set of nodes N_s^q (computed as $\{d \in n_i | n_i \in N_s^q\}$); and the set of documents which are classified in the nodes from the set Cl^q and which satisfy Formula 8 (computed as $\{d \in n_i | n_i \in Cl^q, C^d \sqsubseteq C^q\}$). We have therefore:

$$A_s^q = \{d \in n_i | n_i \in N_s^q\} \cup \{d \in n_i | n_i \in Cl^q, C^d \sqsubseteq C^q\} \tag{10}$$

Under the given definition, the answer to a query is not restricted to the documents classified in the nodes, whose concepts are equivalent to the concept of the query. Documents from nodes, whose concepts are more specific than the query concept are also returned. For instance, a result for the above mentioned query may also contain documents about Java beans.

Note that the proposed approach to query answering allows it to search by comparing the *meaning* of the query, of the nodes, and of the documents by means of propositional reasoning on their formulas. For instance, in our approach documents about "Ethiopian villages" will be returned as the result of the user searching for "African settlements". This makes a fundamental difference with the standard search techniques based on information retrieval and word indexing. These are based on exact term matching and on ranking the results following relative term frequencies; no query semantics is taken into account in these approaches.

Example 6 (Query answering). Suppose that the user defines a query to the Amazon NFC which is translated to the following concept: $C^q = $ java#3 $\sqcup$ cobol#1, where cobol#1 is "a common business-oriented language". It can be shown, that $N_s^q = \{n_7, n_8\}$ (see Figure 3 for the Amazon classification). However, this set does not include node n_5, which contains the book "Java for COBOL Programmers (2nd Edition)". The relevance of node n_5 to the query can be identified by computing the query classification set for query q, which in fact consists of the single node n_5, i.e., $Cl^q = \{n_5\}$. However, n_5 may also contain irrelevant documents, which are excluded from the query result by computing Formula 10. $\qquad\square$

For what regards the complexity of the query answering and document classification algorithms, since both are reduced to the validity problem, they represent co-NP-complete problems. However, as discussed in [10], in most of the cases the time complexity is (or can be reduced to) polynomial.

8   Related Work

In our work we adopt the notion of the concept at a node as first introduced in [6] and further elaborated in [7]. Moreover, the notion of label of a node in a FC, semantically corresponds to the notion of the concept of a label introduced in [7]. In [7] these notions play the key role in the identification of semantic mappings between nodes of two schemas. In this paper, these are the key notions needed to define NFCs which can be used for document classification and query answering in a completely new way.

This work as well as the work in [6,7] mentioned above is crucially related and depends on the work described in [2,17]. In particular, in [2], the authors, for the first time, introduce the idea that in classifications, natural language labels should be translated in logical formulas, while, in [17], the authors provide a detailed account of how to perform this translation process. The work in [6,7] improves on the work in [2,17] by understanding the crucial role that concepts at nodes have in matching heterogeneous classifications and how this leads to a completely new way to do matching. This paper, for the first time, recognizes the crucial role that the ideas introduced in [2,6,7,17] have in the construction of a new theory of classification, and in introducing the key notion of FC.

In [24], the authors propose a very similar approach to converting natural language labels in classifications to concept language formulas. Our approach is different in at least two respects. First, the target application in [24] is matching, whereas in the present paper we focus on document classification and query answering. Second, DL roles are used in [24] to encode the meaning of labels. The advantage of our approach is in that, while using a simpler subset of DLs, we are able to explicitly capture the semantics of a large portion of the label data in a real classification.

A related approach to converting generic thesauri and related resources from their native format to RDF(S) and OWL was recently proposed in [30]. In that work, the authors discuss a set of guidelines for how to perform a conversion of syntactic elements (e.g., structure, entity names) and semantic elements (e.g., property types) from the native format to RDF(S) and OWL. Our approach is different because it aims at extracting semantic information implicitly encoded in the classification schema (by using NLP) in order to enable the automation through reasoning, and not to perform meaning-preserving structure conversion from one format to another in order to improve interoperability as it is the case in [30].

The approach presented in this paper can potentially allow for automatic classification of objects into user-defined hierarchies with no or little intervention of the user. This, in turn, provides the user with less control over the classification process. Therefore, for any classified object, the user may want to be given explanatory details for why the object was classified in one and not another way. From this perspective, the work presented in [18] is particularly relevant to our approach, as it allows to monitor the reasoning process and present the user with the trace of the main reasoning steps which led to the obtained conclusion.

A lot of work in information theory, and more precisely on formal concept analysis (see for instance [31]) has concentrated on the study of concept hierarchies. NFCs are very similar to what in formal concept analysis are called concept hierarchies with no attributes. The work in this paper can be considered as a first step towards providing a computational theory of how to transform the "usual" natural language classifications into concept hierarchies.

The document classification and query answering algorithms, proposed in this paper, are similar to what in the Description Logic (DL) community is called *realization* and *retrieval* respectively. The fundamental difference between the two approaches is in that in the DL approach the underlying structure for the classification is *not* predefined by the user, but is built *bottom-up* from atomic concepts by computing the partial order on the subsumption relation. Interested readers are referenced to [12], where the authors propose sound and complete algorithms for realization and retrieval. In our approach, classifications are built in the *top-down* fashion by the user and in the way decided by the user. Therefore, after their conversion to NFCs, the order of labels imposed by the edges does not necessarily represent the partial order, which requires algorithms and optimizations different from those used in the DL approach.

In Computer Science, the term *classification* is primarily seen as the *process* of arranging a set of objects (*e.g.*, documents) into *categories* or *classes*. There exist a number of different approaches which try to build classifications *bottom-up*, by analyzing the contents of documents. These approaches can be grouped in two main categories: *supervised classification*, and *unsupervised classification*. In the former case, a small set of training examples needs to be pre-populated into the categories in order to allow the system to automatically classify a larger set of objects (see, for example, [5,20]). The latter approach uses various machine learning techniques to classify sets of objects (*e.g.*, data clustering [13]), and it usually has much lower precision than the former one. There exist some approaches that apply (mostly) supervised classification techniques to the problem of documents classification into hierarchies [15,26]. The classifications built following our approach are better and more natural than those built following these approaches. They are in fact constructed *top-down*, as chosen by the user and not constructed bottom-up, as they come out of the document analysis. Moreover, in our approach there is no need to have a pre-populated set of documents in order to classify another, larger set. Last but not least, our approach has the ability to classify documents one-by-one and not only in sets by contrasting reciprocal properties of documents in the set as it is done in the above approaches.

9 Future Work and Conclusions

In this paper we have introduced the notion of Formal Classification, namely of a classification where labels are written in a propositional concept language. Formal Classifications have many advantages over standard classifications all deriving from the fact that formal language formulas can be reasoned about far more easily than natural language sentences. In this paper we have highlighted how this can be done to perform automatic document classification and semantics-aware query answering. Our approach has the potential, in principle, to allow for the automatic classification of (say) the Yahoo! documents into the Yahoo! directories.

The primary goal of this paper is to present the theory of how to translate classifications into Lightweight Ontologies and how they can be used for the automation of essential tasks on classifications. Therefore, large-scale experiments are out of the scope of the present paper even if the first experiments show the proof of concept of our approach. However, the results shown in the related approach of semantic matching allow us to expect promising results for our approach. In fact, in both cases, the core underlying technologies are NLP (applied to classifications) and propositional reasoning, which gives us a reason to think that the results of the two approaches will be comparable. Note that semantic matching outperforms other similar approaches in some primary indicators [8].

However much more can be done. Our future work includes testing the feasibility of our approach with very large sets of documents, such as those classified in the DMOZ directory, as well as the development of a sound and complete query answering algorithm. Apart from this, we will explore the ways of combining the proposed approach to query answering with those based on document indexing and keywords-based search. Our future work also includes a study of how dynamic changes made to classifications can be fully supported at the level of the corresponding FCs and NFCs.

References

1. Franz Baader, Diego Calvanese, Deborah McGuinness, Daniele Nardi, and Peter Patel-Schneider. *The Description Logic Handbook : Theory, Implementation and Applications.* Cambridge University Press, 2003.
2. P. Bouquet, L. Serafini, and S. Zanobini. Semantic coordination: a new approach and an application. *In Proc. of the 2nd International Semantic Web Conference (ISWO'03). Sanibel Islands, Florida, USA*, October 2003.
3. Lois Mai Chan and J.S. Mitchell. *Dewey Decimal Classification: A Practical Guide.* Forest P.,U.S., December 1996.
4. eCl@ss: Standardized Material and Service Classification. see http://www.eclass-online.com/.
5. G.Adami, P.Avesani, and D.Sona. Clustering documents in a web directory. *In Proceedings of Workshop on Internet Data management (WIDM-03)*, 2003.

6. F. Giunchiglia and P. Shvaiko. Semantic matching. *Knowledge Engineering Review*, 18(3):265–280, 2003.

7. F. Giunchiglia, P. Shvaiko, and M. Yatskevich. S-match: An algorithm and an implementation of semantic matching. *In Proceedings of ESWS'04*, 2004.

8. F. Giunchiglia, P. Shvaiko, and M. Yatskevich. Semantic schema matching. In *CoopIS*, 2005.

9. F. Giunchiglia and M. Yatskevich. Element level semantic matching. In *Meaning Coordination and Negotiation workshop, ISWC*, 2004.

10. F. Giunchiglia, M. Yatskevich, and E. Giunchiglia. Efficient semantic matching. In *ESWC*, 2005.

11. A.D. Gordon. *Classification*. Monographs on Statistics and Applied Probability. Chapman-Hall/CRC, Second edition, 1999.

12. Ian Horrocks, Lei Li, Daniele Turi, and Sean Bechhofer. The instance store: DL reasoning with large numbers of individuals. In *Proc. of the 2004 Description Logic Workshop (DL 2004)*, pages 31–40, 2004.

13. A. K. Jain, M. N. Murty, and P. J. Flynn. Data clustering: a review. *ACM Computing Surveys*, 31(3):264–323, 1999.

14. Johnson-Laird. *Mental Models*. Harvard University Press, 1983.

15. Daphne Koller and Mehran Sahami. Hierarchically classifying documents using very few words. In Douglas H. Fisher, editor, *Proceedings of ICML-97, 14th International Conference on Machine Learning*, pages 170–178, Nashville, US, 1997. Morgan Kaufmann Publishers, San Francisco, US.

16. Douglas B. Lenat. CYC: A large-scale investment in knowledge infrastructure. *Communications of the ACM*, 38(11):33–38, 1995.

17. Bernardo Magnini, Luciano Serafini, and Manuela Speranza. Making explicit the semantics hidden in schema models. *In: Proceedings of the Workshop on Human Language Technology for the Semantic Web and Web Services, held at ISWC-2003, Sanibel Island, Florida*, October 2003.

18. D. L. McGuinness, P. Shvaiko, F. Giunchiglia, and P. Pinheiro da Silva. Towards explaining semantic matching. In *International Workshop on Description Logics at KR'04*, 2004.

19. George Miller. *WordNet: An electronic Lexical Database*. MIT Press, 1998.

20. Kamal Nigam, Andrew K. McCallum, Sebastian Thrun, and Tom M. Mitchell. Text classification from labeled and unlabeled documents using EM. *Machine Learning*, 39(2/3):103–134, 2000.

21. Natalya F. Noy. Semantic integration: a survey of ontology-based approaches. *SIGMOD Rec.*, 33(4):65–70, 2004.

22. The OpenNLP project. See http://opennlp.sourceforge.net/.

23. Fabrizio Sebastiani. Machine learning in automated text categorization. *ACM Computing Surveys*, 34(1):1–47, 2002.

24. Luciano Serafini, Stefano Zanobini, Simone Sceffer, and Paolo Bouquet:. Matching hierarchical classifications with attributes. In *ESWC*, pages 4–18, 2006.

25. J. F. Sowa. *Conceptual Structures: Information Processing in Mind and Machine*. Addison-Wesley, 1984.

26. Aixin Sun and Ee-Peng Lim. Hierarchical text classification and evaluation. In *ICDM*, pages 521–528, 2001.

27. MeSH: the National Library of Medicine's controlled vocabulary thesaurus. see http://www.nlm.nih.gov/mesh/.

28. DMoz: the Open Directory Project. See http://dmoz.org/.
29. Michael Uschold and Michael Gruninger. Ontologies and semantics for seamless connectivity. *SIGMOD Rec.*, 33(4):58–64, 2004.
30. Mark van Assem, Maarten R. Menken, Guus Schreiber, Jan Wielemaker, and Bob Wielinga. A method for converting thesauri to RDF/OWL. In *the Third International Semantic Web Conference (ISWC'04)*, number 3298, pages 17–31, Hiroshima, Japan, November 2004. Lecture Notes in Computer Science.
31. Rudolf Wille. Concept lattices and conceptual knowledge systems. *Computers and Mathematics with Applications*, 23:493–515, 1992.

GeRoMe: A Generic Role Based Metamodel for Model Management

David Kensche[1], Christoph Quix[1], Mohamed Amine Chatti[1], and Matthias Jarke[1,2]

[1] RWTH Aachen University, Informatik V (Information Systems), 52056 Aachen, Germany
[2] Fraunhofer FIT, Schloss Birlinghoven, 53574 St. Augustin, Germany
{kensche,quix,chatti,jarke}@cs.rwth-aachen.de

Abstract. The goal of *Model Management* is the development of new technologies and mechanisms to support the integration, evolution and matching of data models at the conceptual and logical design level. Such tasks are to be performed by means of a set of model management *operators* which work on models and their elements, without being restricted to a particular metamodel (e.g. the relational or UML metamodel).

We propose that generic model management should employ a generic metamodel (GMM) which serves as an abstraction of particular metamodels and preserves as much of the original features of modeling constructs as possible. A naive generalization of the elements of concrete metamodels in generic metaclasses would lose some of the specific features of the metamodels, or yield a prohibitive number of metaclasses in the GMM. To avoid these problems, we propose the *Generic Role based Metamodel GeRoMe* in which each model element is *decorated* with a set of role objects that represent specific properties of the model element. Roles may be added to or removed from elements at any time, which enables a very flexible and dynamic yet accurate definition of models.

Roles expose to operators different views on the same model element. Thus, operators concentrate on features which affect their functionality but may remain agnostic about other features. Consequently, these operators can use polymorphism and have to be implemented only once using *GeRoMe*, and not for each specific metamodel. We verified our results by implementing *GeRoMe* and a selection of model management operators using our metadata system ConceptBase.

1 Introduction

Design and maintenance of information systems require the management of complex models. Research in (data) *model management* aims at developing technologies and mechanisms to support the integration, merging, evolution, and matching of data models at the conceptual and logical design level. These problems have been addressed for specific modeling languages for a long time. Model management has become an active research area recently, as researchers now address the problem of *generic* model management, i.e. supporting the aforementioned tasks without being restricted to a particular modeling language [7,8]. To achieve this goal, the definition of a set of *generic* structures representing models and the definition of *generic* operations on these structures are required.

S. Spaccapietra et al. (Eds.): Journal on Data Semantics VIII, LNCS 4380, pp. 82–117, 2007.

According to the IRDS standard [18], metamodels are *languages* to define models. Examples for metamodels are *XML Schema* or the *UML Metamodel*. The same terminology is adopted in the specifications of the Object Management Group (OMG, http://www.omg.org) for MOF (Meta Object Facility) and MDA (Model Driven Architecture). Models are the description of a concrete application domain. Within an (integrated) information system, several metamodels are used, a specific one for each subsystem (e.g. DB system, application). Thus, the management of models in a generic way is necessary.

1.1   The Challenge: A Generic Mechanism for Representing Models

This paper addresses the first challenge mentioned in [8], the development of a mechanism for representing models. Since the goal is the support of *generic* model management, this has to be done in some generic way. Currently, model management applications often use a generic graph representation but operators have to be aware of the employed metamodel [10,15,23]. A graph representation is often sufficient for the purpose of finding correspondences between schemas, which is the task performed by the model management operator Match [28], but such a representation is not suitable for more complex operations (such as merging of models) as it does not contain detailed semantic information about relationships and constraints. For example, in [27] a generic (but yet simple) metamodel is used that distinguishes between different types of associations in order to merge two models. Consequently, in order to support a holistic model management framework it is necessary to provide a detailed generic metamodel. A more detailed discussion about the related work on the representation of models is given in section 2.

The intuitive approach to develop a truly generic metamodel (GMM) identifies abstractions of the metaclasses of different metamodels. Its goal is to define a comprehensive set of generic metaclasses organized in an inheritance lattice. Each metaclass in a given concrete metamodel then has to be mapped to a unique metaclass of the GMM.

The sketched approach exhibits a prohibitive weak point: elements of particular metamodels often have semantics that overlap but is neither completely different nor equivalent. For example, a generic Merge operator has to merge elements such as classes, relations, entity types and relationship types. All of these model elements can have attributes and should therefore be processed by the same implementation of an operator. In this setting, such polymorphism is only possible if the given model elements are represented by instances of the same metaclass in the GMM, or at least by instances of metaclasses with a common superclass. Thus, one has to choose the features of model elements which are combined in one metaclass.

Actually, in each metamodel there may be elements incorporating an entirely new combination of such aspects. One approach to cope with this problem is to focus on the "most important" features of model elements while omitting such properties which are regarded as less important. But to decide which properties are important and which are not results in loss of information about the model.

All properties of model elements could be retained if the GMM introduced a set of metaclasses as comprehensive as possible and combined them with multiple inheritance such that any combination of features is represented by a distinct metaclass. Despite the modeling accuracy of such a GMM, it will suffer from another drawback, namely that it leads to a combinatorial explosion in the number of sparsely populated intersection classes which add no new state.

1.2   Our Solution: Role Based Modeling

In such cases, a role based modeling approach is much more promising. In role based modeling, an object is regarded as playing roles in collaborations with other objects.

Applied to generic metadata modeling this approach allows to *decorate* a model element with a combination of multiple predefined aspects, thereby describing the element's properties as accurately as possible while using only metaclasses and roles from a relatively small set. In such a GMM, the different features of a model element (e.g. it is not only an *Aggregate* but also an *Association*) are only different views on the same element. During model transformations or evolution, an element may gain or lose roles, thereby adding and revoking features. Thus, the combinatorial explosion in the number of metaclasses is avoided but nevertheless most accurate metadata modeling is possible.

Therefore, the GMM proposed in this work retains these characteristics by employing the *role based* modeling approach, resulting in the *Generic Role based Metamodel GeRoMe* (phonetic transcription: dʒerəʊm). Implementations of model management operators can assert that model elements have certain properties by checking whether they play the necessary roles. At the same time the operator remains agnostic about any roles which do not affect its functionality. Thus, while role based metamodeling allows to formulate accurate models, the models appear to operators only as complex as necessary. *GeRoMe* will be used only by model management applications; users will use their favorite modeling language.

The difference between our and the naive generalization approach is similar to the difference between the local-as-view (LAV) and global-as-view (GAV) approaches in data integration. By defining elements of a GMM as generalization of elements of specific metamodels, an element of the GMM is defined as a view on the specific elements. In contrast, in our approach the definition of the roles in *GeRoMe* is independent of a particular metamodel, and the elements of the concrete metamodels can be characterized as a combination of roles. Thus, our role based approach can be seen as a LAV approach on the meta level, which has similar advantages as the normal LAV approach [22]. The role based metamodel is more "stable" with respect to the concrete metamodels represented, i.e. additional modeling features of other metamodels can be easily added by defining new role classes. Thus, this change would not affect other role classes in *GeRoMe*. In addition, the representations of the concrete metamodels are more accurate as their elements can be described by a combination of role classes.

The definition of the GMM requires a careful analysis and comparison of existing metamodels. Since it has to be possible to represent schemata in various metamodels in order to allow generic model management, we analyzed five popular yet quite different metamodels (Relational, EER, UML, OWL DL, and XML Schema). We identified the common structures, properties, and constraint mechanisms of these metamodels. This part of our work can be seen as an update to the work in [17], in which several semantic database modeling languages have been compared.

The paper is structured as follows. Section 2 provides some background information on model management and role based modeling, and presents a motivating scenario. In section 3, we analyze and compare existing metamodels and derive the *Generic Role based Metamodel GeRoMe*. Section 4 shows several examples of models in different metamodels represented in *GeRoMe*. Section 5 explains how model management operations can be performed using *GeRoMe*. As an example, we describe some atomic operations necessary for the transformation of an EER model into a a relational model. The architecture and implementation of our model management prototype is discussed in section 6. In particular, we present a rule-based approach to import and export models. Finally, section 7 summarizes our work and points out future work.

2   Background and Motivation

The next subsection provides an overview of model management in general. The motivating scenario in section 2.2 should give an idea of the benefits of a model management framework and the usage of a generic metamodel for model management. An overview of work about role based modeling concludes this section.

2.1   Model Management

Model management aims at providing a formalization for the definition and modification of complex models [8]. To achieve this goal, a model management system has to provide definitions for *models* (i.e. schemas represented in some metamodel), *mappings* (i.e. relationships between different models), and *operators* (i.e. operations that manipulate models and mappings). There have been earlier approaches to model management [3,20], which did address especially the transformation of models between different metamodels. Model management has become more important recently, as the integration of information systems requires the management of complex models. The most important operations in model management are Merge (integration of two models), Match (creating a mapping between two models), Diff (finding the differences between two models), and ModelGen (generating a model from another model in a different metamodel representation).

Rondo [23] is the first complete prototype of model management. It represents models as directed labeled graphs. Each node of such a graph denotes one model element, e.g. an XML Schema complex type or relational table. A model is represented by a set of edges between these nodes. A model element's type (Table, Column, Class, ...) is also specified by such an edge with the label *type*. Furthermore, types of attributes are specified by other dedicated edges, e.g. *SQLtype*. For each of the supported metamodels a different set of types is available. Although the models are represented in a generic graph structure, the implementation of the operators is not truly generic. For example, the implementation of the Match operator requires two models of the same type as input, and some operators (such as Extract) have specific implementations for each metamodel.

Another approach to generic model representation has been introduced in [3], expressed in a relational model dictionary [1], and was recently used for the generic ModelGen implementation MIDST [2]. This approach differs from our representation in that it describes a class of model elements as a pattern built up from a set of components such as an EER relationship type which is composed of at least two participators and any number of attributes. A model element belongs to a class of modeling constructs if it matches the given pattern. They map all metamodels to a very small set of modeling constructs. In contrast, we regard the differences in the semantics of modeling constructs in different metamodels as subtle but important. For example, modeling sets with object identity and sets without object identity in the same way results in hiding this knowledge in code of the model management system whereas it should be part of the generic representation. In our representation we describe a model element by the set of roles it plays and their relationships to other elements. A small difference between two constructs can be modeled by adding a role to an element and thereby adding a new feature to the element.

Another rule-based approach to model transformation is presented in [9]. Models are first translated into a universal metamodel and then a sequence of rule-based transformations is applied to generate a model that is valid in the target metamodel. Details about the universal metamodel are not given in [9].

Clio [15] is a tool for creating schema mappings. Whereas schema matching algorithms just discover correspondences between schemas, Clio goes one step further and derives a mapping from a set of correspondences. The mapping is a query that transforms the data from one schema into another schema. However, Clio supports only XML and relational schemas.

More sophisticated model management operators such as Merge (integration of two models according to a given mapping, resulting in a new model) require even more semantic information about the models involved. For example, in [27] a meta model with several association types (e.g. has-a, is-a) is used.

The various approaches to model management show that each operator requires a different view on a model. Schema matching focuses on labels and structure of schema elements, whereas merging and transformation of models require more detailed information about the semantics of a model (e.g. association types, constraints). These different views are supported by our role based approach, as operators will see only those roles which are relevant in their context.

2.2 Scenario

The following simplified scenario should provide an idea of what model management is about and of the benefits of utilizing a generic metamodel for model management.

Complex information systems undergo regular changes due to changes of the requirements, of the real world represented by the information system, or of other systems connected to the information system. As an example, we consider the following eBusiness scenario: a supplier of an automotive manufacturer receives orders from a business partner in some XML format (XS1). The orders are entered into the ERP system of the supplier by a transformation program, which uses a mapping between the XML schema and the relational DB (RM2) of the ERP system.

In order to generate this mapping, the two models are represented as models in a generic metamodel (GM1 and GM2). A Match operator can then be used to create a mapping GM1_GM2 between the two models, which can be further translated into the

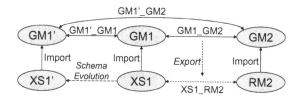

Fig. 1. Schema evolution using *GeRoMe* and Model Management

desired mapping XS1_RM2 between the original models, e.g. by exporting the mapping with an operator which generates a set of data access objects for RM2 and a parser for XML documents conforming to XS1 as well as glue code which uses the mapping information for adapting these classes to each other.

Due to a change in the system of the manufacturer, the schema of the orders has changed. This change has to be propagated to the mapping between the XML schema and the relational DB. Focusing on the models, this scenario can be seen as an example of schema evolution (Fig. 1). The original XML schema XS1 is mapped to the relational model (RM2) of the DB using the mapping XS1_RM2. The schema evolution generates a new version of the XML schema, namely XS1'.

Again, instead of applying the model management operators to the level of specific schemas, we will first generate a corresponding representation of the specific model in *GeRoMe* (GM1'). Then, we have to apply the Match operator to GM1 and GM1', resulting in a mapping GM1'_GM1 between these models. This match operation should be simpler than matching the new version GM1' with GM2 directly, as two versions of the same model should be quite similar. Then, we can compose the mappings GM1'_GM1 and GM1_GM2 to a new mapping GM1'_GM2. Note, that this operation has just to consider mappings between models represented in *GeRoMe*, which should simplify the implementation of such an operator. The result of this step is a mapping from GM1' to GM2 of those elements which are also present in GM1.

In order to map elements which have been added during the schema evolution a Diff operator has to be used on GM1' and GM1 which takes into account the mapping GM1'_GM1. The difference then has to be mapped individually.

The important difference to other approaches is that the operations in *GeRoMe* are truly generic, they do not have to take into account different representations of models. Therefore, the operators have to be implemented only once, namely for the *GeRoMe* representation. In the example the same match operator can be used in both cases, to match the two versions of the XML Schema and to match the XML Schema with the relational model.

2.3   Role Based Modeling

The concept of role (or aspect) based modeling has first been described in detail in the context of the network model [4] and later on in several works on object-oriented development and object-oriented databases [11,29,30].

Different formalizations have been proposed, which exhibit significant differences, but all have in common that a role extends the features of an existing object while being a view on the object and *not* an object in its own right. In [11] *multiple direct class membership* is considered as a solution to the problem of artificial intersection classes. That is, instead of defining an intersection class, the combination of state and behavior is achieved by defining an object to be instance of several classes at the same time, which are not necessarily on the same specialization path.

In [29] the notion of aspects of objects is discussed. It is stated that at any given moment an entity may have many different types that are not necessarily related. Often this issue cannot be handled by multiple inheritance since this would lead to a large number of sparsely populated "intersection classes" which add no new state. This approach is different from multiple direct class membership in that each object can have multiple aspects of the same type, e.g. a person can at the same time be a student at more than one university while still being the same individual.

[6] presents an approach to avoid large class hierarchies in chemical engineering applications that is also based on aspects. Aspects divide a class into separately instantiatable partitions. Thus, aspects are a "part" of the object whereas roles are more "external" objects attached to another object, thereby providing different views on that object. A comparison of aspects and roles and issues concerning their implementation are discussed in [14].

Other approaches, such as the one considered in [30], treat the different features of an object as roles, which are themselves instances of so called *role classes* and have identity by state. This representation also allows model elements to play directly or implicitly more than one instance of the same role. In addition, [30] introduces the concept of *role player qualification* which means that not every object may play every role but that certain conditions have to hold.

3   The Generic Role Based Metamodel *GeRoMe*

In this section, we will first explain the role model which we have employed to define *GeRoMe*. Based on our analysis of existing metamodels (section 3.2), we have derived the *Generic Role based Metamodel*, which is described in detail in section 3.3.

3.1   Description of the Role Model

GeRoMe employs the following role model. A model element is represented by an object which has no characteristics in its own right. Roles can be combined to describe a model element encompassing several properties. Thus, the model element is *decorated* with its features by letting it *play* roles. A role maintains its own identity and may be player of other roles itself. Because a model element without roles does not have any features, every model element has to play at least one role. Every role object has exactly one player. In our model, some role classes may be used more than once by an element, e.g. an *Attribute* may play the role of a *Reference* to more than one other *Attribute*. Thus, the complete representation of a model element and its roles forms a tree with the model element as its root.

We used three different relationships between role classes, namely *inheritance*, *play*, and *precondition*. The *play* relationship defines which objects may be player of certain roles. For example, an *Attribute* role may play itself the role of a reference. In addition, a role may be a precondition of another role. Thus, in order to be qualified to play a role of a certain class, the player must be already the player of another role of a certain other class. Except for namespaces, all links between model elements are modeled as links between roles played by the elements.

To tap the full power of role modeling, we have to define role classes in such a way that each of them represents an "atomic" property of a model element. Then roles can be combined to yield the most accurate representation of an element.

3.2   Role Based Analysis of Concrete Metamodels

A generic metamodel should be able to represent both the structures and constraints expressible in any metamodel. Thus, to define such a metamodel it is necessary to analyze and compare the elements of a set of metamodels. Our choice of metamodels comprises the relational model (RM) [12] and the enhanced entity relationship model (EERM) [12] because these two models are rather simple and are in widespread use. The metamodel of the Unified Modeling Language (UML, version 1.5) has been analyzed as an example for object-oriented languages. The description logics species of the Web Ontology Language (OWL DL, http://www.w3.org/2004/OWL/) has been included since it follows different description paradigms due to its purpose. For example, properties of concepts are not defined within the concepts themselves but separately. Finally, XML Schema (http://www.w3.org/XML/Schema) has been analyzed as it is the most important metamodel for semistructured data.

We analyzed the elements and constraints available in these five metamodels and identified their differences and similarities. In doing so, we determined the role classes, which constitute our role based metamodel. In total, we compared about seventy structural properties and elements and twenty types of constraints. Some of them are very easily abstracted, such as data types or aggregates. Others, such as the XML Schema *element* or OWL object properties, are rather intricate and need closer inspection. The XML Schema element is an association (associating a parent element with its children). The root element of a document is a special element which does not have a parent. Furthermore, an XML Schema may allow different types of root elements for a document. Another problematic example are object properties in OWL DL: the *Association* role is played by a "pair of properties" and the *ObjectAssociationEnd* role is played by object properties. Furthermore, some metamodels provide redundant options for representing the same semantics, e.g. there is no semantic difference between an XML Schema attribute and a simple-typed XML Schema element with a maximum cardinality of 1. Thus, it is difficult to represent such specific model elements in a GMM. In section 4, we describe some of the representation problems in more detail.

Table 1 shows a selection of role classes and states the related model elements in the considered metamodels. The table contains roles which are used to define structural model elements (e.g. relation, class) and roles to define relationships and constraints (e.g. association, disjointness). Due to space constraints, the table does not embody all metamodel elements and correspondences in the different metamodels.

Table 1. Roles played by concrete metaclasses

Role	EER	Relational	OWL DL	XML Schema	UML
Domain	domain	domain	xsd datatype	any simple type	datatype
Aggregate	entity/rel.-ship type, comp. attr.	relation	class	complex type	class, association class, struct
Association	relationship type	-	a pair of inverse object properties	element	association, association class
ObjectSet	entity/rel.-ship type	-	class	complex type, schema	class, ass. class, association, interface
Base-Element	supertype in isA, subset in Union	base of anonymous domain	superclass, superproperty	base simple / complex type	superclass, implemented interface
Derived-Element	subtype in isA or union type	anonymous domain constraint	subclass, subproperty	derived simple / complex type	subclass, subinterface, implementation
Union	derivation link of union type	-	derivation link of union class	derivation link of union type	-
IsA	isA derivation link	-	subclassing derivation link	restriction / extension derivation link	subclassing, implementation
Enumeration	enumerated domain restriction	enumerated domain restriction	enumeration	enumeration	enum, constants in interface (constant inheritance)?
Attribute	(composite / multivalued) attribute	column	data type property	attribute, element with simple type	attributes in struct, member variables, properties
Object-Association-End	link between relationship type and its participator	-	object property	link between element and its nested or enclosing complex type	point where association meets participator
Literal-Association-End	-	-	-	link between an element and its nested simple type	-
Literal	instance of a domain	domain value	data type value	simple type value	constant, value of simple type
Structured-Instance	instance of a structured type	tuple	individual	valid XML	value of struct, object
Visible	entity type, rel.-ship type, attr.	relation, column	named class, property	named type, attribute element	anything not anonymous
Reference	-	foreign key comp.	-	keyref component	-
Foreign Key	-	foreign key	-	keyref	-
Disjointness	constraint on subtypes	-	constraint on classes	-	constraint on classes
Injective	primary/partial key	unique, primary key	inverse functional	unique, key	-
Identifier	primary/partial key	primary key	-	key	-
Universal	anonymous domain of attribute	anonymous domain constraint of column	allValuesFrom	restriction of complex type	- (covariance breaks polymorphism)
Existential	-	-	someValuesFrom	-	-
Default	-	default value	-	default value	default value

3.3 Description of *GeRoMe*

Figure 2 presents the Generic Role based Metamodel *GeRoMe* at its current state, based on the analysis of the previous section. All role classes inherit from *RoleObject* but we omitted these links for the sake of readability. Although we use here the UML notation to describe the *metamodel GeRoMe*, it has to be stressed that UML or the related MOF standard (http://www.omg.org/mof/) are not suitable for expressing *models* for *generic* model management applications, since – as we discussed above – the use of multiple inheritance instead of a role based approach would lead to a combinatorial explosion of classes in the metamodel. Below, we will describe the elements of *GeRoMe* according to their basic characteristics: structural elements, derivations, and constraints.

Structural Elements. Every model element representing a primitive data type plays the role of a *Domain*. *GeRoMe* contains a collection of predefined domains such as *int* and *string*. In contrast, model elements which may have attributes play an *Aggregate* role (e.g. entity and relationship types, composite attributes in EER; relations, classes and structs in other metamodels).

Thus, the *Aggregate* role is connected to a set of *Attribute* roles. Each of these *Attribute* roles is part of another tree-structured model element description. An *Attribute* role is a special kind of *Particle* and has therefore the *min* and *max* attributes which can be used to define cardinality constraints. Every attribute has a *Type*, which may be a primitive type or an *Aggregate* in the case of composite attributes.

The *Aggregate* role and the *Domain* role are specializations of *Type*. *Type* is a specialization of *DerivableElement* which is the abstract class of roles to be played by all model elements which may be specialized. Another kind of *DerivableElement* is the *Association* role. Properties of associations are *AssociationEnd* roles. For example, association roles are played by EER relationship types, UML associations, or UML association classes. A model element which provides object identity to its instances may participate in one or more associations. This is modeled by specifying the element's *ObjectSet* role to be the participator of one or more *ObjectAssociationEnd* roles. Thus, an association end is a model element in its own right, and the association is a relationship between objects and values. In addition, the roles *AggregationEnd* and *CompositionEnd* can be used to model the special types of associations available in UML. In order to be able to represent the aforementioned special case of XML Schema elements having a simple type, we had to introduce the *LiteralAssociationEnd* as a role class. Furthermore, an *Attribute* or *LiteralAssociationEnd* role may itself play the role of a *Reference*, which defines a referential constraint referencing another *Attribute* of the same type.

The *Association* and *Aggregate* role classes are an intuitive example of two role classes that can be used in combination to represent similar concepts of different metamodels. If the represented schema is in a concrete metamodel which allows relationship types to have attributes, such as the EER metamodel, then every model element playing an *Association* role may play additionally an *Aggregate* role. If associations may not have attributes, which is the case in OWL, a model element may only play either of both roles. On the other hand, the representation of a relational schema may not contain *Association* roles at all. Thus, these two roles can be combined to represent the precise semantics of different metamodel elements. Of course any of these combinations can

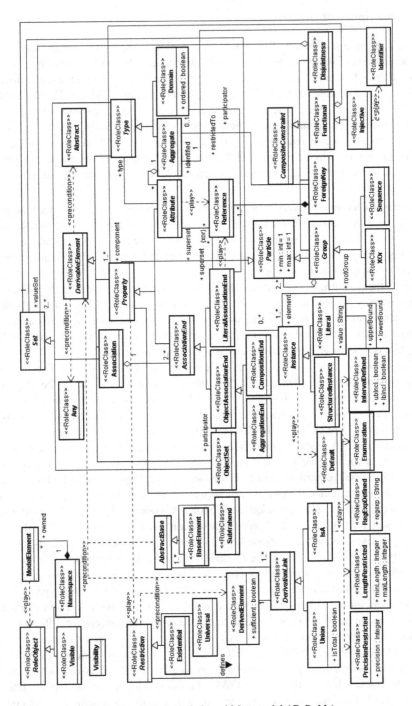

Fig. 2. The Generic Role based Metamodel (*GeRoMe*)

be further combined with other roles, such as the *ObjectSet* role, to yield even more description choices.

We have defined a formal semantics for models represented in *GeRoMe* that allows to specify *Instances* for model elements which play a *Set* role. Values of *Domains* are modeled as elements playing a *Literal* role. On the other hand values of elements playing *ObjectSet*, *Aggregate*, or *Association* roles, or combinations thereof are represented by elements playing a *StructuredInstance* role. These are for example rows in a table, values of structs in UML, or instances of classes or association classes. An *Abstract* role marks a *Set* as being not instantiable. The *Any* role is used as a wildcard, in cases where types or associations or attributes are not constrained. This is commonly used in XML Schema where you can specify components of a complex type with `anyAttribute` or `anyElement`, for instance. Each *Instance* can also play the role of a *Default* value with respect to any number of properties. Our formal semantics defines also the shape of the structured instance such that it conforms to the structure defined by its value set. But we abstain here from further elaborating on that issue since this topic abandons the model level for the instance level.

Finally, model elements can be *Visible*, i.e. they can be identified by a name. The *name* attribute of a *Visible* role has to be unique within the *Namespace* it is defined in. Furthermore, a visibility can be chosen for a *Visible* element from a predefined enumeration. A model's root node is represented by a model element which plays a *Namespace* role.

Derivation of New Elements. A *BaseElement* role is played by any model element that is a superset in the definition of a derived element. Thus, a *DerivedElement* can have more than one *BaseElement* and vice versa. These roles can be played by any *DerivableElement*.

The *BaseElement* and *DerivedElement* roles are connected via dedicated model elements representing the *DerivationLink*. Each *DerivationLink* connects one or more *BaseElements* to one *DerivedElement*. The *IsA* role can be used to define specialization relationships. It extends the definition of a superclass by adding new properties (e.g. inheritance in UML). A *DerivedElement* role which is connected to an *IsA* role with more than one *BaseElement* role can be used to define a type which is the intersection of its base elements. A *Subtrahend* is an element whose instances are never instances of the derived element (e.g. a `complementOf` definition in OWL).

We identified two different kinds of *isA* relationships which are often not distinguished from each other. All surveyed metamodels allow *extension* (i.e. the subtype defines additional attributes and associations) if they allow specialization at all. In EER and OWL, model elements can specialize base elements also by constraining the ranges of inherited properties. In EER, this is called *predicate defined specialization* [12, p.80], whereas in OWL it is called *restriction* and comprises a very important description facility for inheritance. Such derivations can be expressed in our metamodel by deriving the constrained property from the original one and letting it play the role of a *Universal* or *Existential* restriction. This *Restriction* role must reference the *DerivedElement* role of the respective subclass. These restrictions cannot be used in UML. For example defining a universal restriction on an association would amount to covariance, that is specialization of a property when specializing a class. Covariance breaks polymorphism in UML (or object oriented programming languages); it is therefore not allowed.

Special kinds of derivations are for example enumerations and intervals. We model such derivations by letting the *IsA* link play additional roles. This is similar to the facets of XML Schema simple types and allows to orthogonally specify conditions of the derived *Set*. Obviously some of these roles may only be applied when deriving *Domains*. You can define new structural elements by using an *Enumeration* role and enumerating those *Instances* which are element of the new *Set*. Furthermore, derivations may define intervals of existing *Domains* or restrict the length and precision of their values. In case the base element is the built-in domain *string* or a subtype thereof a regular expression can define a new subtype. In XML Schema, named domains can be derived from others whereas in the relational metamodel derived domains occur only as an anonymous type of attributes with enumeration or interval domains.

Constraints. Constraints are represented by separate model elements. For example, a disjointness constraint on a set of derived elements (or any other types) has to be defined by a model element representing this constraint. The element has to play a *Disjointness* role which references the types to be disjoint. In the case of OWL or UML, any collection of classes can be defined to be disjoint. When representing an EER model, this constraint can be used to define a disjoint *isA* relationship by referencing at least all of the derived elements.

Another constraint is the *Functional* constraint which declares a property or a set of properties to have the characteristics of be a function (uniqueness and completeness) and is used for example to represent certain OWL properties. Correspondingly, an *Injective* property is a functional property that specifies a one-to-one relationship. Such an *Injective* role is equivalent to a uniqueness constraint in XML Schema or SQL. It can also define a composite key by being connected to multiple properties. An injective constraint playing an *Identifier* role defines a primary key. This reflects the fact that a primary key is only a selected uniqueness constraint, and thus, only one of multiple candidate keys.

The *ForeignKey* constraint is a collection of *Reference* roles which defines a (possibly composite) reference to an *Identifier*. This is used to model foreign keys in the relational model or key references in XML Schema.

Additional restrictions on the structure of *Aggregates* or *Associations* can be given by *Group* constraints which reference a set of *Particles*. For instance, the *Sequence* constraint defines the order of appearance of properties. The *XOr* constraint is a modeling feature that is available in the UML metamodel or in XML Schema. It states that an object may participate only in one of the related associations or that only one of referenced attributes occurrs. Such *Group* constraints can also be nested which corresponds to the nesting of the respective model groups in XML Schema and allows to define them recursively together with cardinality constraints.

We are aware that there are subtle differences in the semantics of constraints for the various metamodels. However, these differences stem from the objectives of the respective modeling languages and apply only to the data level. In contrast, the goal of *GeRoMe* is to represent models and to provide a generic data structure for manipulating them. For instance, in a relational database a uniqueness constraint is checked whenever a row is inserted or updated whereas in an ontology such a constraint will only narrow the interpretation of the model such that individuals with the same value for the unique property are classified as being equal. On the model level the constraint is just a statement about the property.

Another issue are constraints that can be attached as an expression in some formal constraint language to the model (e.g. OCL constraints or SQL assertions). Such constraints cannot be represented in a generic way, as this would require a language that unifies all features of the various constraint languages. Thus, a generic constraint language would be difficult to interpret because of the complexity of the language or it would be undecidable whether a constraint can be satisfied or not. Currently, we are able to express constraints as first-order logic formulas (using predicates referring to the instance level as defined in appendix A.1) which certainly cannot cover all constraints (e.g., SQL assertions with aggregations or functions). Therefore, a translation of existing contraint languages into our language could be done only partially. The opposite way, however, will be possible, e.g. generating executable code from these constraints. This is especially important for mappings between different models as these mappings will be used to transform data from one model into another model.

GeRoMe can be extended with new role classes representing other features of constraints and structures while existing models and operators still remain correct.

4   Representation Examples

This section presents some example models based on a small airport database in [12, p.109] (see fig. 3). We represented EER, XML Schema and OWL DL models for this example. The model contains simple entity types composed of attributes as well as some advanced features, which are not supported by all metamodels (e.g. composite attributes, *isA* relationship).

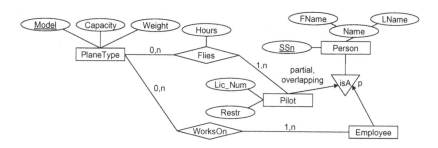

Fig. 3. Part of an airport EER schema

4.1   Representation of an EER Schema

Fig. 4 shows a part of the representation of the airport model in *GeRoMe*. The *GeRoMe* representation shows each model element as a *ModelElement* object (gray rectangle) which plays a number of roles (white squares) directly or by virtue of its roles playing roles themselves. Each such role object may be connected to other roles or literals, respectively. Thus, the roles act as interfaces or views of a model element. The links

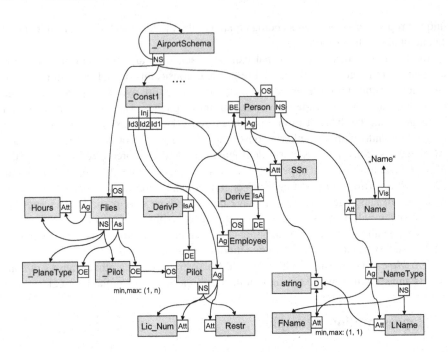

Fig. 4. *GeRoMe* representation of an EER schema

between role objects connect the model element descriptions according to the semantics of the represented schema.

For the sake of readability, we refrain here from showing the whole model and omitted repeating structures with the same semantics such as links from namespaces to their owned elements or *Visible* roles. A model element plays a *Visible* role if it has a name. We represent this in the following figures by assigning a simple label to the gray box resembling the element. In case of anonymous elements, which do not play a *Visible* role, we prefix the label with an underscore.

The root model element of the airport schema is a model element representing the schema itself (*_AirportSchema*). It plays a *Namespace* role (NS) referencing all model elements directly contained in this model.

The *Name* attribute is a visible model element and therefore its model element object plays the *Visible* role (Vis). The role defines a name of the element as it could be seen in a graphical EER editor (note that we omitted other occurrences of the *Visible* role class).

Since entity types are composed of attributes, every object representing an entity type plays an *Aggregate* role (Ag). Furthermore, instances of entity types have object identity. Consequently, representations of entity types also play an *ObjectSet* role (OS). The *Aggregate* role is again connected to the descriptions of the entity type's attributes.

The EER model defines a primary key constraint on the *SSn* attribute. Therefore, a model element representing the constraint (*_Const1*) and playing an *Injective* role (Inj) is connected to this attribute. This is a uniqueness constraint which is special in the sense that it has been chosen to be a primary key for the entity type *Person*. This fact is represented by the constraint playing an *Identifier* role (Id1) connected to the identified aggregate. Since *Person*'s subtypes must have the same identifier, the injectiveness constraint plays also *Identifier* roles (Id2, Id3) with respect to these model elements.

In the EER model, it is usually not possible to specify domain constraints, but the addition of default domains does not hurt. Therefore, attributes always have a type in *GeRoMe*. Domains are themselves represented as model elements playing domain roles (D) (e.g. string). It is also possible to derive new types from existing ones as this is also possible in most concrete metamodels.

In addition, note that the composite attribute *Name* has not a domain but another *Aggregate* as type. Unlike the representation of an entity type, *_NameType* is not player of an *ObjectSet* role. Consequently, this element cannot be connected to an *Association-End*, which means that it cannot participate in associations. Furthermore, *_NameType* is not visible as it is an anonymous type. However, the representation is very similar to that of entity types and this eases handling both concepts similarly. For example, in another schema the composite attribute could be modeled by a weak entity type. If these two schemata have to be matched, a generic Match operator would ignore the *ObjectSet* role. The similarity of both elements would nevertheless be recognized as both elements play an *Aggregate* role and have the same attributes.

Furthermore, the figure shows the representation of the *isA* relationship. Since every instance of *Pilot* and *Employee* is also an instance of *Person*, the *Person* model element plays a *BaseElement* role (BE) referenced by two *IsA* roles (IsA). These roles define two children, namely the *DerivedElement* roles (DE) which are played by the respective subtypes *Employee* and *Pilot*. Any attribute attached to the *Aggregate* roles of the subtypes defines an extension to the supertype. The children could also be defined as predicate-defined subtypes by associating to the *DerivedElement* roles a number of *Restriction* roles.

The subtype *Pilot* participates in the relationship type *Flies*. The representation of this relationship contains an *Association* role (As) which is attached to two *Object-AssociationEnd*s (OE) (i.e. a binary relationship). Furthermore, the relationship has an attribute, and consequently, it plays the role of an *Aggregate*. The representations of the two association ends define cardinality constraints and are linked to the *ObjectSet* roles (OS) of their respective participators. They also may play a *Visible* role which assigns a name to the association end.

4.2   Representation of an XML Schema

Figure 6 shows part of an XML Schema for the airport domain whereas figure 5 shows the representation of this example schema in *GeRoMe*. The XML Schema element is a relationship between its enclosing type and the complex type of the nested element. But it is always a 1:n relationship since an XML document is always tree structured. Cross links between elements in different subtrees have to be modeled by references.

But what about root elements in a schema? These elements are related to the schema itself which in our role based model is represented by the *http://../Airport* model element. This is just one example of a concrete model element which is not obviously mapped to a generic metamodel.

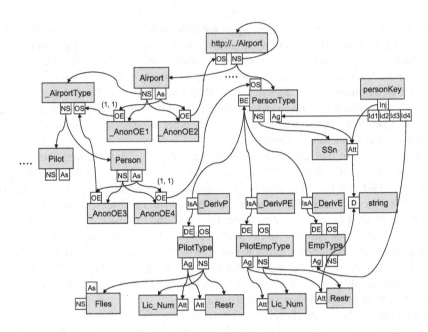

Fig. 5. Representation of a similar XML Schema

An XML document conforming to an XML Schema can have any element as root element which is defined in the schema file as a direct child of the schema element. Consequently, any such element is represented in *GeRoMe* as a model element playing an association role with its complex type as one participator and the schema node as the other participator. In the example, *Airport* is the only such element. This element is visible and its name is "Airport". *AssociationEnd*s of XML elements have no names attached and therefore are anonymous. Complex types may be anonymously nested into an element definition. In the example, this is the case for *_AirportType*. Since definitions of keys have labels in XML Schema, the identifier of *Person* plays a *Visible* role with its label "personKey" assigned to it.

Model elements defined within other model elements such as attributes and XML elements are referenced by the *Namespace* role of the containing element. For example, the element *Flies* is owned by the *Namespace* role of *PilotType*. Another consequence of the structure of semistructured data is that the *AssociationEnd* of the nested type always has cardinality (1, 1), i.e. it has exactly one parent. Finally, the model element *PilotEmpType* has been introduced as it is not possible to represent overlapping types in XML Schema.

4.3   Representation of an OWL DL Ontology

In table 1, we stated that OWL DL object properties are represented by model elements playing *ObjectAssociationEnd* roles and that a pair of these model elements is connected by an *Association*. This is another good example for the problems which occur when integrating heterogenous metamodels to a GMM. The reasons for the sketched

```
<xsd:schema xmlns="http://../Airport">
  <xsd:element name="Airport">
    <xsd:complexType>..</xsd:complexType>
    <xsd:key name="personKey">
      <xsd:selector xpath="./Person" />
      <xsd:field xpath="@SSn" />
    </xsd:key>
  </xsd:element>
  <xsd:complexType name="PersonType">
    <xsd:attribute name="SSn" type="xsd:string" />
  </xsd:complexType>
  <xsd:complexType name="PilotType">
    <xsd:complexContent>
      <xsd:extension base="PersonType">
        <xsd:sequence>
          <xsd:element name="Flies">
            <xsd:complexType>...</xsd:complexType>
          </xsd:element>
        </xsd:sequence>
        <xsd:attribute name="Lic_Num" type="xsd:string" />
        <xsd:attribute name="Restr" type="xsd:string" />
      </xsd:extension>
    </xsd:complexContent>
  </xsd:complexType>
  <xsd:complexType name="PilotEmpType">
    ...
  </xsd:complexType>
</xsd:schema>
```

Fig. 6. An XML Schema for the airport domain

representation can be explained with the semantics of the relationship type *WorksOn* in fig. 3. The representation of the corresponding OWL DL elements is shown in figure 7.

Intuitively and correctly, one represents *WorksOn* as a model element playing an *Association* role. *WorksOn* has two *ObjectAssociationEnd*s: one with cardinality (0,n) pointing on *PlaneType* and one with cardinality (1,n) pointing on *Employee*. This is represented analogous to *Flies* in fig. 4. Now what are the problems if you would regard an object property *WorksOn* as corresponding to the given relationship type?

Firstly, an object property always has domain and range. Thus, it has a direction. But the direction of a relationship type is only suggested by its name. On the other hand, an association end has a direction. The role name describes the role which the participator plays in the relationship type with respect to the participator at the opposite end. Furthermore, these role names are often phrasal verbs as are the names of object properties in OWL. Actually, in description logics object properties are often called *roles*. Thus, "WorksOn" should be the role name assigned to the link between the relationship type and the entitiy type *PlaneType*.

Secondly, an object property may have one cardinality restriction, whereas a relationship type has at least two (one for each participating entity). This shows that an object property corresponds to an association end, and that a pair of object properties (one of which is the inverse of the other) is correctly represented as a binary association. Note that OWL DL allows only binary relationships.

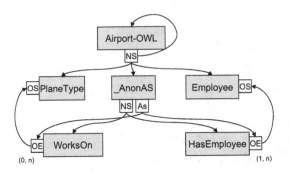

Fig. 7. Representation of OWL object properties

In order to allow other constraints, such as *Symmetric*, new roles can be added to *GeRoMe*. Adding a new role to the metamodel will render existing models and operator implementations valid and correct. Thus, it is also easy to extend *GeRoMe* if this is necessary in order to include new modeling constructs.

5   Model Management Using *GeRoMe* Models

In this section, we show how model management operators can make use of *GeRoMe*. Transformation of models is a typical task for model management applications. Our implementation of generic ModelGen operators is comparable to the approach described in [26] which is imperative as well. Another approach is the rule-based model transformation of [2]. We implemented our Import and Export operators based on equivalence rules between the concrete metamodels and *GeRoMe* (cf. section 6.3). A rule based approach is particularly useful for this task as equivalence rules enable consistent import and export of models since they are applicable in both directions.

We will explain the transformation of the EER model of fig. 4 into a relational schema. Therefore, the original representation has to undergo several transformations in order to become a representation of a relational schema. Fig. 8 shows the final result of the transformation steps which will be discussed in detail in the following.

5.1   Transformation of *GeRoMe* Models

In model management, transformation of models is performed by a ModelGen operator, i.e. the operator generates a model from another existing model. We have implemented the transformation of constructs such as composite attributes or inheritance from an EER schema by several ModelGen_X operators. Each operator transforms the modeling constructs not allowed in the relational model into modeling elements of the relational model. The decomposition of the operators into several "atomic" operators has the advantage that they can be reused in combination with other operators to form new operators. Note that the following operators are not aware about the original representation of the models, i.e. the operators just use the *GeRoMe* representation. Thus, they could also be used to transform a UML model into XML Schema if similar transformation tasks are required (e.g. transformation of associations to references).

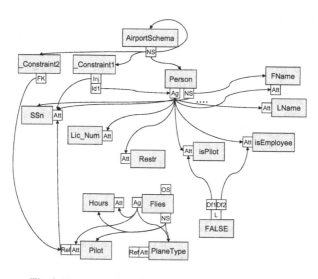

Fig. 8. Representation of the resulting relational schema

It has to be emphasized that mapping of models from one metamodel to another is just one popular example application of model management. The goal of our generic metamodel is *not only* to provide a platform for schema translation but to provide a generic model representation that serves as a foundation for the polymorphic usage of *any* model management operator. Thereby, other applications of model management, such as schema evolution, are also supported in a generic way.

Transformation of Relationship Types. Relationship types are not allowed in the relational metamodel. According to properties such as cardinality constraints, they have to be transformed to relations by executing the operator ModelGen_AssocToRef for each *Association* role. First, it looks for attached *ObjectAssociationEnd* roles, the arity of the association, and cardinality constraints. Depending on these constraints the transformation is either performed automatically or the user is asked for a decision before the operator can proceed. Copies of all attributes in the participators' identifiers are attached to the relationship's *Aggregate* role. An *Aggregate* role has to be created first, if not yet available. Furthermore, these copies play *Reference* roles (Ref) referencing the original attributes, and thereby defining referential constraints. These reference roles constitute a foreign key (FK). After performing all these transformations, the association ends and the relationship's *Association* role are deleted.

The result yet contains *ObjectSet* roles (OS), which are not allowed in a relational model. These roles can now be removed directly, as the associations have been transformed to attribute references. This yields an intermediate result which cannot be interpreted as a valid schema in the EER or relational metamodel, since it now contains constructs disallowed in both metamodels. An Export operator to the Relational or EER metamodel would have to recognize this invalidity and reject to export.

Transformation of IsA Relationships. The *isA* relationships also have to be removed depending on their characteristics (partial and overlapping), the attributes of the extensions *Pilot* and *Employee* thereby become attributes of the supertype.

The operator *ModelGen_FlattenIsA* fulfills this task by receiving a *BaseElement* role as input. It first checks for disjointness of connected *isA* relationships and whether they are total or not. Depending on these properties, the user is presented a number of choices on how to flatten the selected *isA* relationships. In the example, the base type *Person* and its subtypes *Pilot* and *Employee* have been selected to be transformed to one single aggregate due to the fact that the *isA* relationship is neither total nor disjoint. The resulting aggregate contains all attributes of the supertype and of the subtypes. Additionally, the boolean attributes *isPilot* and *isEmployee* as well as *Default* roles Df1 and Df2 related to these attributes have been introduced.

Transformation of Composite Attributes. The transformation of composite attributes is done by another atomic operator. First, it collects recursively all "atomic" attributes of a nested structure. Then, it adds all these attributes to the original *Aggregate* and removes all the structures describing the composite attribute(s) (including the anonymous type). This operator also needs to consider cardinality constraints on attributes, since set-valued attributes have to be transformed into a separate relation.

In this way, the whole EER schema has been transformed to a corresponding relational schema. Of course, more operators are needed to handle other EER features, such as *Union* derivations of new types.

5.2 Equivalence of Models Represented in Different Metamodels

The preceding sections showed models for the airport domain in different concrete metamodels. It can be seen that, although each of the models is designed for the same domain, their *GeRoMe* representations differ from each other.

Please note that the differences in the representations stem from the constraints and semantics of the concrete metamodels. Nevertheless the representations use the same role classes in all models, while accurately representing the features of the constructs in the concrete modeling languages. For example, the XML Schema *PersonType* plays the same roles as the EER *Person*, since entity types have the same semantics as XML Schema complex types. Furthermore, the relational *Person* does not play the *ObjectSet* and *BaseElement* roles since these are not allowed in the relational model. On the other hand, all these roles play an *Aggregate* role, and therefore they look the same to an operator which is only interested in this role.

In the last section we demonstrated the tranformation of an EER model into a relational model. Because of the aforementioned differences in the semantics of representations in different concrete metamodels a model resulting from such transformations cannot be equivalent to the original model in a formal way. For example, since the relational model does not allow relationship types, these elements have to be transformed to relations with referential constraints. Thus, during the transformation information about the original model is lost because the target metamodel cannot represent these concepts.

Consequently, if you transform the *GeRoMe* representation of an EER model into the *GeRoMe* representation of a relational schema and try to reverse this, the result may be a model which is different from the original schema. For example, it is not possible to identify which model elements stem from entity types or relationship types, respectively.

To summarize, a generic metamodel cannot represent models from different concrete metamodels identically because each concrete metamodel is designed to represent different aspects of real world entities and their relationships. What it can do is to represent models in any metamodel with the same set of modeling elements. This allows to implement model management operators only with respect to these elements of the generic metamodel and to use these operators polymorphically for models from arbitrary metamodels.

6 Architecture and Implementation

Applications dealing with complex models require support for model management in several ways. Therefore, our goal is to provide a library for the management of *GeRoMe* models (including the definition of several operators) that can be reused in various application settings. In the following, we will first present the architecture of our framework. In section 6.3, we will explain how we have realized the import and export of *GeRoMe* models, which is based on a logical formalization presented in section 6.2. More information about the import and export of models and also the transformation of models using a rule based approach in *GeRoMe* can be found in [21].

6.1 Architecture

In order to make the functionalities of *GeRoMe* available to several applications, we developed an API for the manipulation of models represented in *GeRoMe*. Manipulations are performed by a set of model management operators. These can be atomic operators or operators composed of existing operators. Figure 9 presents the structure of our API as well as the general architecture of model management applications based on *GeRoMe*.

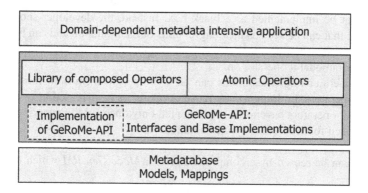

Fig. 9. Architecture of a metadata intensive application based on *GeRoMe*

Our implementation of a model management platform is based on a multi-layered architecture. The lowest layer provides facilities to store and retrieve models in the *GeRoMe* representation and is implemented using the deductive metadatabase system ConceptBase [19]. ConceptBase uses Telos as modeling language [25], which allows to represent multiple abstraction levels and to formulate queries, rules and constraints. Objects are represented using a frame-like or graphical notation on the user side, and a logical representation (triples similar to RDF) based on Datalog⁻ internally. The logical capabilities of ConceptBase can be used to analyze the models or to encode the semantics of models in logical rules (e.g. inheritance of attributes)[1]. In addition, *GeRoMe* models can be stored as and constructed from a set of logical facts which is used for the import and export of models. This will be discussed in more detail below. Furthermore, it is possible to store models represented in *GeRoMe* in an XML format to ease the exchange of metadata.

On top of the storage layer, an abstract object model corresponding to the model in fig. 2 has been implemented as a Java library. This is a set of interfaces and base implementations in Java. An implementation of these interfaces can be chosen by instantiating a factory class. Consequently, the object model is independent from the underlying implementation and storage strategy. The relationship between roles and model elements is represented in member variables and methods which allow to add and delete roles from model elements (or other roles). A role has also a link to its player. A model element can be queried for the roles it plays or all roles of a specific class can be retrieved. Some convenience methods in the model element interface allow direct access to the role object (e.g. `getAggregate()`). The *GeRoMe* API is also independent from any original metamodels; the relationship between models represented in *GeRoMe* and models represented in the original metamodels is established by import and export operators as described below in section 6.3.

The next layer is formed by atomic operators based on the *GeRoMe* API. Operators have to be implemented "as atomically as possible" in order to allow maximum reuse. These atomic operators are not aware of the original metamodel, i.e. their implementations use exclusively roles and structures in *GeRoMe*.

By "atomic" we denote that when implementing an operator such as ModelGen_RM, this shall not be implemented as a black box. Instead, the developer should extract certain steps that can be seen as meaningful units of manipulation and can be reused in other tasks. Such an atomic operator should not implicitly encode any knowledge about the native metamodel it operates on.

Atomic operator implementations can be combined to form new, more complex, composite operators. In doing so, the reuse of operators is increased in two ways. On the one hand, operators have to be implemented only once for the generic metamodel and can be used for different concrete metamodels.

For example an operator for the transformation of association ends to referential constraints can be reused by a composite operator *ModelGen_RM* which computes a

---

[1] We are aware of the fact that Datalog cannot be used to support full reasoning on all modeling languages, especially not OWL DL. However, this is not the goal of *GeRoMe*, it is used to represent the explicit knowledge about models which will be used in model management operators. Full reasoning about models has still to be done by special purpose reasoners for the specific metamodels.

relational model from an EER model and by another composite operator *ModelGen_XS* for computing an XML Schema from an OWL ontology.

On the other hand, operators such as Match or Merge can be reused to compose new operators for solving different metadata related tasks. Thus, a metadata intensive application uses atomic and composite operators to implement its model manipulation functionality.

6.2 Logical Formalization

A logical formalization of *GeRoMe* enables the specification of several model management tasks in a declarative way. As we will describe in the next section, import and export of models can be easily defined by rules using such a formalization. Furthermore, this logical representation enables also more sophisticated reasoning mechanisms on models, for example, to check the consistency of models or the correctness of transformations.

Formally, *GeRoMe* is defined by a set of role types $\mathcal{R} = \{r_1, \ldots, r_n\}$ and a set of attribute types $\mathcal{A} = \{a_1, \ldots, a_m\}$ which can be applied to role types. In addition, $\mathcal{V}$ denotes a set of atomic values which may be used as attribute values. A model M represented in *GeRoMe* is defined by a tuple $M = \langle E, R, type, plays, attr \rangle$, where

- $E = \{e_1, \ldots, e_k\}$ is a set of model elements,
- $R = \{o_1, \ldots, o_p\}$ is a set of role objects,
- $type : R \rightarrow \mathcal{R}$ is a total function that assigns exactly one role class to each role object,
- $plays \subseteq (E \cup R) \times R$ represents the aforementioned relation between model elements (or role objects) and role objects,
- $attr \subseteq (R \times \mathcal{A}) \times (R \cup \mathcal{V})$ represents the attribute values of a role object (i.e. attributes may also refer to other role objects).

To make the representation more human-readable, we have used a simplified notation in the formulation of the import/export rules below. The fact that an object e is a model element ($e \in E$) is represented by the statement `modelElement(e)`. Role objects are not explicitly represented; they are denoted as terms which have the name of their role class as functor and all objects on which they depend as arguments. For example, `objectAssociationEnd(e)` states that the model element e plays the *ObjectAssociationEnd* role. The same term can be used to identify the role object. The *attr* relationship is also reified: a term like `attrName(o,v)` denotes that the object o has the value v for the attribute called `attrName`. For example, `min(objectAssocationEnd(e),1)` specifies that the *min*-attribute of the role object defined above is 1.

We have also defined a formal semantics for *GeRoMe* to characterize data instances (see appendix A.1), which is in line with the logical formalization given above. Data instances are also used at the model level (see role *Instance*), e.g. as default values or boundaries of a type defined by an interval. The main goal of the formal semantics is however the formal definition of mappings between models, which should finally be used to translate data instances from one model to another model. As this is out of the scope of this paper, we do not elaborate on the formal semantics here.

Using the logical representation for *GeRoMe* models and a similar representation for models in specific metamodels, we can use a rule-based approach for the import and export of models as we will present in the next section. Moreover, this representation of a model is a fine grained representation, because each feature (or property) of a model element is represented by a separate fact. This is especially useful for the Diff operator in which we need to identify the differences of model elements.

6.3   Import and Export Operators

We do not continuously synchronize a *GeRoMe* model with underlying native metadata. Instead, we import the native metadata into *GeRoMe* and after manipulating this model we export it into some native format. A process that has also been used in [3]. In general, it is not even possible to enforce consistency of the native schema with the *GeRoMe* model since manipulations may yield an intermediate result that is not valid in neither the source nor the target modeling language. Consider the example of section 5. An EER model in which some of the relationship types have been transformed into foreign keys but others have not, is neither a valid EER model, as it contains references, nor a valid relational schema as it still contains relationship types. Consequently, the *GeRoMe* model cannot be synchronized with a native schema. Instead, only the input and output must be representations of valid native models.

Import and export operators to the native format of the various modeling languages are currently being implemented. The operators use the logical representation presented before and a rule-based approach: the relationship between a concrete metamodel and *GeRoMe* is represented by a set of equivalence rules. The left hand side of a rule refers to elements of the concrete metamodel, the right hand side refers to *GeRoMe* elements.

Using a rule-based approach for specifying the import/export operators has the advantage that the semantics of these operators can be specified in a declarative way and is not hidden in the code of a complex transformation function. Furthermore, our approach is fully generic; it uses reflection and annotations in Java to create objects or to generate facts from an existing *GeRoMe* model. Therefore, the code required to support another metamodel is limited to the generation of the metamodel-specific facts and the specification of the equivalence rules. This reduces the effort for the implementation of import/export operators significantly.

Formally, a *GeRoMe* model is represented by a set of ground facts KB_{GeRoMe} which uses only vocabulary (functions, predicates, ..) from the logical *GeRoMe* representation (e.g. $modelElement(Person)$, $attribute(Person, Name)$, ...). The model itself corresponds to the one and only logical model M of KB_{GeRoMe}. This interpretation is trivial but it has to be noted that there must be only one logical model, otherwise KB_{GeRoMe} is ambigious. This is one requirement that has to be considered when implementing the rules for import and export.

Now, a model in a concrete metamodel (say EER) is also represented by a set of ground facts KB_{EER} about model elements which uses only vocabulary from the concrete metamodel ($UMLAssociationEnd(as, ae, rn, min, max)$, $RMTable(x)$, $EEREntityType(...)$, ...). The import amounts to applying a set of rules to the facts KB_{EER} (say $S_{EER \hookrightarrow GeRoMe}$). The left hand side of the implication contains only vocabulary from the concrete metamodel, the right hand side contains only vocabulary

```
sql_column(ID),
sql_column_table(ID, TableID),
sql_column_name(ID, Name),
sql_column_type(ID, Type) <=>
    modelElement(ID),
    owned(namespace(TableID), ID),
    visible(ID),
    name(visible(ID), Name),
    attribute(ID),
    property(aggregate(TableID), attribute(ID)),
    domain(attribute(ID), domain(Type)),
    max(attribute(ID), 1).

sql_column_nullable(ID, true) <=>
    min(attribute(ID), 0).
```

Fig. 10. Example rules for the Import/Export of SQL models

from *GeRoMe*. The result is a set of ground facts KB_{GeRoMe} (instantiations of the right hand sides). The export of a model is performed the other way around; to have consistent import and export operators, the rules are expressed as equivalence rules which can be interpreted from left to right or vice versa.

Fig. 10 gives an example for such rules. The rules are expressed in standard Prolog syntax, i.e. labels starting with an upper-case letter denote variables. They are evaluated using a meta-program implemented in Prolog, which is able to handle rules with multiple predicates on both sides of the equivalence. The example defines the import of a column of a SQL table into a *GeRoMe* model. The column with the identifier ID belongs to a table and has a name and a type. In *GeRoMe*, we will create a model element with the same ID. The second statement defines the relationship between the namespace role of the table and the newly created model element. The following statements define that the element is visible and has a name. Then, we have to specify that the new model element plays also the attribute role, and link this role to the aggregate role of the model element representing the table. Finally, the domain of the attribute is defined by linking it to the domain role of the type, and the maximum cardinality of the attribute is set to 1. The second rule represents the special case in which NULL-values are allowed for the column, which is represented in *GeRoMe* by a minimum cardinality of 0.

In the example of Fig. 10 we have used terms as arguments of some predicates (e.g. namespace(TableID)). As described above, these terms represent the role objects. With a pure logical view, one could also interpret these terms just syntactically as *Skolem functions*, which have been introduced on the right hand side to replace existentially quantified variables, i.e. variables that would appear only on one side of the rule. As the goal is to construct objects using the *GeRoMe*-API, these functions must return meaningful objects. Therefore, while creating the *GeRoMe* objects from a set of facts, these functions will return the corresponding role objects of the given model elements, e.g. namespace(TableID) returns the *Namespace* role of the model element TableID. By doing so, we make sure that the same objects are used, even if they are referenced in different rules; for example, the attribute role of ID is referenced in both rules of fig. 10. Note that in some cases, objects can play multiple roles of the

```
xs_namespace(NamespaceID),
xs_complextype(ID),
xs_complextype_ns(ID, NamespaceID),
xs_complextype_name(ID, Name) <=>
    modelElement(ID),
    owned(namespace(NamespaceID),ID),
    visible(ID),
    name(visible(ID),Name),
    objectSet(ID).

xs_attribute(ID),
xs_attribute_of(ID, ComplexTypeID) <=>
    aggregate(ComplexTypeId),
    modelElement(ID),
    attribute(ID),
    property(aggregate(ComplexTypeID),attribute(ID)),
    ...
```

Fig. 11. Example rules for the Import/Export of XML Schemas

same type (e.g. attributes may play several reference roles); in this case, these functions have more than one argument (i.e. all objects that are necessary to identify the role).

Fig. 11 presents an example of import/export rules for complex types of XML schemas. The first part of the right hand side of the rule is similar to the example before; it defines a model element which is contained in a namespace and which plays a visible role. In addition, the model element plays also the *ObjectSet* role, as complex types participate in associations. The second rule adds an aggregate rule to the model element of this complex type, if the complex type contains also attributes. The rule creates also a model element (ID) for the attribute and links the attribute role of this object to the aggregate role of the complex type. We omitted further statements for the definition of namespaces, etc.

Note that the rules can be used in both ways. Thus, it is also possible to export *GeRoMe* models using these rules. Depending on the desired target metamodel, the corresponding rule set will be activated and evaluated based on a set of facts representing the *GeRoMe* model. Evaluating the rules is only one step of the export operator: before a model can be exported to a concrete metamodel, the export operator has to check whether all roles used can be represented in the target metamodel. If not, the problematic roles have to be transformed into different elements as described, for example, in section 5.

Due to the role and rule based approach and the generic implementation of the necessary Java classes the effort of supporting a new metamodel is minimized. Since the correspondences are not hidden in imperative code, but are given as a set of equivalence rules, the developer can concentrate on the logical correspondences and does not have to deal with implementation details. Besides, only two classes have to be implemented that produce facts about a concrete model from an API (e.g., the Jena OWL API, see fig. 12) or read facts and produce the model with calls to the API, respectively. These two classes merely produce (or read) a different syntactic representation of the native model and do not perform any sophisticated processing of schemas. Creating and processing of facts about the *GeRoMe* representation is completely done with reflection.

```
public String transformClass(OntClass cls) {
  //...
  List<OntClass> lClasses=cls.listSuperClasses(true).toList();

  for(OntClass superClass : lClasses) {
    sResID = transformClass(superClass);
    Term t=Prolog.term("owl_subclass",plID,Prolog.id(sResID));
    mlFacts.add(t);
  }
}
```

Fig. 12. Example code fragment for importing OWL classes

```
// term is a Java object representing a Prolog term
if(term.arity() == 1) {
  if(!invokeBuilder(term)) {
    throw new ModelManException("No such method");
  }
}
else if(term.arity() == 2 || term.arity() == 3) {
  if(!invokeMethod(term)) {
    throw new ModelManException("No such property");
  }
}
```

Fig. 13. Creating *GeRoMe* objects using reflection

During the export, facts about a *GeRoMe* model are created according to Java annotations in the API. During the import unary facts cause model elements and role objects to be created, binary facts establish relationships between objects and ternary facts do the same for indexed relationships (see fig. 13). This significantly reduces the programming effort for supporting a new metamodel. For example, import and export of SQL requires about 250 lines of Java code for each operator, and about 200 lines of code for the Prolog rules. The relationships between the modeling constructs could be expressed in less than 20 equivalence rules.

6.4   Equivalence of Imported and Reexported Models

The transformations, performed by ModelGen operators such as the ones presented in section 5, in general serve the purpose of removing constructs disallowed in the target metamodel. Therefore, the transformation cannot be reversed automatically as it removed information from the original model which can only be regained by asking the user. At best, suggestions can be made based on heuristics.

However, the import and subsequent export for a generic metamodel should not lose information. It must be emphasized that an import to and an export from *GeRoMe* may result in a model syntactically different from the original model, as there are redundant ways to represent the same modeling construct in specific metamodels. For example, consider an OWL object property described as being functional; this could also be modeled by an *inverseFunctional* statement of the inverse property. In the import/export rules, such ambiguity must be resolved by using negation, e.g. the property will be defined as functional only if there is no (visible) inverse property that could be declared as *inverseFunctional* or vice versa.

On the other hand, semantic equivalence of imported and subsequently reexported models means that the same set of instances (individuals, tuples, XML fragments, ..) satisfies both, the original model and the imported and reexported model. The mapping rules for metamodels described above should be formulated in a way which ensures that this property holds.

Equivalence between models can be defined by means of information capacity [16,24] This definition must be adopted in our case to metamodels. Let f be a mapping between the native metamodel M and *GeRoMe* defined by a set of mapping rules R. A subsequent import and export can only yield the original model if f is invertible, so f^{-1} and f can be composed. Therefore, it must be a total and injective function from the set of valid models in M to the set of valid *GeRoMe* models. Then f is an *information capacity preserving mapping* [16,24] between the sets of models, and *GeRoMe* dominates M via f and, naturally, the composition of f and f^{-1} is the identity function (an *equivalence preserving mapping*) on the set of models in metamodel M. Consequently, the above notion of semantic equivalence would be satisfied.

Thus, the question of whether a model in a native metamodel can be losslessly imported and reexported can only be answered with respect to the allowed modeling constructs and the mapping rules R for the respective metamodel. These mapping rules must translate every native modeling construct uniquely into a corresponding generic modeling construct (or combination thereof) and translate the same generic construct into the same native modeling construct. Indeed, there are some constructs, that still cannot be represented in *GeRoMe*. For instance, as we concentrated on data models, we cannot model methods in *GeRoMe*. But *GeRoMe* is designed to be extendable; if it is not possible to represent a modeling construct in the correct way in *GeRoMe*, new roles can be added to do so. We have made this experience while implementing the mapping rules for XML Schema; it contains several modeling features which are not available in other modeling languages. For instance, the *LiteralAssociationEnd* role has been introduced to model XML elements with simple type. These could as well be modeled as attributes, but then it would not be possible to tell whether an attribute should be exported to an XML Schema attribute or an element.

While implementing the mapping rules for the import and export operators, we have to assert that structures or constraints are uniquely imported into our metamodel and, vice versa, that *GeRoMe* represents these features non-ambigously, so that they can be exported again into the native format. In [2] the authors already argued for their system that a formal proof of losslessness of translations to a generic metamodel is hopeless as even a test for losslessness of translations between two native metamodels is undecidable [5]. However, we tried to ease the formulation of such a mapping by implementing import and export in a way which allows the developer to concentrate on defining the mapping rules in a declarative way rather than distributing the mapping over a set of Java classes.

7   Conclusion

Generic model management requires a generic metamodel to represent models defined in different modeling languages (or metamodels). The definition of a generic metamodel is not straightforward and requires the careful analysis of existing metamodels. In this paper, we have presented the generic role based metamodel *GeRoMe*, which is based on our analysis and comparison of five popular metamodels (Relational, EER, UML, OWL, and XML Schema).

We recognized that the intuitive approach of identifying generic metaclasses and one-to-one correspondences between these metaclasses and the elements of concrete metamodels is not appropriate for generic metamodeling. Although classes of model elements in known metamodels are often similar, they also inhibit significant differences which have to be taken into account. We have shown that role based metamodeling can be utilized to capture both, similarities and differences, in an accurate way while avoiding sparsely populated intersection classes. In addition, the role based approach enables easy extensibility and flexibility as new modeling features can be added easily. Implementations of operators access all roles they need for their functionality but remain agnostic about any other roles. This reduces the complexity of models from an operator's point of view significantly. Furthermore, the detailed representation of *GeRoMe* models is used only by a model management application, users will still use their favorite modeling language.

Whereas role based modeling has yet only been applied to the model level, we have shown that a generic metamodel can benefit from roles. In particular, *GeRoMe* enables *generic* model management. As far as we know, the role based approach to the problem of generic metadata modeling is new. It has been validated by representing several models from different metamodels in *GeRoMe*.

We implemented a framework for the management of models including an object model for *GeRoMe* models that allows operators to manipulate, store, and retrieve models. Atomic model management operators are implemented based on our generic metamodel and can be combined to composite operators. In particular, the usage of a generic metamodel allows to apply operator implementations polymorphically to models represented in various modeling languages which increases the reusability of operators. As a first evaluation of *GeRoMe*, we have implemented some ModelGen operators.

We have developed a *rule-based* approach for import and export operators which is based on a logical formalization of *GeRoMe* models. These operators will also be used to verify that the model elements of different metamodels can be represented accurately and completely in *GeRoMe*.

Future work will concentrate on the development of further model management operators. We have started working on the implementation of a Match operator for *GeRoMe* models and are investigating how the generic representation can be exploited by this operator. We have defined a formal semantics for *GeRoMe* which was necessary to describe the structure of instances of *GeRoMe* models. The semantics is also used for a formal definition of mappings between *GeRoMe* models which we are currently designing. The mapping representation will be used by model management operators such as Merge and Compose.

While it might be necessary to integrate new modeling features of other languages, or features which we did not take into account so far, we are confident that our work is a basis for a generic solution for model management.

Acknowledgements. This work is supported in part by the EU-IST project SEWASIE (http://www.sewasie.org) and the EU Network of Excellence ProLearn (http://www.prolearn-project.org).

References

1. P. Atzeni, P. Cappellari, P. A. Bernstein. A Multilevel Dictionary for Model Management. L. M. L. Delcambre, C. Kop, H. C. Mayr, J. Mylopoulos, O. Pastor (eds.), *Proc. 24th International Conference on Conceptual Modeling (ER), Lecture Notes in Computer Science*, vol. 3716, pp. 160–175. Springer, Klagenfurt, Austria, 2005.
2. P. Atzeni, P. Cappellari, P. A. Bernstein. Model-Independent Schema and Data Translation. Y. E. Ioannidis, M. H. Scholl, J. W. Schmidt, F. Matthes, M. Hatzopoulos, K. Böhm, A. Kemper, T. Grust, C. Böhm (eds.), *Proc. 10th International Conference on Extending Database Technology (EDBT), Lecture Notes in Computer Science*, vol. 3896, pp. 368–385. Springer, Munich, Germany, 2006.
3. P. Atzeni, R. Torlone. Management of Multiple Models in an Extensible Database Design Tool. P. M. G. Apers, M. Bouzeghoub, G. Gardarin (eds.), *Proc. 5th International Conference on Extending Database Technology (EDBT), Lecture Notes in Computer Science*, vol. 1057, pp. 79–95. Springer, Avignon, France, 1996.
4. C. W. Bachman, M. Daya. The Role Concept in Data Models. *Proceedings of the Third International Conference on Very Large Data Bases (VLDB)*, pp. 464–476. IEEE-CS and ACM, Tokyo, Japan, 1977.
5. D. Barbosa, J. Freire, A. O. Mendelzon. Information Preservation in XML-to-Relational Mappings. Z. Bellahsene, T. Milo, M. Rys, D. Suciu, R. Unland (eds.), *Proc. of the Second International XML Database Symposium, XSym 2004, Toronto, Canada, Lecture Notes in Computer Science*, vol. 3186, pp. 66–81. Springer, August 2004.
6. M. Baumeister, M. Jarke. Compaction of Large Class Hierarchies in Databases for Chemical Engineering. *8. GI-Fachtagung fr Datenbanksysteme in Bro, Technik und Wissenschaft (BTW)*, pp. 343–361. Springer, Freiburg, 1999.
7. P. A. Bernstein. Applying Model Management to Classical Meta Data Problems. *Proc. First Biennial Conference on Innovative Data Systems Research (CIDR2003)*. Asilomar, CA, 2003.
8. P. A. Bernstein, A. Y. Halevy, R. Pottinger. A Vision for Management of Complex Models. *SIGMOD Record*, **29**(4):55–63, 2000.
9. P. A. Bernstein, S. Melnik, P. Mork. Interactive Schema Translation with Instance-Level Mappings. K. Böhm, C. S. Jensen, L. M. Haas, M. L. Kersten, P.-Å. Larson, B. C. Ooi (eds.), *Proc. 31st International Conference on Very Large Data Bases (VLDB)*, pp. 1283–1286. ACM Press, Trondheim, Norway, 2005.
10. P. A. Bernstein, S. Melnik, M. Petropoulos, C. Quix. Industrial-Strength Schema Matching. *SIGMOD Record*, **33**(4):38–43, 2004.
11. E. Bertino, G. Guerrini. Objects with Multiple Most Specific Classes. *Proc. European Conference on Object-Oriented Programming (ECOOP), Lecture Notes in Computer Science (LNCS)*, vol. 952, pp. 102–126. Springer, Aarhus, Denmark, 1995.
12. R. A. Elmasri, S. B. Navathe. *Fundamentals of Database Systems*. Addison-Wesley, Reading, Mass., 3rd edn., 1999.
13. R. Fagin, P. G. Kolaitis, L. Popa, W. C. Tan. Composing schema mappings: Second-order dependencies to the rescue. *ACM Transactions on Database Systems*, **30**(4):994–1055, 2005.
14. S. Hanenberg, R. Unland. Roles and Aspects: Similarities, Differences, and Synergetic Potential. *Proc. 8th International Conference on Object-Oriented Information Systems, Lecture Notes in Computer Science (LNCS)*, vol. 2425, pp. 507 – 520. Springer, Montpellier, France, 2002.

15. M. A. Hernández, R. J. Miller, L. M. Haas. Clio: A Semi-Automatic Tool For Schema Mapping. *Proc. ACM SIGMOD Intl. Conference on the Management of Data*, p. 607. ACM Press, Santa Barbara, CA, 2001.

16. R. Hull. Relative Information Capacity of Simple Relational Database Schemata. *SIAM Journal of Computing*, **15**(3):856–886, August 1986.

17. R. Hull, R. King. Semantic Database Modeling: Survey, Applications, and Research Issues. *ACM Computing Surveys*, **19**(3):201–260, 1987.

18. ISO/IEC. Information technology – Information Resource Dictionary System (IRDS) Framework. *International Standard ISO/IEC 10027:1990*, DIN Deutsches Institut für Normung, e.V., 1990.

19. M. A. Jeusfeld, M. Jarke, H. W. Nissen, M. Staudt. ConceptBase – Managing Conceptual Models about Information Systems. P. Bernus, K. Mertins, G. Schmidt (eds.), *Handbook on Architectures of Information Systems*, pp. 265–285. Springer-Verlag, 1998.

20. M. A. Jeusfeld, U. A. Johnen. An Executable Meta Model for Re-Engineering of Database Schemas. *Proc. 13th Intl. Conference on the Entity-Relationship Approach (ER94)*, *Lecture Notes in Computer Science (LNCS)*, vol. 881, pp. 533–547. Springer-Verlag, Manchester, U.K., 1994.

21. D. Kensche, C. Quix. Transformation of Models in(to) a Generic Metamodel. submitted for publication.

22. M. Lenzerini. Data Integration: A Theoretical Perspective. L. Popa (ed.), *Proceedings of the Twenty-first ACM Symposium on Principles of Database Systems (PODS)*, pp. 233–246. ACM Press, Madison, Wisconsin, 2002.

23. S. Melnik, E. Rahm, P. A. Bernstein. Rondo: A Programming Platform for Generic Model Management. *Proc. ACM SIGMOD Intl. Conference on Management of Data*, pp. 193–204. ACM, San Diego, CA, 2003.

24. R. J. Miller, Y. E. Ioannidis, R. Ramakrishnan. The Use of Information Capacity in Schema Integration and Translation. R. Agrawal, S. Baker, D. A. Bell (eds.), *Proc. 19th International Conference on Very Large Data Bases (VLDB)*, pp. 120–133. Morgan Kaufmann, Dublin, Ireland, 1993.

25. J. Mylopoulos, A. Borgida, M. Jarke, M. Koubarakis. Telos: Representing Knowledge About Information Systems. *ACM Transactions on Information Systems*, **8**(4):325–362, 1990.

26. P. Papotti, R. Torlone. Heterogeneous Data Translation through XML Conversion. *Journal of Web Engineering*, **4**(3):189–204, 2005.

27. R. Pottinger, P. A. Bernstein. Merging Models Based on Given Correspondences. J. C. Freytag, P. C. Lockemann, S. Abiteboul, M. J. Carey, P. G. Selinger, A. Heuer (eds.), *Proc. 29th International Conference on Very Large Data Bases (VLDB)*, pp. 826–873. Morgan Kaufmann, Berlin, Germany, 2003.

28. E. Rahm, P. A. Bernstein. A Survey of Approaches to Automatic Schema Matching. *VLDB Journal*, **10**(4):334–350, 2001.

29. J. Richardson, P. Schwarz. Aspects: extending objects to support multiple, independent roles. *Proc. ACM SIGMOD Intl. Conference on Management of Data*, pp. 298–307. Denver, CO, 1991.

30. R. K. Wong, H. L. Chau, F. H. Lochovsky. A Data Model and Semantics of Objects with Dynamic Roles. *Proc. 13th Intl. Conference on Data Engineering (ICDE)*, pp. 402–411. IEEE Computer Society, Birmingham, UK, 1997.

A   Appendix

A.1   Formal Semantics of *GeRoMe*

The formalization of *GeRoMe* in section 6.2 described how *GeRoMe* models can be represented as a set of logical facts, and how this representation can be used to implement the import and export operators.

To describe the semantics of a *GeRoMe* model, we have to characterize what are the valid instances of a *GeRoMe* model. For example, we have to define for a model element *Person* how intances of this model element may look like and which are valid relationships between persons and other instances. In the following, we will first define the formal semantics of *GeRoMe*, and a simplified notation for instances of *GeRoMe* models that is used in data mappings.

Semantics

Definition 1 (Atoms and Object Identifiers)

- *A denotes a set of atoms, which are literal values of simple datatypes, e.g. "HLX", "Boeing-747", "John", "Smith", "5.2".*
- *O denotes a set of object identifiers, which are used to distinct two instances with the same component values from each other if they are instances of an ObjectSet.*

Definition 2 (*GeRoMe* Interpretation). *An interpretation $\Im$ in GeRoMe is a tuple $\Im =< \mathcal{I}, \mathcal{O}, \mathcal{P}, \mathcal{V}, A, O, \epsilon >$ where O is a set of object identifiers and A is a set of atoms (literals, ..) as defined before. $\epsilon \notin O \cup A$ is the null value, which can be used for null data values (for attributes), null participators (for association ends), or null object identifiers (for elements without object identity).*

$\mathcal{I}$ is the interpretation mapping which maps a model element (specifying a data set, not a constraint) to a set of instances.
$\mathcal{O}$ maps a model element to the set of its object identifiers.
$\mathcal{P}$ maps a model element to a set of Association instantiations.
$\mathcal{V}$ maps a model element to a set of data values.
The interpretation mapping is defined as follows:

- *If m is a Domain then $\mathcal{I}[m] \subseteq A$ is the set of atoms in m.*
- *If m is an ObjectSet, an Association, an Aggregate, or any combination of these then*
  $\mathcal{I}[m] \subseteq [\mathcal{O}[m] \times \mathcal{V}[m] \times \mathcal{P}[m]]$ where
  - *If m is an ObjectSet then $\mathcal{O}[m] \subseteq O$ is the set of object identifiers of instances of m, otherwise $\mathcal{O}[m] = \{\epsilon\}$.*
  - *If m is an Association with AssociationEnds $AE_i\ i = 1, \ldots, n$ then*
    $\mathcal{P}[m] \subseteq [(\mathcal{O}[AE_1.participator] \cup \epsilon) \times \ldots \times (\mathcal{O}[AE_n.participator] \cup \epsilon)]$,
    otherwise $\mathcal{P}[m] = \{\epsilon\}$. The participator of an AssociationEnd is always an ObjectSet. Consequently, this defines a set of tuples of object identifiers. If an association end may be null, ϵ may be the value of this participator. If an association end may participate more than once, each participation is instantiated by another tuple, that is, another element of $\mathcal{I}[m]$. Thus, multiple participations of one participator are multiple instances of the association.
  - *If m is an Aggregate with Attributes $A_i\ i = 1, \ldots, n$ then*
    $\mathcal{V}[m] \subseteq [\mathbb{P}(\mathcal{I}[A_1.type]) \times \ldots \times \mathbb{P}(\mathcal{I}[A_n.type])]$,
    otherwise $\mathcal{V}[m] = \{\epsilon\}$. Infinite, recursive structures are not allowed, i.e. an element x of $\mathcal{V}[m]$ must not contain any element in which x occurs. The cardinality of a component of $\mathcal{V}[m]$ must be within the (min,max) constraints of the attribute.

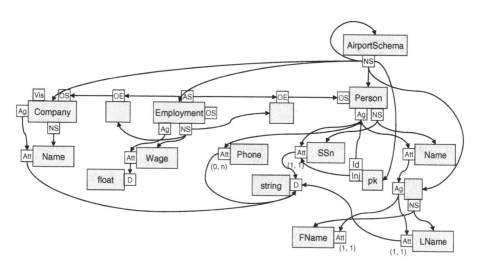

Fig. 14. An example schema about persons and companies

Examples. Figure 14 gives an example schema containing various combinations of the *ObjectSet, Asssociation* and *Aggregate* roles. A possible interpretation are the following:
$O = \{1, 2, 3\}$,
$A = \{"InsuranceCorp.", "0815", "John", "Smith", 2500.00\}$,
$\mathcal{O}[Company] = \{1\}$,
$\mathcal{O}[Person] = \{2\}$,
$\mathcal{O}[Employment] = \{3\}$,
$\mathcal{O}[\_theAnonType] = \{\epsilon\}$,
$c \in \mathcal{I}[Company]$ with $c =< 1, \epsilon, < "InsuranceCorp." >>$,
$p \in \mathcal{I}[Person]$ with $p =< 2, \epsilon, < "0815", < \epsilon, \epsilon, < "John", "Smith >>>$,
$n \in \mathcal{I}[\_theAnonType]$ with $c =< \epsilon, \epsilon, < "John", "Smith" >>$,
$e \in \mathcal{I}[Employment]$ with $c =< 3, < 1, 2 >, < 2500.00 >>$,

Simplified Notation. For the formulation of constraints, queries, and mappings, we choose a simpler representation that uses flat logical predicates instead of the complex terms used before.

Definition 3 (Notation of instances as logical facts). *The interpretation $\mathfrak{J}$ of a model M is represented by a set of facts $\mathcal{D}_M$ as described below.*

- *The interpretation of a model element $\mathcal{I}[m]$ is represented by a set of abstract identifiers $\{id_1, \ldots, id_n\}$. The set of all abstract identifiers is denoted by $\mathcal{T}$. $inst(id_i, m) \in \mathcal{D}_M$ means that the object represented by id_i is an instance of m.*
- *$\forall$ model elements m playing a Domain role and $\forall v \in \mathcal{I}[m] : value(id_i, v) \in \mathcal{D}_M$ and $inst(id_i, m) \in \mathcal{D}_M$.*
- *$\forall$ model elements m playing an ObjectSet role and $\forall o \in \mathcal{O}[m]$: $oid(id_i, o) \in \mathcal{D}_M$ and $inst(id_i, m) \in \mathcal{D}_M$. Each id_i has at most one object identifier o, and each object identifier o is related to exactly one id_i. There is no $oid(id_i, o) \in \mathcal{D}_M$ with $o = \epsilon$.*

- ∀ *model elements m playing an Aggregate role and having the attribute a (model element), and this instance has the value* $v \in T$ *for that attribute:* $attr(id_i, a, v) \in \mathcal{D}_M$ *and* $inst(id_i, m) \in \mathcal{D}_M$.
- ∀ *model elements m playing an Association role in which the object with identifier o participates for the association end ae:* $part(id_i, ae, o) \in \mathcal{D}_M$ *and* $inst(id_i, m) \in \mathcal{D}_M$.
- *There are no other elements in* $\mathcal{D}_M$.

Please note that the existence of a predicate like $attr(id, a, v)$ or $part(id, ae, o)$ in $\mathcal{D}_M$ requires the existence of other predicates in $\mathcal{D}_M$ to assure a consistent model (e.g., an attribute value has to be an instance of the type of that attribute).

The "artificial" identifiers id_i are introduced here to reify the complex tuples of an interpretation $\mathfrak{J}$ in order to have flat tuples.

Example. The example given above is represented by the following set of facts ($T = \{\#1, \#2, \#3, \ldots\}$):

$$oid(\#1, 1) \qquad\qquad oid(\#2, 2)$$
$$oid(\#3, 3)$$
$$attr(\#1, Name, \#5) \qquad attr(\#2, SSN, \#6)$$
$$value(\#5, "InsuranceCorp") \; value(\#6, "0815")$$
$$attr(\#2, Name, \#4) \qquad attr(\#4, FName, \#7)$$
$$\qquad\qquad\qquad\qquad\qquad value(\#7, "John")$$
$$attr(\#4, LName, \#8) \qquad attr(\#3, Wage, \#9)$$
$$value(\#8, "Smith") \qquad value(\#9, "2500")$$
$$part(\#3, EmployedBy, \#1) \quad part(\#3, Employs, \#2)$$
$$inst(\#1, Company) \qquad inst(\#2, Employee)$$
$$inst(\#3, Employment) \qquad inst(\#4, \_theAnonType)$$
$$inst(\ldots) \text{ for values}$$

A.2   Queries and Mappings in *GeRoMe*

Using the formal semantics of *GeRoMe* models, it is straightforward to represent formulas over *GeRoMe* models that can be used as queries or mappings.

A query in *GeRoMe* is a conjunctive query using the predicates defined above in definition 3. A mapping is basically a relationship of queries over two different models. As it has been proven in [13], mappings expressed second-order tuple generating dependencies (SO tgds) are closed under composition, but first-order tgds are not. Therefore, we use SO tgds to express mappings between models.

Definition 4 (*GeRoMe* model mapping). *A* GeRoMe *model mapping (or, in short, mapping) is a triple* $\mathcal{M} = (\mathbf{S}, \mathbf{T}, \Sigma)$, *where* $\mathbf{S}$ *and* $\mathbf{T}$ *are the source model and the target model respectively, and* Σ *is a finite set of formulas of the form*

$$\exists \mathbf{f}((\forall \mathbf{x_1}(\varphi_1 \to \psi_1)) \land \ldots \land (\forall \mathbf{x_n}(\varphi_n \to \psi_n)))$$

where each member of $\mathbf{f}$ *is a function symbol, and where each* φ_i *is a conjunction of atomic formulas and/or equalities over* $\mathbf{S}$ *and* ψ_i *is a conjunction of atomic formulas over* $\mathbf{T}$ *as defined in definition 3. Furthermore, the variables of* $\mathbf{x_i}$ *appear in at least one atomic formula of* φ_i.

The predicates from definition 3 can also be used in first-order logic formulas to express constraints on models. For example, the following formula states that employees working at "Insurance Corp." earn more than 2000 EUR.

$$\forall x, y, z, v, n \quad inst(x, Employment) \land attr(x, Wage, y) \land value(y, v) \land$$
$$part(x, EmployedBy, z) \land attr(z, Name, n) \land n = "InsuranceCorp."$$
$$\Rightarrow v > 2000$$

As it would be very inefficient to transform data into the *GeRoMe* representation, it is not intended that these queries, mappings, and constraints are actually evaluated on the *GeRoMe* models. Instead, these expressions will be translated into the native query format of the original metamodel (e.g. SQL for a relational database schema) and executed by the specific query evaluation engines.

Metadata Management in a Multiversion Data Warehouse

Robert Wrembel and Bartosz Bębel

Institute of Computing Science, Poznań University of Technology, Poznań, Poland
{Robert.Wrembel, Bartosz.Bebel}@cs.put.poznan.pl

Abstract. A data warehouse (DW) is a database that integrates data from external data sources (EDSs) for the purpose of advanced analysis. EDSs are production systems that often change not only their contents but also their structures. The evolution of EDSs has to be reflected in a DW that integrates the sources. Traditional DW systems offer a limited support for the evolution of their structures. Our solution to this problem is based on a multiversion data warehouse (MVDW). Such a DW is composed of the sequence of persistent versions, each of which describes a schema and data within a given time period. The management of the MVDW requires a metadata model that is much more complex than in traditional data warehouses. In our approach and prototype MVDW system, the metadata model contains data structures that support: (1) monitoring EDSs with respect to content and structural changes, (2) automatic generation of processes monitoring EDSs, (3) applying discovered EDS changes to a selected DW version, (4) describing the structure of every DW version, (5) querying multiple DW versions at the same time and presenting the results coming from multiple versions.

1 Introduction

A data warehouse (DW) is a large database (often exceeding a size of dozens of terabytes) that integrates data from multiple external data sources (EDSs). The content of a DW includes historical, current, and summarized data. Data warehouses are important components of decision support systems. Data stored in a DW are analyzed by the so-called On-Line Analytical Processing (OLAP) applications for the purpose of discovering trends (e.g., demand and sales of products), discovering patterns of behavior (e.g., customer habits, credit repayment history) and anomalies (e.g., credit card usages) as well as for finding dependencies between data (e.g., market basket analysis, suggested buying, insurance fee assessment). The process of good decision making often requires forecasting future business behavior, based on present and past data as well as based on assumptions made by decision makers. This kind of data processing is called a 'what-if' analysis. In this analysis, a decision maker uses a DW for simulating changes in the real-world, creates virtual possible business scenarios, and explores them with OLAP queries. To this end, a DW must provide means for creating and managing various DW alternatives. This feature often requires changes to the structure of a DW.

S. Spaccapietra et al. (Eds.): Journal on Data Semantics VIII, LNCS 4380, pp. 118–157, 2007.

Two examples illustrating the need for the 'what-if' analysis include: simulating changes in a pay rate of fines as well as simulating changes in taxing of parking lots. In the first example, the police maintains an official pay rate of fines where every offense is categorized to a particular pay rate. They might need to simulate a hypothetical increase in fines (impacting an income to a budget) by increasing by 10% the rate of the most frequent offenses. Such a simulation requires changes in a dimension that stores the pay rate. In the second example, a city leases parking places to someone, who pays a tax from the whole leased parking area. The city managers might decide to simulate changes in income from parking places by changing the taxation policy. Instead of taxing the whole parking area they may want to tax every single parking place. Such a simulation will require changes to the DW schema, in particular, to a dimension describing the taxation scheme.

An inherent feature of external data sources is their autonomy, i.e., they may evolve in time independently of each other and independently of a DW that integrates them [65,71]. The changes have an impact on the structure and content of a DW. The evolution of EDSs can be characterized by content changes, i.e., insert/update/delete data, and schema changes, i.e., add/modify/drop a data structure or its property. Content changes result from user activities that perform their day-to-day work on data sources by means of different applications. On the contrary, schema changes are caused by: (1) changes of the real-world being represented in EDSs (e.g., changing the borders of countries/regions, changing the administrative structure of institutions, changing legislations); (2) new user requirements (e.g., storing new kinds of data); (3) new versions of software being installed, and (4) system tuning activities.

Several real-world examples illustrating the need for a DW evolution come from Poland. The first case concerns changes in the administrative division of Poland that until 1998 was composed of 49 regions. In 1999, the number of regions was reduced to 19. Some regions retained their old names, but their borders changed substantially. Such an administrative change has a strong impact, for example, on the analysis of past and present sales of products in regions. The second case concerns reclassification of building materials from 7% to 22% tax category that happened when Poland joined the EU. Comparing a gross sales of these materials in consecutive months of 2004 will result in a remarkable increase in gross sales starting from May, as compared to previous months. In practice, this increase is mainly caused by tax increase rather than by actual increase in sales. Although these cases can be handled by the solution based on slowly-changing dimensions (SCD) Type 2 or Type 3 [46] it is recommended to separate these different DW states as they describe different real-world scenarios. SCD Type 2 and 3 store all (past and current) data in the same data structure.

As yet another example let us consider a DW storing various data on unemployed, maintained by a city hall. Until 2004 they analyzed unemployment per city and education in every month. Since 2005 they started analyzing the impact of vocational trainings (partially supported by the EU) on unemployment rate. Such an analysis requires changes to a DW schema in order to register unemployed taking vocational trainings. This case can not be handled by the solutions proposed for SCDs. Other examples of various change scenarios can be found in [10,9,25,52].

The consequence of content and schema changes at EDSs is that a DW built on such EDSs becomes obsolete and needs to be synchronized. In practice, content changes are monitored and propagated to a DW often by means of materialized views [35] and the history of data changes is supported by applying temporal extensions, e.g., [18,30,52]. Temporal extensions use timestamps on modified data in order to create temporal versions.

Schema changes of EDSs are often handled in a DW by applying schema evolution, e.g., [12,42] and versioning extensions [13,33,52]. Schema evolution approaches maintain one DW schema and the set of data that evolve in time. In versioning extensions, a DW evolution is managed partially by means of schema versions and partially by data versions. These approaches solve the DW evolution problem partially. Firstly, they do not offer a clear separation between different DW states. Secondly, the approaches do not support modeling alternative, hypothetical DW states required for the 'what-if' analysis.

In our approach, we propose a multiversion data warehouse (MVDW) as a framework for handling content and schema changes in EDSs as well as for simulating and managing alternative business scenarios. The MVDW is composed of a sequence of its versions, each of which corresponds either to the real-world state (representing the content of EDSs within a given time period) or to a simulation scenario applied to the 'what-if' analysis.

In order to support the life-cycle of a DW, from its initial loading by ETL processes and then periodical refreshing, to OLAP processing and query optimization, a DW has to manage metadata. Metadata are data about various aspects of a DW. They are used for improving a DW management and exploitation. There are two basic types of metadata, namely business and technical ones. Business metadata include among others: dictionaries, thesauri, business concepts and terminology, predefined queries and report definitions. They are mainly used by end-users. Technical metadata include among others: a DW schema description and the definitions of its elements, physical storage information, access rights, statistics for a query optimizer, ETL process descriptions, and data transformation rules [77].

In the case of a multiversion data warehouse, metadata are much more complex than in traditional DWs and have to provide additional information. Industry standard metamodels, i.e., the Open Information Model and the Common Warehouse Metamodel [77] as well as research contributions, e.g., [40,61] do not support metadata describing the evolution of a DW.

The focus of this paper and its **contribution** includes the development of the two following metamodels: (1) a metamodel for managing multiple versions of a DW and (2) a metamodel for detecting changes in EDSs.

The first metamodel supports:

– the management of multiple versions of schemas and data in the MVDW;
– the execution of queries that address several DW versions;

- the presentation (visualization) of query results, coming from different DW versions, and their comparison;
- the augmentation of query results with metadata that describe changes made to adjacent DW versions. These metadata allow to properly interpret the obtained results.

The second metamodel supports:

- the automatic detection of structural and content changes in EDSs;
- the automatic generation of software for monitoring EDSs;
- the automatic generation of operations in the multiversion data warehouse in response to the detected changes.

Based on the developed concepts and the metamodel, a prototype MVDW system was implemented in Java and Oracle PL/SQL language. Data and metadata are stored in an Oracle Database 10g. To the best of our knowledge, this is the first approach and implemented system that: (1) supports managing multiple, persistent, and separate DW versions; (2) supports modeling alternative business scenarios as DW versions; (3) uses metadata to augment query results.

This paper extends our previous paper [78] with respect to: (1) the abstract description of the model of the MVDW; (2) an algorithm for processing multiversion queries; (3) the performance evaluation of processing multiversion queries.

The reminder of this paper is organized as follows. Section 2 presents basic definitions in the field of the DW technology. Section 3 overviews our concept of the multiversion data warehouse, presents its abstract model, and outlines operations that modify a DW. Section 4 presents the implementation metamodel of the MVDW and a graphical user interface for managing the MVDW. Section 5 illustrates the usage of metadata in queries addressing multiple DW versions, presents the execution algorithm of a multiversion query, and compares our query language to a temporal OLAP query language called TOLAP. Section 6 outlines fundamental implementation issues concerning the MVDW and presents preliminary performance evaluation results. Section 7 presents the system architecture, mechanism, and underlying metamodel for detecting changes in EDSs. Section 8 discusses existing approaches to: handling changes in structures and contents of databases and data warehouses, detecting structural changes in data sources as well as approaches to metadata management. Finally, Section 9 summarizes the paper.

2   Basic Definitions

A DW takes advantage of a multidimensional data model [36,37,40,49] with **facts** representing elementary information being the subject of analysis. A fact contains numerical features, called **measures** that quantify the fact and that allow to compare different facts. Examples of measures include: quantity, income, turnover, duration time.

Facts are organized in n-dimensional spaces, called data cubes. Values of measures in these spaces depend on a context set up by **dimensions**. The structure of a dimension is defined by its schema. A **dimension schema** Dim_{Schema} is a direct acyclic graph composed of a fixed set of nodes L (further called levels) and a fixed set of edges E between levels [49], thus $Dim_{Schema} = (L, E)$. The dimension schema has the following properties:

- L contains a distinguished top level, noted as l_{All}, and a terminal/bottom level, noted as l_{Term};
- relation $\rightarrow$ on L relates a child level (lower level) to its direct parent level (upper level), i.e. for each pair of levels $(l_i, l_j) \in L$: $l_i \rightarrow l_j$ there is no level l_q such that $l_i \rightarrow l_q \rightarrow l_j$;
- for each level $l_i \in L$ the following holds: $l_{Term} \rightarrow l_i \rightarrow l_{All}$;
- every level l_i has associated a domain of values, noted as $dom(l_i)$; the finite subset of $dom(l_i)$, noted as $inst_{l_i}$, constitutes the set of **level instances**; in particular $dom(l_{all}) = all$.

A typical example of dimension called *Geography* is shown in Fig. 1a. It is composed of four levels, namely *Shops*, *Cities*, *Regions*, and l_{All}, where $Shops \rightarrow Cities \rightarrow Regions \rightarrow l_{All}$. The instances of level *Shops* include $\{shopA, shopB, shopC, shopD\}$; the instances of level *Cities* include $\{Edinbourgh, Glasgow, Swansea\}$, cf. Fig. 1b.

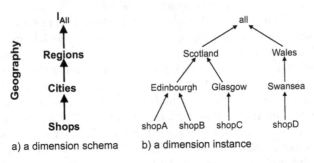

a) a dimension schema   b) a dimension instance

Fig. 1. An example *Geography* dimension schema and dimension instance

A **dimension instance** $Dim_{Instance}$ of $Dim_{Schema} = (L, E)$ is a direct acyclic graph composed of the set of level instances L_I and the set of edges E_I between level instances, thus $Dim_{Instance} = (L_I, E_I)$. The dimension instance has the following properties:

- L_I consists of pairwise disjoint sets of level instances $inst_{l_i} \cup inst_{l_k} \cup \ldots inst_{l_q}$, where $l_i, l_k, \ldots, l_q \in L$;
- for each pair of levels $(l_i, l_j) \in L$: $l_i \rightarrow l_j$ every instance of l_i is connected to an instance of l_j.

An example of the instance of dimension *Geography* is shown in Fig. 1b. In queries, dimensions specify the way measures are aggregated. A child level of a dimension rolls-up to its parent level, yielding more aggregated data.

Data cubes can be implemented either in MOLAP (multidimensional OLAP) servers or in ROLAP (relational OLAP) servers. In the former case, a cube is stored either in a multidimensional array [67,68] or in a hash table (e.g., SQL Server) or as the value of a binary large object (e.g., Oracle) or as another specialized data structure like Quad tree or K-D tree [58].

In a ROLAP implementation, a data cube is stored in relational tables, some of them represent levels and are called **level tables** (e.g., *Categories* and *Items* in Fig. 2), while others store values of measures, and are called **fact tables** (*Sales* in Fig. 2). Two basic types of ROLAP schemas are used for the implementation of a data cube, i.e., a star schema and a snowflake schema [19]. In a star schema, a dimension is composed of only one level table (e.g., *Time* in Fig. 2). In a snowflake schema, a dimension is composed of multiple level tables connected by foreign key - primary key relationships (e.g., dimension *Location* with level tables *Shops*, *Cities*, and *Regions*). In practice, one also builds the so called star-flake schemas where some dimensions are composed of multiple level tables and some dimensions are composed of one level tables, cf. Fig. 2.

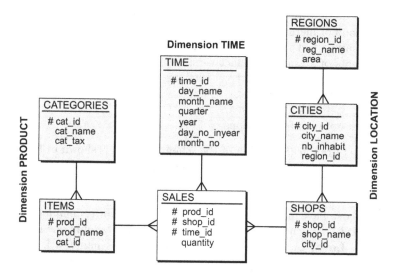

Fig. 2. An example star-flake schema of a data warehouse on sales of products

In the reminder of this paper, we will focus our discussion on the ROLAP implementation of the multidimensional data model, but our concepts can also be used in the MOLAP implementation.

3   Multiversion Data Warehouse

This section overviews our concept of the multiversion data warehouse, informally presents the elements of the MVDW model and its graphical representation, as well as outlines operations that are used for modifying the MVDW. The formal and comprehensive description of the MVDW can be found in [8,53].

3.1 Basic Concepts

The **multiversion data warehouse** is composed of the sequence of its versions. A DW version is in turn composed of a schema version and an instance version. The DW **schema version** describes the structure of a DW within a given time period, whereas the DW **instance version** represents the set of data described by its schema version.

The DW schema version is composed of:

- multiversion dimensions, composed of dimension versions,
- multiversion levels, composed of level versions,
- multiversion hierarchies, composed of hierarchy versions,
- multiversion facts, composed of fact versions,
- attributes,
- integrity constraints,
- assignments of level versions to hierarchy versions,
- assignments of hierarchy versions to dimension versions,
- assignments of fact versions to level versions, forming versions of data cubes,
- assignments of attributes to fact versions,
- assignments of attributes to level versions,
- mappings between attributes,
- mappings between level versions,
- mappings between fact versions.

An abstract graphical notation of the schema version is shown in Fig. 3. Each dimension can have many versions that belong to a *multiversion dimension*, noted as **MV_Dimension**. In a given schema version SV_i, there may be only one dimension version $DV_i \in$ **MV_Dimension**.

Each level can have many versions that belong to a *multiversion level*, noted as **MV_Level**. In a given schema version SV_i, there may be only one level version $LV_i \in$ **MV_Level**. A level version is described by its name, a key attribute (used in roll-up operations) and, optionally, by descriptor attributes (not used in roll-up operations).

In a given schema version SV_i, level versions $\{LV_i, LV_j, ..., LV_q\}$ form a hierarchy version that belongs to a *multiversion hierarchy*, noted as **MV_Hierarchy**. In a given schema version SV_i, there may be only one hierarchy version $HV_i \in$ **MV_Hierarchy**. For a given level version LV_i, function **LV**$_{ChildLV}^{ParentLV}$ $\rightarrow$**HV** assigns the level version to an indicated hierarchy version, at a position indicated by its parent level version ($ParentLV$) and child level version ($ChildLV$).

A hierarchy version belongs to a dimension version. Dimension versions belong to a *multiversion dimension*, noted as **MV_Dimension**. In a given schema version SV_i, there may be only one dimension version $DV_i \in$ **MV_Dimension**. For a given hierarchy version HV_i, function **HV**$\rightarrow$**DV** assigns the hierarchy

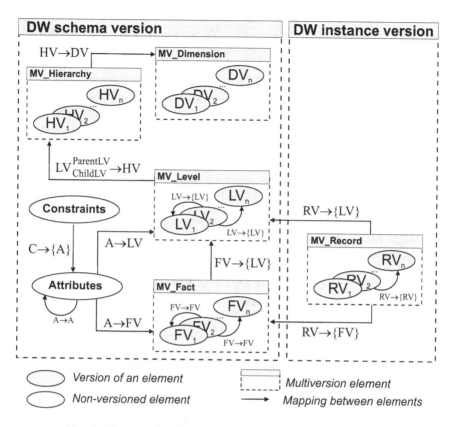

Fig. 3. The graphical abstract representation of the MVDW

version to an indicated dimension version. A given dimension version may include several hierarchy versions, starting at the same bottom level version and ending at the same top level version.

A data cube (storing fact data) is represented by a *fact version*. Versions of the same data cube belong to a *multiversion fact*, noted as **MV_Fact**. In a given schema version SV_i, there may be only one fact version $FV_i \in$ **MV_Fact**. For a given fact version FV_i, function **FV→{LV}** assigns FV_i to the set of level versions $\{LV_i, \ldots, LV_m\}$.

As mentioned earlier, level versions are composed of attributes. The same applies to fact versions. The set of attributes used in level versions and fact versions is noted as **Attributes**. Attributes are assigned to level versions and to fact versions by means of assignment functions **A→LV** and **A→FV**, respectively. An attribute can have several integrity constraints defined. The set of all integrity constraints is noted as **Constraints**. An integrity constraint is assigned to one or more attributes by an assignment function, noted as **C→{A}**. Notice that attributes and integrity constraints are not versioned in order to keep the model simple but powerful enough to provide the versioning functionality.

When the name or the definition of some attributes in a level version changes, a new level version is created in a new DW version. For the purpose of querying multiple DW versions under schema changes, the previous and the newly-created level versions are mapped to each other by a mapping function, noted as **LV→{LV}**. An old level version LV_i can be mapped to a few new level versions in case of creating a new parent level version LV_k based on its child level version LV_i (cf. Section 3.4), i.e. child level LV_i transforms to a new child level LV_j and its newly-created parent level LV_k.

Similarly, when the name or the structure of a fact version changes, a new fact version is created in a new DW version. The previous and the newly-created fact versions are mapped to each other by a mapping function, noted as **FV→FV**. Changes to attribute names and their definitions are mapped by a mapping function, noted as **A→A**.

Example 1. As a simple example illustrating our model, let us consider a DW schema version *V1*, as shown in Fig. 4. This version is composed of the *Sales* fact table in version *V1*. It is associated with the three following level tables *Items*, *Time*, and *Shops*, all in version *V1*. Function **FV→{LV}** executed for $Sales_{V1}$ returns $\{Items_{V1}, Time_{V1}, Shops_{V1}\}$.

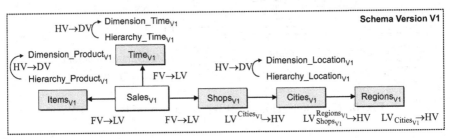

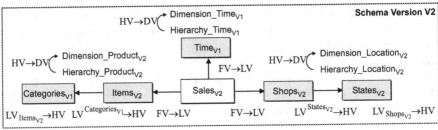

Fig. 4. An example presenting two DW schema versions with their components

$Items_{V1}$ belongs to the *Product* hierarchy in version *V1*. As stated earlier, function $\mathbf{LV}_{ChildLV}^{ParentLV} \rightarrow \mathbf{HV}$ executed for a given level version assigns this level version to an indicated hierarchy version at an indicated position. If *ParentLV* and *ChildLV* are null then the function returns the name and the version of a hierarchy a level belongs to as well as its direct parent and child levels. The function executed for $Items_{V1}$ returns the following tuple:

$Items_{V1}.LV{\rightarrow}HV = \langle Hierarchy\_Product_{V1}, null, null\rangle$,

where the first value is the version hierarchy $Items_{V1}$ belongs to, the second value ($null$) is a child level versions of $Items_{V1}$ and the third value ($null$) is its parent level version.

$Time_{V1}$ belongs to the $Time$ hierarchy in version $V1$, i.e.

$Time_{V1}.LV{\rightarrow}HV = \langle Hierarchy\_Time_{V1}, null, null\rangle$,

$Shops_{V1}$, $Cities_{V1}$, and $Regions_{V1}$ belong to the $Location$ hierarchy in version $V1$, i.e.:

$Shops_{V1}.LV{\rightarrow}HV = \langle Hierarchy\_Location_{V1}, null, Cities_{V1}\rangle$,

$Cities_{V1}.LV{\rightarrow}HV = \langle Hierarchy\_Location_{V1}, Shops_{V1}, Regions_{V1}\rangle$,

$Regions_{V1}.LV{\rightarrow}HV = \langle Hierarchy\_Location_{V1}, Cities_{V1}, null\rangle$.

Hierarchy version $Hierarchy\_Product_{V1}$ belongs to its dimension $Dimension\_Product_{V1}$. Thus, function **HV→DV** executed on $Hierarchy\_Product_{V1}$ returns $Dimension\_Product_{V1}$. Similarly, the function executed for the two remaining hierarchies returns their dimensions.

Let us assume that new schema version $V2$ was derived from $V1$. The schema in $V2$ was changed as described below. Firstly, level $Regions$ was renamed to $States$. This change resulted in creating new version of this level, i.e. $States_{V2}$. Secondly, level $Cities$ was removed from dimension $Location$. It resulted in creating a new version of the hierarchy ($HierarchyLocation_{V2}$) and a corresponding dimension ($DimensionLocation_{V2}$). Moreover, a new version of level $Shops$ was created in order to handle the removal of $Cities$, i.e. $Shops_{V2}$ became a child of $States_{V2}$. Next, a new level $Categories$ was created as a parent level of $Items$. This change resulted in creating a new version of $Items$, i.e. $Items_{V2}$ that became a child of $Categories_{V1}$.

Since level $Regions$ was renamed, $Regions_{V1}$ is mapped to $States_{V2}$ by means of the **LV→LV** function. The function executed for $Regions_{V1}$ returns $States_{V2}$.

Notice that dimension $Time$ has not changed and it is shared by both schema versions.

The DW instance version is composed of (cf. Fig. 3):

- multiversion records, composed of record versions,
- assignments of record versions to level versions,
- assignments of record versions to fact versions.

Versions of records represent either versions of level instances or versions of fact data. Versions of records belong to a *multiversion record*, noted as **MV_Record**. On the one hand, in a given DW instance version IV_i there may be only one version of multiversion record $RV_i \in$ **MV_Record**. On the other hand, the same version of a record may be shared by multiple DW instance versions.

A given version of record RV_i is assigned to one or more level versions by means of an assignment function, noted as **RV→{LV}**. Similarly, a record version is assigned to one or more fact versions by means of an assignment function, noted as **RV→{FV}**.

Level instances and dimension instances can be modified by multiple operations, as outlined in Section 3.4. For the purpose of querying the MVDW under such changes, record version RV_i (being the instance of one level version, say LV_i), is mapped to one or more newly-created record versions (being the instances of newly-created level version, say LV_j, derived from LV_i). Such mappings are represented by a mapping function, noted as $\mathbf{RV \rightarrow \{RV\}}$.

3.2   Types of DW Versions

We distinguish two types of DW versions, namely real and alternative ones. **Real versions** are created in order to keep up with changes in a real business environment, like for example: changing user needs concerning the context of an analysis (adding dimensions to or removing dimensions from a cube), changing the way a business is done (changing the structure of servicing customers from regional offices to city offices), changing the organizational structure of a company, changing the geographical borders of countries/regions, changing the prices/taxes of products. Real versions are linearly ordered by the time they are valid within. **Alternative versions** are created for simulation purposes, as part of the 'what-if' analysis. Such versions represent virtual business scenarios. Alternative versions may branch. All DW versions are connected by version derivation relationships, forming a **version derivation graph**. The root of this graph is the first real version.

Fig. 5 schematically shows real and alternative versions. $R1$ represents an initial real version. Based on $R1$, new real version $R2$ was created. Similarly, $R3$ was derived from $R2$ and $R4$ was derived from $R3$. $A2.1$ and $A2.2$ are alternative versions derived from $R2$, and $A4.1$ is an alternative version derived from $R4$.

One may consider applying a multiversion data warehouse for a company selling and hosting DWs for multiple customers, each of which needs slightly customized DW structure. This scenario can be handled in our approach only by creating a real 'base' version and deriving from it customized alternative versions for every customer.

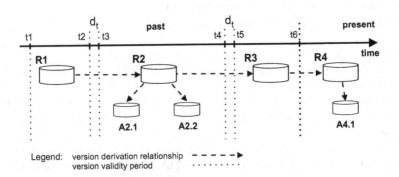

Fig. 5. An example derivation graph including real and alternative versions

3.3   Constraints on DW Versions

Every DW version is valid within certain period of time represented by two timestamps, i.e., **begin validity time** (BVT) and **end validity time** (EVT) [9]. This concept is similar to the concept of valid time in temporal databases [34,72,73].

As an example let us consider again DW versions from Fig. 5. Real version $R1$ is valid within time $t1$ (BVT) and $t2$ (EVT), $R2$ is valid within $t3$ ($t3=t2+d_t$) and $t4$, whereas $R4$ is valid from $t6$ until present. Alternative versions $A2.1$, $A2.2$, and $A4.1$ are valid within the same time period as the real versions they were derived from.

DW versions in the version derivation graph must fulfill the three following constraints:

- *Real Versions Validity Time* - the begin validity time of a child real version is greater by time d_t than the end validity time of its parent real version (cf. Fig. 5);
- *Real-Alternative Versions Validity Time* - the validity time of any alternative DW version is within the validity time of its parent real version;
- *Alternative Parent-Child Versions Validity Time* - the validity time of a child alternative DW version is within the validity time of its parent alternative version. This constraint allows the existence of multiple alternative versions valid within the same time period.

Versions of schema elements (dimensions, hierarchies, levels, facts) and versions of instance elements (records) form version derivation graphs. As dimension versions and fact versions can be shared by multiple DW versions, derivation graphs of these schema elements may differ from the DW version derivation graph. The version derivation graph of a dimension and the version derivation graph of its hierarchies must be identical since we do not allow the existence of dimensions without hierarchies and hierarchies without dimensions.

3.4   DW Version Change Operations and Version Creation

A DW version is created/derived explicitly by a DW designer/administrator. Then a newly-derived DW version is modified by means of operations that have an impact on a schema, further called schema change operations, as well as by means of operations that have an impact on dimension instances, further called instance change operations.

Schema change operations include among others: adding a new attribute to a level table, removing an attribute from a level table, creating a new fact table, associating a given fact table with a given dimension, renaming a fact or a level table, creating a new level table with a given structure, including a parent level table into its child level table, and creating a parent level table based on its child level table. The last three operations are applicable to snowflake schemas.

Instance change operations include among others: inserting a new level instance into a given level, deleting a level instance, changing the association of a child level instance to another parent level instance, merging several instances of a given level into one instance of the same level, splitting a given level instance into multiple instances of the same level.

Notice that multiple schema change operations and instance change operations may be included into one set of operations and executed on the same DW version. The full list of schema and dimension change operations with their formal semantics, their application to the MVDW, and their outcomes can be found in [8].

Our experience in DW version management comes from the electricity supply business. Our findings in this area show that the required number of real DW versions within 5-8 years will not be greater than 10. It results from slowly changing legislation and structural changes in the electricity supply business that impact the information systems and data warehouses already applied. The number of alternative versions will not be greater than 3-5 per year. It is caused by the need for simulating the business (in particular, simulating different modes of computing a depreciation). Thus, the maximum number of DW versions required within 5-8 years should not be greater than 30.

4   Metamodel of the MVDW

The metamodel of the MVDW is general and is applicable to ROLAP and MOLAP implementation. Regardless the implementation, a data structure storing dimension data will further be noted as DIMENSION and a data structure storing fact data (a data cube) will further be noted as FACT.

4.1   MVDW Implementation Metaschema

The core metaschema of our prototype MVDW [79] is shown in Fig. 6. It is designed in the Oracle notation [6] where: a dashed line means an optional foreign key, a solid line means a mandatory foreign key, a line end that is split into three means a relationship of cardinality many, whereas a simple line end means a relationship of cardinality one.

The *Versions* dictionary table stores data about all existing DW versions, i.e., a unique version identifier, name, begin and end validity times, status (whether a version is committed or under development), type (a real or an alternative one), parent-child (derivation) dependencies between versions.

Metadata about FACT versions are stored in the *Fact_Versions* dictionary table. It contains a unique FACT identifier, name, the identifier of a multiversion FACT a given FACT belongs to, FACT implementation name, DW version identifier a given FACT belongs to, the identifier of a transaction that created a given FACT.

Metadata about DIMENSION versions are stored in *Dim_Versions*. It contains a DIMENSION version identifier, name, the identifier of a multiversion DIMENSION a given DIMENSION belongs to, DW version identifier a given DIMENSION belongs to, the identifier of a transaction that created a given DIMENSION.

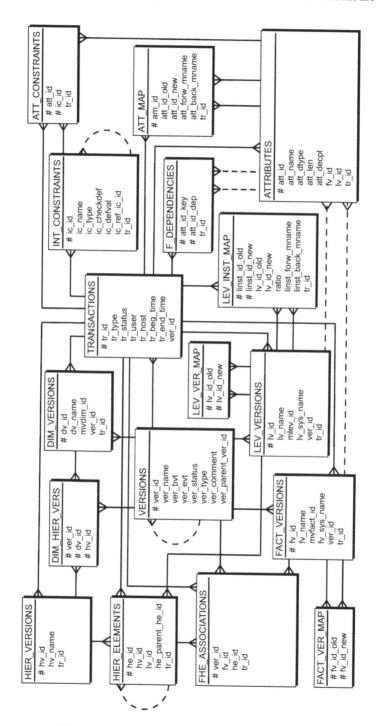

Fig. 6. The metaschema of our prototype MVDW

Metadata describing versions of DIMENSION hierarchies and their associations to DIMENSION versions are stored in *Hier_ Versions* and *Dim_ Hier_ Versions*, respectively. Versions of hierarchies are composed of level versions, whose descriptions are stored in *Lev_ Versions*. This dictionary table stores a level identifier, name, the identifier of a multiversion level a given level belongs to, level implementation name, DW version identifier a given level belongs to, the identifier of a transaction that created a given level. Versions of level hierarchies are composed of level versions. These associations are stored in *Hier_ Elements*.

FACT versions are associated with DIMENSION versions via level versions. The associations are stored in *FHE_ Associations*. Every record in this dictionary table contains the identifier of a FACT version, and the identifier of the version of a hierarchy element (an association with the lowest level in a level hierarchy), the identifier of a DW version this association is valid in, and the identifier of a transaction that created this association.

Every FACT version and level version includes the set of its attributes, that are stored in the *Attributes* dictionary table. As mentioned earlier, attributes are not versioned in order to keep the model simple. As a consequence, a single attribute can't be shared by multiple DW versions.

Integrity constraints that may be defined for FACTS and level versions are stored in the *Int_ Constraints* and *Att_ Constraints* dictionary tables. *Int_ Constraints* stores, among others, the name of an integrity constraint, its type and definition. Our prototype system supports the following types of integrity constraints: primary key, foreign key, null/not null, and check. Attributes of fact as well as level tables that have integrity constraints defined, are registered in *Att_ Constraints*. Functional dependencies between attributes in level versions are stored in *F_ Dependencies*.

Table *Att_ Map* is used for storing mappings between an attribute existing in DW version V_o and its corresponding attribute in a child version V_p. This kind of mappings are necessary in order to track attribute definition changes between versions, i.e., changing an attribute name, data type, length, and integrity constraints. Some changes in attribute domain between two consecutive DW versions, say V_o and V_p (e.g., changing a university grading scale from the Austrian one to the Polish one) will require data transformations, if the data stored in V_o and V_p are to be comparable. To this end, forward and backward conversion methods have to be provided. Their names are registered in *Att_ Map* as the values of *att_ forw_ mname* and *att_ back_ mname*, respectively.

In our prototype system, conversion methods are implemented as Oracle PL/SQL functions. The input argument of such a function is the name of an attribute whose value is being converted and the output is the converted value. Conversion methods are implemented by a DW administrator and they are registered in the metaschema by a dedicated application. In the current implementation a conversion method may accept only one input argument, i.e., an attribute name. From a conceptual and technical point of view, extending conversion methods with multiple arguments will require minor extension of the metamodel, minor modification of a user interface for associating conversion methods with attributes, and an extension of our multiversion query parser (the most complicated task).

The *Fact_Ver_Map* dictionary table is used for storing mappings between a given FACT in DW version V_o and a corresponding FACT in version V_p, directly derived from V_o. This kind of mappings are necessary in order to track FACT definition changes between versions, i.e., changing a FACT name or splitting a FACT. The purpose of *Lev_Ver_Map* is to track changes of levels between versions, i.e., changing a level name, including a parent level into its child level, creating a parent level based on its child level, cf. [8].

As outlined in Section 3.4, the instances of level versions can be modified by changing associations to parent level instances as well as by merging and splitting them. Operations of this type result in a new structures of a dimension instance. In order to allow querying multiple DW versions under such modifications, the system has to map level instances in version V_o into their corresponding instances that were modified in version V_p. To this end, the *Lev_Inst_Map* data dictionary table is used.

The prototype MVDW is managed in a transactional manner and the *Transactions* dictionary table stores the information about transactions used for creating DW versions and modifying them.

Example 2. In order to illustrate the idea and usage of mapping tables, let us consider a DW schema from Fig. 2 and let us assume that initially, in a real version from February (R^{FEB}) to March (R^{MAR}) there existed 3 shops, namely *ShopA*, *ShopB*, and *ShopC* that were represented by appropriate instances of the *Location* dimension. In April, a new DW version was created, namely R^{APR} in order to represent a new reality where *ShopA* and *ShopB* were merged into one shop - *ShopAB*. This change was reflected in the *Location* dimension instances. To this end, the two following records were inserted to the *Lev_Inst_Map* dictionary table:

$$\langle id\_ShopA, id\_ShopAB, id\_ShopsR^{MAR}, id\_ShopsR^{APR},$$
$$100, null, null, tr\_11\rangle$$
$$\langle id\_ShopB, id\_ShopAB, id\_ShopsR^{MAR}, id\_ShopsR^{APR},$$
$$100, null, null, tr\_11\rangle$$

The first and the second value in the above records represents the identifier of *ShopA* and *ShopAB*, respectively. The third and fourth value represents the *Shops* level identifier in version R^{MAR} and R^{APR}, respectively.

The fifth value (attribute *Ratio* in *Lev_Inst_Map*, cf. Fig. 6) is the merging/splitting ratio. It is used in cases when an entity (e.g., branch, division, faculty, shop) splits into multiple new entities. Typically, each of these new entities contains a fraction of its original entity (e.g., the number of employees, funds, assets). The merging/splitting ratio stores the percent of an original entity that constitutes a new entity. The same applies to merging. A new entity can be created by merging whole or only parts of old entities. In our example, the ratio equals to 100%, meaning that the whole *ShopA* and *ShopB* constitute *ShopAB*.

For more advanced splitting or merging operations it will be necessary to provide a backward and a forward transformation methods for converting facts from an old to a new DW version. If such methods are explicitly implemented and provided by a DW administrator, then their names are registered as the values of *linst_ back_ mname* and *linst_forw_ mname*, respectively.

The last value (attribute *tr_ id*) in both of the above records stores the identifier of a transaction that carried out the modifications.

The dictionary tables discussed above implement abstract elements of the model presented in Section 3.1. The mappings between dictionary tables and model elements are summarized in Table 1.

Table 1. The correspondence between dictionary tables and model elements

Model elements	Dictionary tables
DV_i	DIM_VERSIONS
LV_i	LEV_VERSIONS
HV_i	HIER_VERSIONS
FV_i	FACT_VERSIONS
RV_i, RV→{LV}, RV→{FV}	stored in implementation tables created by the system; their names are stored as the values of: FACT_VERSIONS.FV_SYS_NAME LEV_VERSIONS.LV_SYS_NAME
Constraints	INT_CONSTRAINTS F_DEPENDENCIES
Attributes	ATTRIBUTES
LV→HV	HIER_ELEMENTS
HV→DV	DIM_HIER_VERSIONS
FV→{LV}	FHE_ASSOCIATIONS
LV→{LV}	LEV_VER_MAP
FV→FV	FACT_VER_MAP
RV→{RV}	LEV_INST_MAP
C→{A}	ATT_CONSTRAINTS
A→LV	ATTRIBUTES
A→FV	ATTRIBUTES

4.2 MVDW vs. SCD

It may be tempting to apply to the scenario discussed in Example 2 and to other scenarios the mechanism of slowly changing dimension (SCD) proposed by R. Kimball [46,70]. The author proposed the so-called *Type 2 SCD* and *Type 3 SCD* that are capable of handling data evolution. In *Type 2 SCD*, every time data record R_i in table T is changed, an old and a new record are stored in T. Thus, the whole history of record changes is stored in a database. In *Type 3 SCD*, for each column C_i whose value changes are to be tracked, there is a corresponding column $C_{i_{current}}$. C_i stores an initial value, whereas $C_{i_{current}}$ stores a current value. Additionally, for each pair of attributes C_i and $C_{i_{current}}$ there exists also a column $D_{i_{active}}$ that stores the date when the current value becomes active.

The main limitation of *Type 2 SCD* is that: (1) all versions of records (coming from different time periods) are stored in the same table that may cause a decrease in query processing efficiency; (2) sharing versions records between multiple DW states requires further extensions to the *Type 2 SCD* mechanism, namely, for each record its validity times need to be stored. The limitations of the *Type 3 SCD* are as follows. First of all, it does not allow to store the whole history of data changes since only the initial and the last value of an attribute are stored. Second of all, a DW designer has to know in advance which attributes will change their values and he/she has to create for every such an attribute two additional attributes, namely $C_{i_{current}}$ and $D_{i_{active}}$. This causes that any evolving table stores numerous additional attributes, even if some of them may not be used at all. Moreover, neither *Type 2 SCD* nor *Type 3 SCD* support schema changes. What is more, neither of the techniques is capable of handling level instance splitting or level instance merging since they do not allow to register the semantics of instance change operations.

On the contrary, in our approach:

– the whole history of data changes is stored and managed by the system without the need of extending original tables;
– multiple, logically consistent data and schema changes can be separated in different DW versions;
– versions of data can be shared between multiple DW versions;
– the system registers all schema and instance changes in the data dictionary that allows to interpret the obtained query results in the context of the registered changes.

4.3 Metadata Visualization – MVDW User Interface

A MVDW administrator manages the structure and content of the MVDW via a graphical application, implemented in Java. Its main management window is shown in Fig. 7. It is composed of the *version navigator*, located in the left hand side panel and the *schema viewer*, located in the right hand side panel. Both visualize the content of the MVDW metaschema.

The main functionality of the application includes:

– the derivation of a new (real or alternative) version of a DW;
– the modification of a schema version by means of schema change operations (cf. Section 3.4);
– the modification of the structure of dimension instances by means of dimension change operations (cf. Section 3.4);
– loading data from EDSs into a selected DW version (any ODBC data sources, sources accessible via a gateway, or text files can be used);
– visualizing the schema of a selected DW version;

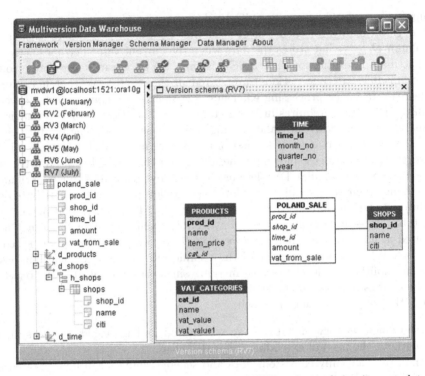

Fig. 7. The user interface for managing the MVDW and visualizing its metadata

- visualizing the DW version derivation graph;
- querying multiple DW versions;
- presenting results of queries on multiple DW versions and augmenting the results with metadata.

5   Metadata in Multiversion Queries

The content of the MVDW can be queried either by a query that addresses a single version – further called a **single-version query** (SVQ) or by a query that addresses multiple versions – further called a **multiversion query** (MVQ).

In the MVDW, data of user interest are usually distributed among several versions and a user may not be aware of the location of particular set of data. Moreover, DW versions being addressed in multiversion queries may differ with respect to their schemas. For these reasons, querying the MVDW is challenging and requires intensive usage of metadata.

5.1   Querying Multiple DW Versions

For the purpose of querying the MVDW, a traditional SQL **select** command has to be extended. To this end, we proposed clauses that allow querying: (1) a single DW version that can be either a real or an alternative one, (2) the set of real DW versions, (3) the set of alternative DW versions.

The set of versions addressed in a MVQ can be provided by a user in a query in the two following ways:

- implicitly – by specifying a time interval (represented by version begin and version end validity times);
- explicitly – by specifying the set of version identifiers.

To this end, the `version from 'beg_date' to 'end_date'` and `version in` $(VID_1, \ldots, VID_n)$ clauses are used, respectively.

The detail description of the clauses as well as a user interface for specifying multiversion queries and visualizing their results is presented in [54].

A user's multiversion query is processed by our MVQ parser and executor in the four following steps.

1. **Constructing the set of DW versions**

   The set $S^V = \{V_1, V_2, \ldots, V_n\}$ of versions that is to be addressed in a multiversion query is constructed by the MVQ parser by using version begin validity times and version end validity times (cf. Section 3.1) if a user specified a time interval in his/her query. Otherwise, explicitly provided version identifiers are used.

2. **Decomposing MVQ**

   Next, for every DW version $\{V_1, V_2, \ldots, V_n\} \in S^V$, the parser constructs an appropriate single-version query $\{SVQ_1, SVQ_2, \ldots, SVQ_n\}$. In this process, the differences in version schemas are taken into consideration. If some tables and attributes changed their names from one version to another version, then appropriate names are found in metadata dictionary tables and are used in these SVQs.

   If an attribute used in the `select` clause is missing in DW versions V_i, V_j, V_k, then the attribute is excluded from single-version queries addressing V_i, V_j, V_k. If an attribute used in the `group by` clause is missing in DW versions V_i, V_j, V_k, then SVQs are not executed in these versions. They are executed only in these versions where the attribute exists or has its corresponding attribute. In both of these cases a user is notified about missing attributes by means of meta-information that is attached to the result of a SVQ. For example, if queried attribute *Gross_price* was removed from table *Sale* in queried DW version V_i then the result of SVQ_i will have attached the following meta-information:

   `Attribute Gross_price removed from Sale`

   The data dictionary tables searched in this step include among others: *Versions, Fact_ Versions, Dim_ Versions, Hier_ Versions, Dim_Hier_ Versions, Hier_ Elements, FHE_ Associations, Lev_ Versions, Fact_ Ver_ Map, Lev_ Ver_ Map, Attributes, Att_ Map*.

3. **Executing SVQs**

   Every single version query $\{SVQ_1, SVQ_2, \ldots, SVQ_n\}$ constructed in step 2 is next executed in its own DW version $\{V_1, V_2, \ldots, V_n\}$. Then, the result set

of every SVQ is returned to a user and presented separately. Additionally, every result set is annotated with:
- an information about a DW version the result was obtained from,
- metadata about schema and dimension instance changes between adjacent DW versions being addressed by the MVQ. The metadata information attached to a SVQ result allow to analyze and interpret the obtained data appropriately.

4. **Integrating SVQ results**

Result sets of single-version queries $\{SVQ_1, SVQ_2, \ldots, SVQ_n\}$ obtained in step 3 may be in some cases integrated into one common data set. This set is represented with respect to the schema of a DW version specified by a user (the current real version by default). The integration of SVQs results will be possible if the MVQ addresses attributes that are present (or have corresponding attributes) in all queried DW versions and if there exist transformation methods between adjacent DW versions (if needed).

For example, it will not be possible to integrate the results of a MVQ addressing DW version V_o and V_p, computing the sum of products sold (select sum(amount) ...), if attribute *amount* exists in version V_o and it was dropped in version V_p.

While integrating result sets the following dictionary tables are used among others: *Fact_Versions*, *Fact_Ver_Map*, *Lev_Versions*, *Lev_Ver_Map*, *Attributes*, *Att_Map*, *Lev_Inst_Map*.

Example 3. In order to illustrate annotating result sets of SVQs with metadata (step 3) let us consider a DW schema from Fig. 2. Let us further assume that initially in a real version from April 2004 R^{APR} there existed 3 shops, namely *ShopA*, *ShopB*, and *ShopC*. These shops were selling *porotherm bricks* with 7% of VAT (tax). Let us assume that in May, *porotherm bricks* were reclassified to 22% VAT category (which is a real case of Poland after joining the European Union). This reclassification was reflected in a new real DW version R^{MAY}.

Now we may consider the below user's MVQ that addresses DW versions from April till May and that computes gross and net total sales of products.

```
select sum(ps.amount * pr.item_price * vc.vat_value1) gross_sales,
       sum(ps.amount * pr.item_price) net_sales,
       pr.name product
from poland_sale ps, products pr, vat_categories vc
where ps.prod_id=pr.prod_id
and pr.cat_id=vc.cat_id
group by pr.name
version from '01-04-2004' to '30-04-2004'
```

The query is decomposed into two SVQs: one for version R^{APR} and one for R^{MAY}. After executing the SVQs in their proper versions, the result set of SVQ addressing version R^{MAY} is augmented and returned to a user with metadata describing changes in the structure of the *Product* dimension instance between versions R^{APR} and R^{MAY}, as follows:

```
Reclassified key [br1(porotherm)→vc7(VAT 7%) to
[br1(porotherm))→vc22(VAT 22%)
in table PRODUCTS
```

In this way a sales analyst will know that a gross sales increase from April to May was at least partially caused by VAT increase.

A screen shot of the result of this query in our MVDW prototype system is shown in Fig. 8. *RV*4 and *RV*5 are version identifiers and they represent versions from April and May, respectively. Query results can be displayed either in a text form (available under the *View data* buttons) or as charts (available *View chart* buttons).

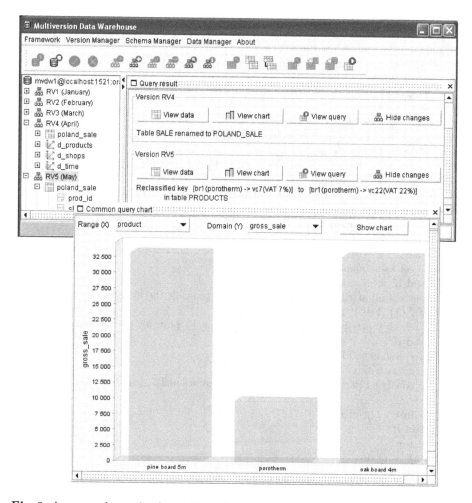

Fig. 8. An example result of a multiversion query addressing real versions from April and May

5.2 MVQ Processing Algorithm

While parsing a cross-version query, the query executor uses information stored in the metaschema. The pseudo-code of parsing and executing a multiversion query is shown as Algorithm 1.

Algorithm 1. Parsing and executing a multiversion query
___

1: input: multiversion query MVQ
2: $Q=\{\}$ {the set of partial queries}
3: $V=\{\}$ {the set of versions being addressed in MVQ}
4: $T=\{\}$ {the set of tables being addressed in MVQ}
5: $A=\{\}$ {the set of attributes used in MVQ}
6: get the set of DW versions MVQ addresses: $V=\{V_i, ..., V_m\}$
7: get the set of tables used in MVQ: $T=\{T_k, ..., T_q\}$
8: get the set of attributes used in MVQ: $A=\{a_k, ..., a_q\}$
9: **for** $V_j \in V$ **do**
10:    $T_{temp}=\{\}$
11:    $A_{temp}=\{\}$
12:    *construct* BOOLEAN=TRUE
13:    check if all tables in T exist in V_j {consult the metadata}
14:    **if** NOT TRUE **then**
15:       check if table names were changed in V_j {consult the metadata}
16:       **if** NOT TRUE **then**
17:          *construct*=FALSE {skip constructing partial query Q_j}
18:       **else**
19:          get table names into T_{temp}
20:       **end if**
21:    **else**
22:       get table names into T_{temp}
23:    **end if**
24:    check if all attributes in A exist in T_{temp} {consult the metadata}
25:    **if** NOT TRUE **then**
26:       check if attribute names were changed in V_j {consult the metadata}
27:    **end if**
28:    **if** *construct*=TRUE **then**
29:       get attribute names into A_{temp}
30:       construct partial query Q_j using table names in T_{temp} and attributes in A_{temp}

31:       insert Q_j into Q
32:    **end if**
33: **end for**
34: **for** $Q_j \in Q$ **do**
35:    execute Q_j
36:    get result of Q_j
37:    return and display Q_j
38: **end for**

5.3   Multiversion Query Language vs. TOLAP

Our Multiversion Query Language and its implemented parser and executor [54,79] offer similar functionality as a temporal OLAP query language called TOLAP [52,75]. Both languages are capable of querying multiple DW states that differ with respect to the schema of dimensions and schema of fact tables. Moreover, both can provide consistent query results under changes to the structure of dimension instances. Query results can be presented in a way as if they were at certain indicated time period (version). In our language, the merge into clause is used for this purpose [54]. TOLAP allows to explicitly query metadata on DW changes. Our query language does not allow to explicitly query metadata but the query parser and executor implicitly queries metadata, so that every query result is augmented with metadata describing changes to adjacent queried DW versions.

6   Implementation Issues

Two or more versions of a DW may share fact as well as dimension data. In order to implement this functionality, we proposed a data sharing mechanism (further called *BitmapSharing*). It consists in storing with every record, in a fact table or a dimension level table, information about all DW versions this record is shared by [11]. At the implementation level, sharing information is stored in the set of bitmaps (bit vectors) attached to a shared table, where one bitmap represents one DW version. The number of bits in a bitmap equals to the number of records in a shared table. The ith bit in bitmap V_m, describing version V_m, is set to 1 if the ith record is shared by DW version V_m. Otherwise the bit is set to 0. The association between a given DW version and its corresponding bitmap is stored in another dedicated data structure.

Currently, the efficiency of *BitmapSharing* is being experimentally evaluated and compared to two prominent data sharing techniques proposed in the literature, i.e., [17,66]. Some of the obtained results are reported below.

Fig. 9 presents the results of the experiment that measured time overhead for constructing the content of a single DW version. Two different versions were queried, namely version number 5 (in the middle of the version derivation graph) and version number 10 (at the end of the graph). Each version (except the initial one) shared all its data records with its parent version. The number of records physically stored (not shared) in each version was parameterized and equaled to 10000, 50000, and 100000. The techniques proposed in [17] and [66] are noted in Fig. 9 as *DBVA* and *Framework*, respectively.

As we can observe from Fig. 9, the *BitmapSharing* offers better performance than the two other techniques. It results from a simpler data sharing mechanism that we use as compared to the *Framework* and *DBVA*. In the *BitmapSharing*, in order to find the required records, the program executes simple table scans in appropriate DW versions, retrieving records with their sharing information. Then, the final selection of records is done by AND-ing appropriate version bitmaps. The *BitmapSharing* performance can be further improved by using indexes.

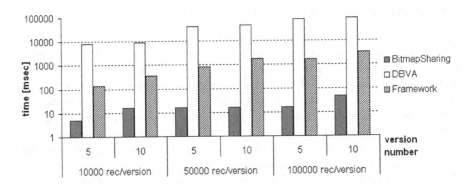

Fig. 9. Constructing the content of a version for version number 5 and version number 10 (percent of records shared by a child and its parent version equals to 100%; number of records physically stored in each version: 10000, 50000, 100000)

Similar performance characteristics to the one shown in Fig. 9 were obtained also for the lower number of shared records. The number (percent) of shared records does not influence the processing time as the system processes the same number of bitmaps, regardless of the number of shared records.

In order to test the scalability of the *BitmapSharing* we executed queries selecting various number of records from every DW version in the test set. The set was composed of 10, 20, 40, 60, 80, and 100 DW versions. The number of records locally stored in every version equaled to 100000. Additionally, a parent DW version shared 100% of its records with its child version.

Table 2 presents execution time for queries selecting 50% of records from every DW version as well as time increase coefficients. The coefficients are computed as $t_{m+\Delta}/t_m$, where t_m is the execution time of a query addressing m (e.g., 40) consecutive DW versions, and $t_{m+\Delta}$ is the execution time of a query addressing $m + \Delta$ consecutive DW versions (e.g., 60). As we can observe from the table, increase time coefficients range from 1.55 to 2.65.

Fig. 10 shows the performance characteristic from Table 2. As we can observe from the chart, although the characteristic is not ideally linear it is close to a linear one.

One of the most important research and technological issues in the field of data warehousing is DW performance in terms of query processing, no matter whether a standard, temporal, or multiversion DW is applied. OLAP applications heavily

Table 2. *BitmapSharing* performance: selecting records from multiple DW versions

Nb of queried versions	10	20	40	60	80	100
Time ID	t_{10}	t_{20}	t_{40}	t_{60}	t_{80}	t_{100}
Response time [msec]	140	312	828	1438	2625	4063
Time increase coefficient		t_{20}/t_{10}	t_{40}/t_{20}	t_{60}/t_{40}	t_{80}/t_{60}	t_{100}/t_{80}
Coefficient value		2.23	2.65	1.74	1.82	1.55

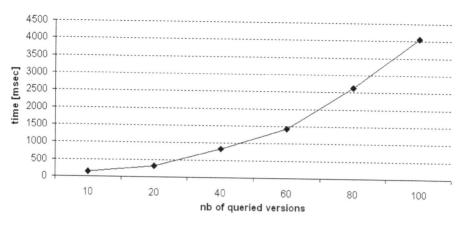

Fig. 10. *BitmapSharing*: selecting records from multiple DW versions (the number of queried versions equals to: 10, 20, 40, 60, 80, and 100; the number of records selected from every version equals to 50%; versions are sharing 100% of their records; the number of records locally stored in every version equals to 100000)

use the so-called *star queries* that join fact tables with multiple dimension tables. Reducing execution time of such joins is crucial to a DW performance. To this end, a special data structure, called a *join index* was developed [76]. This index is typically organized as a B-tree and stores a precomputed join of a fact and a dimension table.

In order to optimize multiversion star queries in the MVDW, we propose a *multiversion join index* [16]. The index joins multiple versions of a fact table with versions of a dimension table that are physically stored in separate DW versions. Its internal structure combines two indexes, namely *Value index* and *Version index*. Both of them are B$^+$-tree based. *Value index* is created on a join attribute. Its leaves store values of an indexed attribute and pointers to *Version index*. *Version index* is used for indexing versions of a data warehouse. Its leaves store lists of ROWIDs, where ROWIDs in one list point to rows (of a fact and a dimension table) in one DW version. Thus, a multiversion star query can be answered by searching *Value index* first, and then, by searching *Version index* in order to find appropriate DW versions storing records of interest. The performance of the multiversion join index has been evaluated by multiple experiments [16]. Their results are currently under reviewing.

7 Detecting Changes in EDSs

In order to ease the detection of content and structural changes in EDSs we use an operational data store (ODS) as a buffering layer between EDSs and the MVDW. Notice that the system architecture and functionality presented in this section focuses on automatic detection of changes in EDSs that have an impact mainly on dimension schemas, fact schemas and structures of dimension instances, rather than on supporting fully functional ETL processes.

7.1 System Architecture

The basic architecture of our system is shown in Fig. 11. External data sources (EDS_1, EDS_2, and EDS_3) are connected in a standard way to the ODS via wrappers [64] that are software modules responsible for data model transformations.

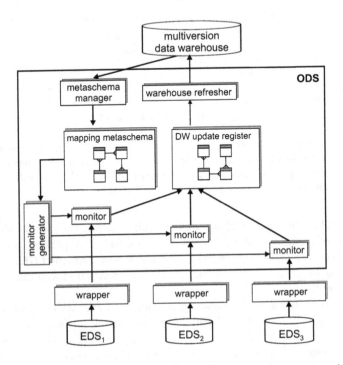

Fig. 11. The ODS architecture supporting the detection of content and structural changes in EDSs

Wrappers are connected to monitors. Monitors are responsible for detecting the occurrences of predefined events on EDSs. In response to an event detection, monitors generate actions that will be applied to an indicated DW version, cf. Section 7.2. The set of EDSs events being detected and their corresponding actions are described in the so-called mapping metaschema, cf. Section 7.3. The content of the mapping metaschema is used for the automatic generation of executable code of monitors, cf. Section 7.4. Actions generated by monitors are stored in a dedicated data structure called the DW update register.

7.2 Events and Actions

For the purpose of synchronizing a DW version with changes in EDSs, for each EDS supplying the MVDW we define the set of events being monitored and the set of actions associated with every event.

We distinguish two types of events, namely: structure events and data events. A **structure event** signalizes changes in an EDS's structure, that include: adding an attribute, modifying the name or domain of an attribute, dropping an attribute, adding a new data structure (table, class), dropping a data structure, changing the name of a data structure. A **data event** signalizes changes in an EDS's content, that include: adding, deleting, or modifying a data item. The set of events being monitored at EDSs is explicitly defined by a DW administrator and is stored in the so-called **mapping metaschema**, cf. Section 7.3.

For every event in the set, a DW administrator explicitly defines one or more ordered **actions** to be performed in a particular DW version. We distinguish two kinds of actions, namely messages and operations. **Messages** represent actions that can not be automatically applied to a DW version, e.g., adding an attribute to an existing data structure at an EDS, creating a new data structure. These events may not necessarily require DW version modification if a new object is not going to store any information of user's interest. Messages are used for notifying a DW administrator about certain source events. Being notified by a message, an administrator can manually define and apply appropriate actions into a selected DW version. **Operations** are generated for events whose outcomes can be automatically applied to a DW version, e.g., the insertion, update, and deletion of a record, the modification of an attribute domain or name, the change of a data structure name. The associations between events and actions are stored in the mapping metaschema.

Notice that actions do not create new DW versions automatically. They are either (1) applied to a DW version explicitly selected by a DW administrator during an action definition or (2) are logged in a special data structure (cf. Section 7.4) for manual application.

From the implementation point of view, operations are represented by SQL DML and DDL statements or stored procedures addressing an indicated DW version. The executable code of operations and bodies of messages are automatically generated by monitors, cf. Section 7.4.

7.3   Mapping Metaschema

The structure of the mapping metaschema is shown in Fig. 12 (represented in the Oracle notation). The *SRC_SOURCES* dictionary table stores descriptions of external data sources. It contains among others connection parameters for accessing every EDS. Data about EDSs data structures whose changes are to be monitored are registered in two dictionary tables: *SRC_OBJECTS* and *SRC_ATTRIBUTES*. All monitored events at EDSs are stored in *SRC_EVENTS*.

DW_AC_SRC_EV_MAPPINGS stores mappings between events detected at EDSs and their associated actions that are to be executed in a given DW version. Action definitions, i.e., an action type and a data warehouse object the action is to be performed on, are stored in *DW_ACTIONS*. MVDW object descriptions (i.e., attributes, versions of fact and dimension level tables,

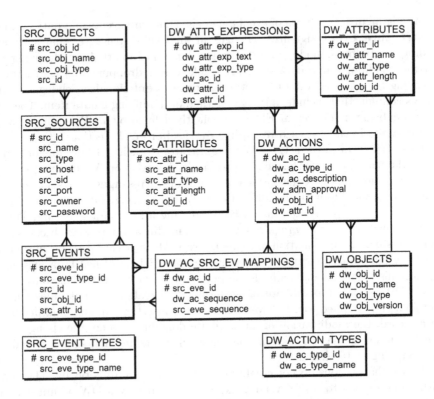

Fig. 12. The structure of the mapping metaschema

versions of dimensions and hierarchies) are stored in the *DW_ATTRIBUTES* and *DW_OBJECTS* dictionary tables.

Values taken from EDSs may need transformations (e.g., conversion of GBP into Euro) before being loaded into a DW version, as it is typically done within the Extraction-Translation-Loading processes [45]. Expressions that transform/compute values of attributes are stored in the *DW_ATTR_EXPRESSIONS*.

A DW administrator defines the content of the mapping metaschema (i.e., mappings between events and actions) by means of a graphical Java application, called the metaschema manager. The mapping metaschema is stored in an Oracle Database 10g.

7.4   Automatic Generation of Monitors

Every EDS is connected to the ODS by its own wrapper and monitor. For each EDS, the code of its monitor is automatically generated by a software module called the **monitor generator**. The monitor generator uses the content of the mapping metaschema. In the current prototype system, monitors are implemented in the Oracle PL/SQL language as stored packages and as triggers detecting defined events. The current implementation allows to automatically generate monitors for data sources implemented on Oracle databases only.

After being installed at EDSs, monitors register predefined events at EDSs and they generate actions (executable code of operations and bodies of messages) in response to the events. Generated actions are stored in a special data structure called the **DW update register**. Every action is described by: (1) its type (message or DML statement), (2) its content (e.g., SQL statement or stored procedure) addressing particular objects in a particular DW version, and (3) its sequence. An action sequence reflects the order of action executions. When an administrator decides to refresh a DW version, he/she selects actions for execution and runs a dedicated process, called the **warehouse refresher**. This process reads operations stored in the DW update register and applies them to a specified DW version.

8   Related Work

This section overviews related work in multiple research areas that are relevant to the work presented in this paper. These areas include: evolution in databases, evolution in data warehouses, detecting structural changes at data sources, and metadata.

8.1   Managing Evolution in Databases

The support for managing the evolution of data and schemas turned up as an important feature in object-oriented databases, mediated and federated database systems as well as in standard relational databases.

The need for schema and data evolution resulted from applying object-oriented databases to Computer Aided Design, Engineering, and Manufacturing systems. This evolution problem was intensively investigated and resulted in the development of various approaches and prototypes, [2,3,17,32,44,63], to list only a few of them. These and many other approaches were proposed for versioning complex objects or complex schemas stored in a database of moderate size.

The problem of managing schema changes appeared also in mediated and federated database systems that were used for interconnecting heterogeneous data sources, e.g., [15,26]. In this field, research has focused on handling schema changes and propagating them into a global schema, e.g., [50,51].

In the area of standard relational databases, research and technological work concentrate on temporal extensions [31,34,39,41,72] and data versioning [1,66].

Versioning mechanisms proposed for object-oriented databases support either versioning of objects or data structures (classes). In mediated and federated databases, the proposed solutions focus on handling schema changes only. In relational databases the proposed solutions support the evolution/versioning of multiple states of data only but not data structures. Our framework supports handling both structural changes and data changes of a DW. Thus we provide a more comprehensive solution.

8.2   Managing Evolution in Data Warehouses

Handling schema changes in external data sources and propagating them into a data warehouse is a natural extension of the solutions presented above. However, DW systems have different characteristics requiring new approaches to this problem.

On the contrary to the approaches managing evolution in the object-oriented field, in data warehouse systems objects being versioned have very simple structure (several fact or dimension tables) but the size of a database is much larger. Therefore, the versioning mechanisms developed in the object-oriented field are not suitable for versioning traditional (relational) data warehouses.

On the contrary to the approaches managing evolution in mediated and federated database systems, in data warehouse systems a final DW schema is usually totally different from schemas of external data sources. Moreover, a DW stores not only elementary data but also data aggregated at many levels. These aggregated data have to be transformed/updated/recomputed as the result of updates to a DW schema and to the structure of dimension instances. This recomputation should be efficient, therefore it is often required to apply an incremental recomputation [35]. These facts pose new challenges in propagating changes from EDSs to DWs.

Four eligible solutions for handling changes in data warehouses have been proposed in the literature. The solutions can be categorized as follows: (1) *schema and data evolution* [12,37,38,42], (2) *simulation* [4,5,7], (3) *temporal extensions* [18,27,30,49,69], and (4) *versioning extensions* [13,14,33,52,75].

Schema and data evolution approaches maintain one DW schema and the set of data that evolve in time. Schema modifications (e.g., dropping an attribute, changing the length or domain of an attribute) require data conversions and, as a consequence, historical DW states are lost. Modifications of the structure of dimension instances are implemented by simple updates of attribute values. This also causes that old values are lost.

Simulation approaches use virtual data structures in order to simulate or to screen DW evolution. In the approach proposed in [4,5] a virtual DW structure, called scenario, is constructed for hypothetical queries, for the purpose of the 'what-if' analysis. Then, the system using substitution and query rewriting techniques transforms a hypothetical query into an equivalent query that is run on a real DW. As this technique computes new values of data for every hypothetical query, based on virtual structures, performance problems will appear for large DWs. The approach proposed in [7] simulates changes in a DW schema by means of views. The approach supports only simple changes in source tables (add, drop, modify an attribute) and it does not deal either with typical multidimensional schemas or evolution of facts or dimensions.

Temporal extensions use timestamps on modified data in order to create temporal versions. Most of the approaches focus mainly on handling changes in the structure of dimension instances, cf. [18,27,30,49,69]. In the approach presented in [18] the authors propose to timestamp hierarchical assignments between level instances. At the implementation level, the assignments are represented as a matrix whose rows and columns store level instances whereas cells store validity times of hierarchical assignments between level instances. Similar concept of time stamping level instances and their hierarchical assignments was presented in [27,30]. Additionally, this concept supports transformations of fact instances as a consequence of changes to dimension instances. To this end, system conversion methods are applied. The methods are expressed as matrices defining recalculations of facts. In order to represent the history of changes to level instances, the system associates and stores timestamps along with level instances. In [69], a similar concept is used, but in this approach, a timestamped history of changes to dimension instances is stored in an additional separate data structure. The paper by [49] proposes consistency criteria that every evolving dimension has to fulfill. It gives an overview how the criteria can be applied to a temporal DW. All the discussed approaches from this category are suitable for representing historical versions of data, but not versions of a schema.

In *versioning extensions*, depending on the approach, a DW evolution is managed partially by means of schema versions and partially by data versions. The versioning mechanism presented in [13,14] supports explicit, timestamped persistent versions of data. The proposed concept also uses timestamps on level instances and their hierarchical assignments. Additionally, fact data are timestamped. The version of a data cube that is valid within a given time period is conceptually represented by the so-called *Temporally Consistent Fact Table*. At the implementation level, one central fact table is used for storing all versions of data. As a consequence, only changes to dimension schemas and dimension instance structures are supported. In [33] an explicit DW schema versioning mechanism is presented. A new persistent schema version is created for handling schema changes. The approach supports only four basic schema modification operators, namely adding/deleting an attribute as well as adding/deleting a functional dependency. A persistent schema version requires a population with data, but this issue is not addressed in the paper. The approach described in [52,75] supports versioning a DW schema and data. To this end, the structures of levels as well as fact tables are timestamped. All schema elements within the same range of their timestamps constitute a temporal schema version. Similar concept is used for versioning dimension instances and fact data that are stored in a temporal dimension schema and a temporal fact table, respectively. The proposed language (TOLAP) is able to query multiple temporal versions that differ with respect to their structures.

Implicit versioning of data was proposed in [43,47,60,65,74]. In all of these approaches versions are used for avoiding conflicts and mutual locking between OLAP queries and transactions refreshing a data warehouse.

Commercial DW systems existing on the market (e.g., Oracle Database 9i/10g, IBM DB2 UDB, Sybase IQ, Computer Associates CleverPath OLAP, NCR Teradata Database, Hyperion Essbase OLAP Server, MS SQL Server, SAP Business Warehouse, SAS Enterprise BI Server) do not offer advanced mechanisms for managing DW evolution or handling multiple DW states. Some functionality supporting a DW evolution is offered by:

- SAP Business Warehouse – it is capable of handling only simple changes (value updates) in dimension instances;
- Oracle Database 10g – it supports flashback queries; this mechanism can only be used for managing data versions provided that a database schema remains unchanged; moreover, it supports querying data from a specific point in time;
- SQL Server 2005 – it supports dimension instances updates; the updates are implemented by the mechanism of Slowly Changing Dimensions of Type 1 and/or Type 2; in this server, dimension schema changes are not supported.

Our approach supports all basic schema and dimension change operations. Fundamental changes, reflecting either new real-world states or simulation scenarios are clearly separated in DW versions. Thus, a user can address only a DW version of interest without the necessity of accessing the whole DW. As a consequence, less data are searched that, in turn, impacts a system's performance. A unique feature of our framework and prototype system is the augmentation of multiversion query results with data describing changes made to queried adjacent DW versions, unlike in [52,75]. These data allow to interpret the obtained results appropriately.

8.3   Detecting Structural Changes in Data Sources

Schema changes of EDSs were originally investigated in the context of adjusting materialized view definitions after changing the structure of their base tables. The EVE framework [48] represents a pioneering work in this area. It allows to include in a materialized view definition rules for its evolution/changes. To this end, EVE uses the so-called View Knowledge Base (VKB) and Meta Knowledge Base (MKB). VKB stores view definitions and MKB stores metadata describing abilities of data sources to co-operate with the EVE framework. Using the content of both knowledge bases, a view is rewritten as the result of changes to an EDS. Further extensions to the EVE framework were proposed in [55] and [56].

The approach presented in [20,22] uses a meta relation whose content describes a data source schema and its changes. The meta relation is stored in a wrapper associated with a data source. This mechanism is capable of handling only basic schema changes, i.e. the creation, deletion, and renaming of an attribute. [80] discusses the SDCC system that is used for synchronizing materialized views maintenance under source changes. SDCC collects and timestamps messages sent by a data source to DW when the source needs to change its schema or data. In this system, every change to a data source has to be approved by a DW before being applied.

Another algorithm, called Dyno [21,23], allows to detect the so-called dangerous dependencies among data source updates, i.e. updates that cause a broken query anomaly [22]. Dyno tries to find such an order of data source updates that eliminates dangerous dependencies. To this end, it constructs a dependency graph with vertices representing update operations. The graph is next topologically sorted in order to detect cycles that signalize dangerous dependencies. If there is a cycle in the graph then every update is executed atomically. Otherwise, multiple updates are executed as a transaction.

The work described in [28,29] focuses on detecting structural changes in dimension instances. To this end, the authors propose to analyze the so-called slices of data. A data slice represents fact data coming from consecutive time periods. Data slice analysis applies various data mining techniques. The drawback of this solution is that the discovered changes not always represent real changes made in a DW.

Most of the discussed approaches focuses on view maintenance under structural changes of data sources. The focus of our work is on propagating changes to a DW schema and dimension instances (which are basis for DW view creation) rather than to materialized views themselves. Moreover, our approach contributes a mapping mechanism between source changes and DW changes. The mappings are defined by a DW administrator and are stored in the mapping metaschema. Based on the mappings, our prototype system automatically generates: (1) wrappers detecting changes for every EDS of interest and (2) commands modifying a DW.

8.4   Metadata Management

The need for metadata describing multiple areas of a DW system design, development, deployment, and usage as well as the need for data exchange between different heterogeneous systems resulted in two industrial metadata standards, namely the *Open Information Model* (OIM) [40,77] and the *Common Warehouse Metadata* (CWM) [40,57,77]. **OIM** was developed by the **Meta Data Coalition** (MDC) for the support of all phases of an information system development. OIM is based on UML, XML, and SQL92. It includes the following models: (1) object-oriented analysis and design, (2) object and component development life-cycles, (3) business engineering, (4) knowledge management tool, as well as (5) database and data warehousing model, including: database and multidimensional schema elements, data transformations, non-relational source elements, report definitions. OIM was supported among others by Microsoft, Brio Technologies, Informatica, and SAS Institute.

On the contrary, **CWM** was developed by the **Object Management Group** (OMG) for the support of integrating DW systems and business intelligence tools. The standard is based on XML, CORBA IDL, MOF, and SQL99. It includes the following models: (1) foundation of concepts and structures, (2) warehouse deployment, (3) relational interface to data, (4) record-oriented structures, (5) multidimensional database representation, (6) XML types and associations, (7) type transformations, (8) OLAP constructs, (9) warehouse process flows, and (10) warehouse day-to-day operations. CWM is supported among others by IBM, Oracle, Hyperion, and SAS Institute.

In 2000, the standard developed by MDC was integrated into the standard developed by OMG. Since then, the integrated standard is developed under OMG [24] and is currently supported by most of software providers.

Although the two standards have been well developed, they do not include either models for detection and propagation of changes from data sources to a DW, or models for schema and data evolution in a DW. Consequently, they do not provide support for temporal or multiversion queries.

From the research approaches discussed in Section 8.2, only [30] presents a metamodel for a temporal DW. Additionally, [61] discusses and presents high level metamodel for handling and assuring data quality in a DW.

Our approach and metamodel substantially extend the metamodel presented in [30] with: (1) the support of not only dimension changes but also with schema changes, (2) the support for querying multiple DW states and annotating query results with metadata.

9   Summary and Conclusions

Handling changes in external data sources and applying them appropriately into a DW became one of the important research and technological issues [59,62]. Structural changes applied inappropriately to a DW schema or to dimension instances may result in wrong analytical results. Research prototypes and solutions to this problem are mainly based on temporal extensions that limit their use. The solution to the so-called slowly-changing dimensions proposed by R. Kimball [46] can be applicable to a limited set of dimension instance changes. Most of commercially available DW systems do not offer mechanisms for managing multiple DW states.

Our approach to this problem is based on a multiversion data warehouse, where a DW version represents the structure and content of a DW within a certain time period. Managing multiple persistent versions of a DW allows to:

– store the history of real-world changes without the loss of any information,
– manage not only changes to dimension instances but also changes to a DW schema,
– create alternative business scenarios for simulation purposes,
– query multiple DW states and compare query results.

A fully-functional DW system needs managing metadata in order to support the full life-cycle of a system. In the case of a multiversion data warehouse, metadata are much more complex than in traditional DWs and have to provide additional information, among others on: the structure and content of every DW version, a trace of schema and dimension instance changes applied to every DW version. The industry standard CWM metamodel and research contributions do not offer metadata describing a DW evolution.

In this paper we contributed by:

1. The development of the MVDW metamodel that is capable of: (1) managing versions of schemas and data in the MVDW, (2) executing queries that address several DW versions, and (3) presenting, comparing, and interpreting results of such queries.

2. The development of the framework for detecting changes in external data sources and propagating them into the MVDW. The functionality offered by the framework includes: (1) automatic generation of software monitoring EDSs, based on metadata, (2) automatic generation of actions to be executed in a DW version in response to EDSs events.

Based on the developed metamodels, the prototype MVDW system was implemented in Java and Oracle PL/SQL language, whereas data and metadata are stored in an Oracle Database 10g.

OLAP queries that run on a data warehouse are typically very complex and their optimization has impact on the performance of the whole DW. In the MVDW, data can be shared by multiple versions that makes querying and query optimization even more difficult. In order to optimize the execution of multiversion queries, we have developed a data sharing technique and a multiversion join index. The multiversion join index has been implemented and evaluated experimentally giving promising results, which are currently under reviewing. The data sharing technique is currently being evaluated and compared experimentally to other techniques proposed in [17,66].

In the future we plan to extend automatic generation of monitors for other database systems including: IBM DB2, Sybase Adaptive Server Enterprise, and MS SQL Server as well as for non-database sources including text and XML files. Future work will also focus on extending our metamodels in order to handle data quality issues in the MVDW. Another interesting task is to extend the accepted industry standard CWM so that it is suitable for describing a multiversion data warehouse.

Acknowledgements. The authors acknowledge anonymous reviewers for their constructive and thorough comments that greatly improved the quality of this paper. The authors would like to thank also the following graduate students from the Poznań University of Technology: Jan Chmiel - for running multiple performance experiments as well as Tomasz Majchrzak and Robert Guzewicz - for developing the MVDW prototype.

References

1. Abdessalem T., Jomier G.: VQL: A query Language for Multiversion Databases. Proc. of Int. Workshop on Database Programming Languages (DBPL), pp. 103-122, 1997, LNCS 1369
2. Agrawal R., Buroff S., Gehani N., Shasha D.: Object Versioning in Ode. Proc. of Int. Conference on Data Engineering (ICDE), pp. 446-455, 1991
3. Ahmed-Nacer M., Estublier J.: Schema Evolution in Software Engineering. In: Databases - A new Approach in ADELE environment. Computers and Artificial Intelligence, 19, pp. 183-203, 2000
4. Balmin A., Papadimitriou T., Papakonstanitnou Y.: Hypothetical Queries in an OLAP Environment. Proc. of Int. Conference on Very Large Data Bases (VLDB), pp. 220-231, 2000

5. Balmin A., Papadimitriou T., Papakonstanitnou Y.: Optimization of Hypothetical Queries in an OLAP Environment. Proc. of Int. Conference on Data Engineering (ICDE), p. 311, 2000

6. Barker R.: Case*Method: Entity Relationship Modelling Addison-Wesley, 1990, ISBN 0201416964

7. Bellahsene Z.: View Adaptation in Data Warehousing Systems. Proc. of Int. Conference on Database and Expert Systems Applications (DEXA), pp. 300-309, 1998, LNCS 1460

8. Bębel B.: Transactional Refreshing of Data Warehouses. PhD thesis, Poznań University of Technology, Institute of Computing Science, 2005

9. Bębel B., Eder J., Konicilia C., Morzy T., Wrembel R.: Creation and Management of Versions in Multiversion Data Warehouse. Proc. of ACM Symposium on Applied Computing (SAC), pp. 717-723, 2004

10. Bębel B., Królikowski Z., Wrembel R.: Managing Multiple Real and Simulation Business Scenarios by Means of a Multiversion Data Warehouse. Proc. of Int. Conference on Business Information Systems (BIS), pp. 102-113, 2006, Lecture Notes in Informatics

11. Bębel B., Wrembel R., Czejdo B.: Storage Structures for Sharing Data in Multiversion Data Warehouse. Proc. of Baltic Conference on Databases and Information Systems, pp. 218-231, 2004

12. Blaschka M., Sapia C., Hofling G.: On Schema Evolution in Multidimensional Databases. Proc. of Int. Conference on Data Warehousing and Knowledge Discovery (DaWaK), pp. 153-164, 1999, LNCS 1676

13. Body M., Miquel M., Bédard Y., Tchounikine A.: A Multidimensional and Multiversion Structure for OLAP Applications. Proc. of ACM Int. Workshop on Data Warehousing and OLAP (DOLAP), pp. 1-6, 2002

14. Body M., Miquel M., Bédard Y., Tchounikine A.: Handling Evolutions in Multidimensional Structures. Proc. of Int. Conference on Data Engineering (ICDE), p. 581, 2003

15. Bouguettaya A., Benatallah B., Elmargamid A.: Interconnecting Heterogeneous Information Systems, Kluwer Academic Publishers, 1998, ISBN 0792382161

16. Buczkowski P., Błaszyk M., Chmiel J., Tucholski M., Wrembel R.: Design, Implementation, Evaluation of a Multiversion Join Index. Research report RA-009/05, Poznań University of Technology

17. Cellary W., Jomier G.: Consistency of Versions in Object-Oriented Databases. Proc. of Int. Conference on Very Large Data Bases (VLDB), pp. 432-441, 1990

18. Chamoni P., Stock S.: Temporal Structures in Data Warehousing. Proc. of Int. Conference on Data Warehousing and Knowledge Discovery (DaWaK), pp. 353-358, 1999, LNCS 1676

19. Chaudhuri S., Dayal U.: An overview of data warehousing and OLAP technology. SIGMOD Record, 26(1), pp. 65-74, 1997

20. Chen J., Chen S., Rundensteiner E.: A Transactional Model for Data Warehouse Maintenance. Proc. of Int. Conference on Conceptual Modeling (ER), pp. 247-262, 2002, LNCS 2503

21. Chen J., Chen S., Zhang X., Rundensteiner E.: Detection and Correction of Conflicting Source Updates for View Maintenance, Proc. of Int. Conference on Data Engineering (ICDE), pp. 436-448, 2004

22. Chen J., Rundensteiner E.: TxnWrap: A Transactional Approach to Data Warehouse Maintenance, Technical Report WPI-CS-TR-00-26, Worcester Polytechnic Institute, 2000, retrieved June 11, 2006, from http://citeseer.ist.psu.edu/384586.html

23. Chen S., Zhang X., Rundensteiner E.: A Compensation-based Approach for Materialized View Maintenance in Distributed Environments. IEEE Transactions on Knowledge and Data Engineering, 18(8), pp. 1068-1081, 2006
24. Competing Data Warehousing Standards to Merge in the OMG. Retrieved August 10, 2005 from http://xml.coverpages.org/OMG-MDC-20000925.html
25. Czejdo B., Messa K., Morzy T., Putonti C.: Design of Data Warehouses with Dynamically Changing Data Sources. Proc. of Southern Conference on Computing, USA, 2000
26. Elmagarmid A., Rusinkiewicz M., Sheth A.: Management of Heterogeneous and Autonomous Database Systems. Morgan Kaufmann Publishers, 1999, ISBN 1-55860-216-X
27. Eder J., Koncilia C.: Changes of Dimension Data in Temporal Data Warehouses. Proc. of Int. Conference on Data Warehousing and Knowledge Discovery (DaWaK), pp. 284-293, 2001, LNCS 2114
28. Eder J., Koncilia C., Mitsche D.: Automatic Detection of Structural Changes in Data Warehouses. Proc. of Int. Conference on Data Warehousing and Knowledge Discovery (DaWaK), pp. 119-128, 2003, LNCS 2737
29. Eder J., Koncilia C., Mitsche D.: Analysing Slices of Data Warehouses to Detect Structural Modifications. Proc of Conference on Advanced Information Systems Engineering (CAiSE), pp. 492-505, 2004, LNCS 3084
30. Eder J., Koncilia C., Morzy T.: The COMET Metamodel for Temporal Data Warehouses. Proc. of Conference on Advanced Information Systems Engineering (CAiSE), pp. 83-99, 2002, LNCS 2348
31. Etzion O., Jajoda S., Sripada S.: Temporal Databases: Research and Practice. 1998, LNCS 1399
32. Gançarski S., Jomier G.: A framework for programming multiversion databases. Data Knowledge Engineering, 36(1), pp. 29-53, 2001
33. Golfarelli M., Lechtenbörger J., Rizzi S., Vossen G.: Schema Versioning in Data Warehouses. Proc. of ER Workshops, pp. 415-428, 2004, LNCS 3289
34. Goralwalla I.A., Tansel A.U., Ozsu M.T.: Experimenting with Temporal Relational Databases. Proc. of ACM Conference on Information and Knowledge Management (CIKM), pp. 296-303, 1995,
35. Gupta A., Mumick I.S. (eds.): Materialized Views: Techniques, Implementations, and Applications. The MIT Press, 1999, ISBN 0-262-57122-6
36. Gyssens M., Lakshmanan L.V.S.: A Foundation for Multi-Dimensional Databases. Proc. of Int. Conference on Very Large Data Bases (VLDB), pp. 106-115, 1997
37. Hurtado C.A., Mendelzon A.O., Vaisman A.A.: Maintaining Data Cubes under Dimension Updates. Proc. of Int. Conference on Data Engineering (ICDE), pp. 346-355, 1999
38. Hurtado C.A., Mendelzon A.O., Vaisman A.A.: Updating OLAP Dimensions. Proc. of ACM Int. Workshop on Data Warehousing and OLAP (DOLAP), pp. 60-66, 1999
39. Microsoft ImmortalDB. Retrieved November 25, 2005 from http://research.microsoft.com/db/ImmortalDB/
40. Jarke M., Lenzerini M., Vassiliou Y., Vassiliadis P.: Fundamentals of Data Warehouses. Springer-Verlag, 2003, ISBN 3-540-42089-4
41. Jensen C.S., Lomet D.B.: Transaction Timestamping in (Temporal) Databases. Proc. of Int. Conference on Very Large Data Bases (VLDB), pp. 441-450, 2001
42. Kaas Ch.K., Pedersen T.B., Rasmussen B.D.: Schema Evolution for Stars and Snowflakes. Proc. of Int. Conference on Enterprise Information Systems (ICEIS), pp. 425-433, 2004

43. Kang H.G., Chung C.W.: Exploiting Versions for On-line Data Warehouse Maintenance in MOLAP Servers. Proc. of Int. Conference on Very Large Data Bases (VLDB), pp. 742-753, 2002

44. Kim W., Chou H.: Versions of Schema for Object-Oriented Databases. Proc. of Int. Conference on Very Large Data Bases (VLDB), pp. 148-159, 1988

45. Kimball R., Caserta J.: The Data Warehouse ETL Tookit. John Wiley & Sons, Inc., 2004, ISBN 0764567578

46. Kimball R., Ross M.: The Data Warehouse Toolkit. John Wiley & Sons, Inc., 2002, ISBN 0-471-20024-7

47. Kulkarni S., Mohania M.: Concurrent Maintenance of Views Using Multiple Versions. Proc. of the Int. Database Engineering and Application Symposium (IDEAS), pp. 254-259 ,1999

48. Lee A., Nica A., Rundensteiner E.: The EVE Framework: View Synchronization in Evolving Environments. Technical Report WPI-CS-TR-97-4, Worcester Polytechnic Institute, 1997, retrieved June 10, 2006, from http://citeseer.ist.psu.edu/100503.html

49. Letz C., Henn E.T., Vossen G.: Consistency in Data Warehouse Dimensions. Proc. of Int. Database Engineering and Applications Symposium (IDEAS), pp. 224-232, 2002

50. McBrien P., Poulovassilis A.: Automatic Migration and Wrapping of Database Applications - a Schema Transformation Approach. Proc. of Int. Conference on Conceptual Modeling (ER), pp. 96-113, 1999, LNCS 1728

51. McBrien P., Poulovassilis A.: Schema Evolution in Heterogeneous Database Architectures, A Schema Transformation Approach. Proc. of Conference on Advanced Information Systems Engineering (CAiSE), pp. 484-499, 2002, LNCS 2348

52. Mendelzon A.O., Vaisman A.A.: Temporal Queries in OLAP. Proc. of Int. Conference on Very Large Data Bases (VLDB), pp. 242-253, 2000

53. Morzy T., Wrembel R.: Modeling a Multiversion Data Warehouse: A Formal Approach. Proc. of Int. Conference on Enterprise Information Systems (ICEIS), pp. 120-127, 2003

54. Morzy T., Wrembel R.: On Querying Versions of Multiversion Data Warehouse. Proc. ACM Int. Workshop on Data Warehousing and OLAP (DOLAP), pp. 92-101, 2004

55. Nica A., Lee A., Rundensteiner E.: CVS: The Complex Substitution Algorithm for View Synchronization. Technical Report WPI-CS-TR-97-8, Worcester Polytechnic Institute, 1997, retrieved June 10, 2006, from http://citeseer.ist.psu.edu/nica97cv.html

56. Nica A., Rundensteiner E.: Using Complex Substitution Strategies for View Synchronization. Technical Report, WPI-CS-TR-98-4, Worcester Polytechnic Institute, 1998, retrieved June 11, 2006, from http://citeseer.ist.psu.edu/35922.html

57. Object Management Group. Common Warehouse Metamodel Specification, v1.1. Retrieved August 10, 2005 from http://www.omg.org/cgi-bin/doc?formal/03-03-02

58. Overmars M.H.,van Leeuwen J.: Dynamic multidimensional data structures based on Quad- and K-D trees. Acta Informatica, (17), pp. 267-285, 1982

59. Panel discussion on "Future trends in Data Warehousing and OLAP" at ACM Int. Workshop on Data Warehousing and OLAP (DOLAP), 2004

60. Quass D., Widom J.: On-Line Warehouse View Maintenance. Proc. of ACM SIGMOD Int. Conference on Management of Data, pp. 393-404, 1997

61. Quix C.: Repository Support for Data Warehouse Evolution. Proc. of Design and Management of Data Warehouses (DMDW), 1999

62. Rizzi S.: Open Problems in Data Warehousing: 8 Years Later. Keynote speech at Design and Management of Data Warehouses (DMDW), 2003
63. Roddick J.: A Survey of Schema Versioning Issues for Database Systems. In Information and Software Technology, volume 37(7), pp. 383-393, 1996
64. Roth M.T., Schwarz P.: Don't scrap it, wrap it. A wrapper architecture for data sources. Proc. of Int. Conference on Very Large Data Bases (VLDB), pp. 266-275, 1997
65. Rundensteiner E., Koeller A., and Zhang X.: Maintaining Data Warehouses over Changing Information Sources. Communications of the ACM, 43(6), 2000
66. Salzberg B., Jiang L., Lomet D., Barrena M., Shan J., Kanoulas E.: A Framework for Access Methods for Versioned Data. Proc. of Int. Conference on Extending Database Technology (EDBT), pp. 730-747, 2004, LNCS 2992
67. Sarawagi S.: Indexing OLAP Data. IEEE Data Engineering Bulletin, 20(1), pp. 36-43, 1997
68. Sarawagi S., Stonebraker M.: Efficient organization of large multidimensional arrays. Proc. of Int. Conference on Data Engineering (ICDE), pp. 328-336, 1994
69. Schlesinger L., Bauer A., Lehner W., Ediberidze G., Gutzman M.: Efficienlty Synchronizing Multidimensional Schema Data. Proc. of ACM Int. Workshop on Data Warehousing and OLAP (DOLAP), pp. 69-76, 2001
70. Slowly Changing Dimension. Retrieved July 24, 2006, from http://www.1keydata.com/datawarehousing/scd-type-1.html
71. Sjøberg D.: Quantifying Schema Evolution. Information Software Technology 35(1), pp. 35-54, 1993
72. Snodgrass R. (ed.): The Temporal Query Language TSQL2. Kluwer Academic Publishers, 1995, ISBN 0-7923-9614-6
73. Tansel A., Gadia J., Jajodia S., Segev A., Snodgrass R. (Eds.): Temporal Databases. Benjamin Cummings, 1993, ISBN 0-8053-2413-5
74. Teschke M., Ulbrich A.:. Concurrent Warehouse Maintenance whithout Compromising Session Consistency. Proc. of Int. Conference on Database and Expert Systems Applications (DEXA), pp. 776-785, 1998, LNCS 1460
75. Vaisman A., Mendelzon A.: A Temporal Query Language for OLAP: Implementation and Case Study. Proc. of Workshop on Data Bases and Programming Languages (DBPL), pp. 78-96, 2001, LNCS 2397
76. Valduriez P.: Join Indices. ACM Transactions on Database Systems (TODS), 12(2), pp. 218-246, 1987
77. Vetterli T., Vaduva A., Staudt M.: Metadata Standards for Data Warehousing: Open Information Model vs. Common Warehouse Metadata. SIGMOD Record, vol. 29(3), pp. 68-75, 2000
78. Wrembel R., Bębel B.: Metadata Management in a Multiversion Data Warehouse. Proc. of Ontologies, Databases, and Applications of Semantics (ODBASE), pp. 1347-1364, 2005, LNCS 3761
79. Wrembel R., Morzy T.: Managing and Querying Versions of Multiversion Data Warehouse. Proc. of Int.f Conference on Extending Database Technology (EDBT), pp. 1121-1124, 2006, LNCS 3896
80. Zhang X., Rundensteiner E.: Integrating the maintenance and synchronization of data warehouses using a cooperative framework. Information Systems 27, pp. 219-243, 2002

SomeRDFS in the Semantic Web

P. Adjiman[1], F. Goasdoué[1], and M.-C. Rousset[2]

[1] LRI, bâtiment 490, Université Paris-Sud 11, 91405 Orsay Cedex, France
[2] LSR-IMAG, BP 72, 38402 St Martin d'Heres Cedex, France

Abstract. The Semantic Web envisions a world-wide distributed architecture where computational resources will easily inter-operate to coordinate complex tasks such as query answering. Semantic marking up of
web resources using ontologies is expected to provide the necessary glue
for making this vision work. Using ontology languages, (communities of)
users will build their own ontologies in order to describe their own data.
Adding semantic mappings between those ontologies, in order to semantically relate the data to share, gives rise to the Semantic Web: data on
the web that are annotated by ontologies networked together by mappings. In this vision, the Semantic Web is a huge semantic peer data
management system. In this paper, we describe the SomeRDFS peer
data management systems that promote a "simple is beautiful" vision of
the Semantic Web based on data annotated by RDFS ontologies.

1 Introduction

The Semantic Web [1] envisions a world-wide distributed architecture where
computational resources will easily inter-operate to coordinate complex tasks
such as query answering. Semantic marking up of web resources using *ontologies*
is expected to provide the necessary glue for making this vision work.

Recent W3C efforts led to recommendations for annotating data with ontologies. The Resource Description Framework (RDF, http://www.w3.org/RDF) allows organizing data using simple taxonomies of classes and properties with RDF
Schema (RDFS), the ontology language that comes with RDF. The Ontology
Web Language (OWL, http://www.w3.org/2004/OWL) is defined on top of RDF
and allows building more complex statements about data. It corresponds in its
decidable versions (OWL-lite and OWL-DL) to expressive description logics.

Using ontology languages, (communities of) users will build their own ontologies in order to describe their own data. Adding semantic mappings between
those ontologies, in order to semantically relate the data to share, gives rise to
the Semantic Web: data on the web that are annotated by ontologies networked
together by mappings. In this vision, the Semantic Web is a huge semantic peer
data management system (PDMS).

Some PDMSs have been developped for the Semantic Web like Edutella [2],
RDFPeers [3], GridVine [4] or SomeOWL [5]. Edutella, RDFPeers and GridVine
use RDF while SomeOWL uses a fragment of OWL.

Edutella is made of a network of super-peers, the topology of which is a hypercube. Super-peers are mediators with the same schema: a reference ontology

S. Spaccapietra et al. (Eds.): Journal on Data Semantics VIII, LNCS 4380, pp. 158–181, 2007.
© Springer-Verlag Berlin Heidelberg 2007

(e.g., http://demoz.org). The data sources of a super-peer are its connected peers. Therefore, data are distributed over the peers while the ontologies are distributed over the super-peers. A peer must annotate its data in terms of the ontology of the super-peer to which it is connected. To answer queries, there is no need of mappings between the super-peer ontologies since they are identical: queries are efficiently routed in the network, using its topology of hypercube, in order to find super-peers that can provides answers with their peers.

In RDFPeers and GridVine PDMSs, the peers are organized according to a Distributed Hash Table using CHORD [6]. As in Edutella, such a fixed structure allows efficient routing of messages between peers. While RDFPeers only addresses the problem of query answering without taking into account the ontologies that annotate the data, GridVine takes into account the ontologies. On each GridVine peer, data are annotated with an RDFS ontology and mappings with ontologies of other peers are stated by equivalences between properties of peer ontologies.

In SomeOWL PDMSs[1] [5], peers are not organized according to a fixed topology: the topology is induced by the mappings between the peers ontologies. SomeOWL PDMSs are based on a simple data model: the ontologies and mappings are expressed in a fragment of OWL-DL that corresponds to the $\mathcal{CLU}$ description logic ($\neg$, $\sqcap$, and $\sqcup$). Query answering takes into account the ontologies and is achieved using a rewrite and evaluate strategy. The rewriting part is reduced to a consequence finding problem in distributed propositional theories. It is performed by SomeWhere, a peer-to-peer inference system that implements DeCA: DEcentralized Consequence finding Algorithm [5]. Query answering in a SomeOWL PDMS is sound, complete and terminates. Moreover, the detailed experiments reported in [7] show that it scales up to 1000 peers.

The contribution of this paper is to show how to deploy a PDMS using a data model based on RDF on top of the SomeWhere infrastructure: we will call such a PDMS a SomeRDFS PDMS. To express the ontologies and mappings, we consider the core fragment of RDFS allowing to state (sub)classes, (sub)properties, typing of domain and range of properties. A mapping is an inclusion statement between classes or properties of two distinct peers, or a typing statement of a property of a given peer with a class of another peer. Therefore, mappings are RDFS statements involving vocabularies of different peers which thus establish semantic correspondances between peers.

Like in a SomeOWL PDMS, the topology is induced by the mappings between the peers' ontologies. We show that query answering in SomeRDFS PDMSs can be achieved using a rewrite and evaluate strategy, and that the corresponding rewriting problem can be reduced to the same consequence finding problem in distributed propositional theories as in [5]. SomeWhere can then be used to compute the rewritings, with the same properties as mentionned above. We thus provide an operational solution for deploying a Semantic Web of data annotated with RDFS ontologies related by mappings. Moreover, the consequence finding

---

[1] In this article, we denote by SomeOWL PDMSs the PDMSs based on OWL that have been designed in [5].

problem resulting from the propositional encoding of the fragment of RDFS that we consider is tractable since the resulting propositional theories are reduced to clauses of length 2 for which the reasoning problem is in P. The experiments reported in [7] show that it takes in mean 0.07s to SOMEWHERE for a complete reasoning on randomly generated sets of clauses of length 2 distributed on 1000 peers.

The paper is organized as follows. Section 2 defines the fragment of RDFS that we consider as data model for SOMERDFS. Section 3 relates the problems of query answering and query rewriting, and shows how query rewriting can be reduced to a consequence finding problem in distributed propositional theories. Section 4 presents the query rewriting algorithm which is built on top of the DECA algorithm of SOMEWHERE. We conclude with related work in Section 5 and a discussion in Section 6.

2   Data Model of a SOMERDFS PDMS

We consider the core constructors of RDFS based on unary relations called *classes* and binary relations called *properties*. Those constructors are: class inclusion, property inclusion, and domain/range typing of a property. We denote this language core-RDFS.

While the logical semantics of the whole RDFS raises non trivial problems [8,9,10,11], core-RDFS has a first-order logical semantics which is clear and intuitive. This semantics can be defined in terms of interpretations or can be given by the first-order formulas expressing the logical meaning of each constructor. Based on the FOL semantics, it can be seen that core-RDFS is a fragment of $DL\text{-}Lite_R$, which is a description logic (DL) of the $DL\text{-}Lite$ family [12,13]. The $DL\text{-}Lite$ family has been designed for allowing tractable query answering over data described w.r.t ontologies.

The following table provides the logical semantics of core-RDFS by giving the DL notation and the corresponding first-order logical (FOL) translation of the core-RDFS constructors.

Constructor	DL notation	FOL translation
Class inclusion	$C_1 \sqsubseteq C_2$	$\forall X(C_1(X) \Rightarrow C_2(X))$
Property inclusion	$P_1 \sqsubseteq P_2$	$\forall X \forall Y(P_1(X,Y) \Rightarrow P_2(X,Y))$
Domain typing of a property	$\exists P \sqsubseteq C$	$\forall X \forall Y(P(X,Y) \Rightarrow C(X))$
Range typing of a property	$\exists P^- \sqsubseteq C$	$\forall X \forall Y(P(X,Y) \Rightarrow C(Y))$

Ontologies, data descriptions and mappings of SOMERDFS peers are stated in core-RDFS. To make the semantics clear, we have chosen to use the FOL notation to denote ontologies, data and mappings as (possibly distributed) sets of FOL formulas. As seen in the previous table, the correspondence with the DL notation is obvious. It is important to note that core-RDFS belongs to the intersection of two logical languages that have been extensively studied: Horn rules without function and description logics. Therefore, core-RDFS is a fragment of DLP [14].

2.1   Peer Ontologies

Peer ontologies are made of core-RDFS statements involving only relations of a *peer vocabulary*. A peer vocabulary is the union of a set of classe names and a set of property names that are disjoint. The class and property names are unique to each peer. We use the notation $\mathcal{P}{:}R$ for identifying the relation (class or property) R of the ontology of the peer $\mathcal{P}$.

2.2   Peer Storage Descriptions

The specification of the data stored in a peer is done through the declaration of assertional statements relating data of a peer to relations of its vocabulary. The DL notation and the FOL translation of assertional statements is the following (a and b are constants):

Constructor	DL notation and FOL translation
Class assertion	$C(a)$
Property assertion	$P(a,b)$

2.3   Peer Mappings

Mappings are the key notion for establishing semantic connections between ontologies in order to share data. We define them as core-RDFS statements involving relations of two different peer vocabularies. The DL notation and the FOL translation of the mappings that are allowed in SomeRDFS are given in the following table.

Mappings between $\mathcal{P}_1$ and $\mathcal{P}_2$	DL notation	FOL translation
Class inclusion	$\mathcal{P}_1{:}C_1 \sqsubseteq \mathcal{P}_2{:}C_2$	$\forall X(\mathcal{P}_1{:}C_1(X) \Rightarrow \mathcal{P}_2{:}C_2(X))$
Property inclusion	$\mathcal{P}_1{:}P_1 \sqsubseteq \mathcal{P}_2{:}P_2$	$\forall X \forall Y(\mathcal{P}_1{:}P_1(X,Y) \Rightarrow \mathcal{P}_2{:}P_2(X,Y))$
Domain typing of a property	$\exists \mathcal{P}_1{:}P \sqsubseteq \mathcal{P}_2{:}C$	$\forall X \forall Y(\mathcal{P}_1{:}P(X,Y) \Rightarrow \mathcal{P}_2{:}C(X))$
Range typing of a property	$\exists \mathcal{P}_1{:}P^- \sqsubseteq \mathcal{P}_2{:}C$	$\forall X \forall Y(\mathcal{P}_1{:}P(X,Y) \Rightarrow \mathcal{P}_2{:}C(Y))$

The definition of *shared relations* follows from that of mappings.

Definition 1 (Shared relation). *A relation is* shared *between two peers if it belongs to the vocabulary of one peer and it appears in a mapping in the second peer.*

2.4   Schema and Data of a SomeRDFS PDMS

In a PDMS, both the schema and data are distributed through respectively the union of the peer ontologies and mappings, and the union of the peer storage descriptions. The important point is that each peer has a partial knowledge of the PDMS. In a SomeRDFS PDMS, a peer just knows its ontology, its mappings with other peers and the relations shared with them, and its own data.

The schema of a SomeRDFS PDMS $\mathcal{S}$, denoted $schema(\mathcal{S})$, is the union of the ontologies and the sets of mappings of all the peers.

The data of a SomeRDFS PDMS $\mathcal{S}$, denoted $data(\mathcal{S})$, is the union of the peers data descriptions.

A SomeRDFS knowledge base is the union of its schema and data.

2.5 Queries

Many query languages have been recently developped for RDF [15] (e.g., RDQL, SPARQL,...). Most of them offer select-project-join queries which are known as the core relational query language in the database literature, namely the *conjunctive queries*.

Conjunctive queries can be expressed in first-order logic as open formulas with free variables $\bar{X}$ and made of conjunction of atoms. The free variables are called the *distinguished variables* of the query and they correspond to the variables of interest for the users. The other variables are existential variables that appear in the atoms of the query. The conjunction of atoms models the request of a user. For example, the following query expresses that the user is interested in knowing which artists have created paintings belonging to the cubism movement. The existential variable Y is just there to denote the existence of paintings created by the artist denoted by the variable X: the user wants to get as answers the instances of X satisfying the formula but he/she is not interested to know the instances of Y.

$$Q(X) \equiv \exists Y\ Artist(X) \wedge Creates(X,Y) \wedge Painting(Y) \wedge BelongsTo(Y, cubism)$$

The FOL translation for a conjunctive query is given in the following table.

Conjunctive query	FOL translation
$Q : \{(\bar{X}) \mid \bigwedge_{i=1}^{n} r_i(\bar{X}_i, \bar{Y}_i)\}$	$Q(\bar{X}) \equiv \exists \bar{Y} \bigwedge_{i=1}^{n} r_i(\bar{X}_i, \bar{Y}_i)$, where $\bar{X} = \bigcup_{i=1}^{n} \bar{X}_i$ are free variables and $\bar{Y} = \bigcup_{i=1}^{n} \bar{Y}_i$ are existential variables.

The most general queries that we will consider, the SOMERDFS *queries*, are conjunctive queries that may involve the vocabularies of several peers. In contrast, the users' queries involve the vocabulary of a single peer, since a user interrogates the PDMS through a peer of his choice.

Definition 2 (Query). *A query is a conjunctive query in terms of relations of peer vocabularies.*

Definition 3 (User query). *A user query is a query in terms of relations of a single peer vocabulary.*

2.6 Semantics

In a SOMERDFS PDMS, ontologies, storage descriptions, mappings, and queries have all a FOL correspondence. From a logical point of view, a SOMERDFS PDMS is a FOL knowledge base made of Horn rules (the schema) and ground atoms (the data). As mentioned before, it could also be equivalently seen as a DL knowledge base made of a Tbox (the schema) and an Abox (the data).

Two main semantics have been investigated for a PDMS based on FOL: the standard FOL semantics and the epistemic FOL semantics (see Section 5). Roughly speaking, the standard FOL semantics does not distinguish mappings from ontology formulae, i.e., they are interpreted in the same way. In contrast, the epistemic FOL semantics restricts the expressivity of mapping formulae.

In a SomeRDFS PDMS, we adopt the standard FOL semantics. As for data, we stick to the usual information integration assumption, namely the *unique name assumption*.

Semantics of a query. While a user query is given in terms of the relations of a single peer, its expected answers may be found all over the PDMS. An answer is a tuple made of constants stored in the PDMS for which it can be logically inferred (from the union of ontologies, storage descriptions and mappings) that it satisfies the expression defining the query. It corresponds to an extension of the notion of *certain answer* in information integration systems.

Definition 4 (Answer set of a query). *Let S be a SomeRDFS PDMS and Q a n-ary query. Let C be a set of constants appearing in $data(S)$. The* answer set *of Q is: $Q(S) = \{\bar{t} \in C^n \mid S \models Q(\bar{t})\}$.*

Subsumption. The *subsumption* (a.k.a. containment) relation allows to compare two relations (classes, properties and queries) of the same arity.

A relation r_1 subsumes (respectively strictly subsumes) a relation r_2, iff for every interpretation I, $r_2^I \subseteq r_1^I$ (respectively $r_2^I \subset r_1^I$).

Given a SomeRDFS PDMS S, a relation r_1 subsumes (respectively strictly subsumes) a relation r_2 w.r.t. S, iff for every model I of $schema(S)$, $r_2^I \subseteq r_1^I$ (respectively $r_2^I \subset r_1^I$).

2.7   Graphical Conventions

In the following, we adopt some graphical conventions in order to represent a SomeRDFS schema.

A class is denoted by a node labeled with the class name. A property is a directed edge labeled with the property name. Such an edge is directed from the domain to the range of the property. A relation inclusion is denoted by a directed dotted edge labeled with the subsumption symbol $\sqsubseteq$. Such an edge is directed from the subsumee to the subsumer. A peer ontology is a subgraph totally contained in a box labeled with a peer name. A mapping is a directed edge from a peer ontology to another peer ontology. The owner of the mapping is the peer the box of which contains the corresponding edge label. Moreover, since there is no ambiguity with the owners of the ontology relations, we omit to prefix a relation name with its owner name in order to alleviate the notations.

For instance, let consider the mapping $\forall X (\mathcal{P}_1{:}Artifact(X) \Rightarrow \mathcal{P}_2{:}Works(X))$ between a peer $\mathcal{P}_1$ and a peer $\mathcal{P}_2$. This mapping is a class inclusion: the class $\mathcal{P}_1{:}Artifact$ of $\mathcal{P}_1$ is contained in the class $\mathcal{P}_2{:}Work$ of $\mathcal{P}_2$. If we suppose that it belongs to $\mathcal{P}_2$, its graphical notation is the one in Figure 1. In that case, $\mathcal{P}_1{:}Artifact$ is a shared relation between $\mathcal{P}_1$ and $\mathcal{P}_2$.

Let consider another mapping $\forall X \forall Y (\mathcal{P}_1{:}paints(X,Y) \Rightarrow \mathcal{P}_2{:}painting(Y))$ between $\mathcal{P}_1$ and $\mathcal{P}_2$. This mapping is a range typing of the property $\mathcal{P}_1{:}paints$

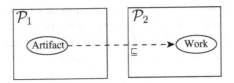

Fig. 1. Class inclusion mapping

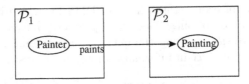

Fig. 2. Range typing mapping

of $\mathcal{P}_1$, the domain of which is typed with the class $\mathcal{P}_1\!:\!Painter$ of $\mathcal{P}_1$. The range typing is made with the class $\mathcal{P}_2\!:\!Painting$ of $\mathcal{P}_2$. If we suppose that this mapping belongs to $\mathcal{P}_1$, its graphical notation is the one in Figure 2. In that case, $\mathcal{P}_2\!:\!Painting$ is a shared relation between $\mathcal{P}_1$ and $\mathcal{P}_2$.

2.8   Illustrative Example

We will illustrate our contributions throughout the article on the following simple SomeRDFS $\mathcal{S}$ consisting of two peers $\mathcal{P}_1$ and $\mathcal{P}_2$.

$\mathcal{P}_1$ can store data about artists (some of them being sculptors and/or painters), artifacts artists have created, and the artistic movements the artifacts belong to. Some artist creations are distinguished according to whether their creators are sculptors or painters. $\mathcal{P}_2$ can store data about works (some of them being paintings, sculptures or musics) and the artistic period they refer to. The FOL notation of their ontologies is given in Figure 3.

$\mathcal{P}_1$ actually stores that Picasso has painted "Les demoiselles d'Avignon" which belongs to the Picasso's pink movement, and has sculpted "La femme au chapeau" which belongs to the Modern art movement. $\mathcal{P}_2$ stores that "Le déjeuner des canotiers" is a painting and that "Les demoiselles d'Avignon" refers to the Cubism

$\mathcal{P}_1$ ontology	$\mathcal{P}_2$ ontology
$\forall X(\mathcal{P}_1\!:\!Sculptor(X) \Rightarrow \mathcal{P}_1\!:\!Artist(X))$	$\forall X(\mathcal{P}_2\!:\!Painting(X) \Rightarrow \mathcal{P}_2\!:\!Work(X))$
$\forall X(\mathcal{P}_1\!:\!Painter(X) \Rightarrow \mathcal{P}_1\!:\!Artist(X))$	$\forall X(\mathcal{P}_2\!:\!Sculpture(X) \Rightarrow \mathcal{P}_2\!:\!Work(X))$
$\forall X \forall Y(\mathcal{P}_1\!:\!creates(X,Y) \Rightarrow \mathcal{P}_1\!:\!Artist(X))$	$\forall X(\mathcal{P}_2\!:\!Music(X) \Rightarrow \mathcal{P}_2\!:\!Work(X))$
$\forall X \forall Y(\mathcal{P}_1\!:\!creates(X,Y) \Rightarrow \mathcal{P}_1\!:\!Artifact(Y))$	$\forall X \forall Y(\mathcal{P}_2\!:\!refersTo(X,Y) \Rightarrow \mathcal{P}_2\!:\!Work(X))$
$\forall X \forall Y(\mathcal{P}_1\!:\!paints(X,Y) \Rightarrow \mathcal{P}_1\!:\!creates(X,Y))$	$\forall X \forall Y(\mathcal{P}_2\!:\!refersTo(X,Y) \Rightarrow \mathcal{P}_2\!:\!Period(Y))$
$\forall X \forall Y(\mathcal{P}_1\!:\!sculpts(X,Y) \Rightarrow \mathcal{P}_1\!:\!creates(X,Y))$	
$\forall X \forall Y(\mathcal{P}_1\!:\!sculpts(X,Y) \Rightarrow \mathcal{P}_1\!:\!Sculptor(X))$	
$\forall X \forall Y(\mathcal{P}_1\!:\!paints(X,Y) \Rightarrow \mathcal{P}_1\!:\!Painter(X))$	
$\forall X \forall Y(\mathcal{P}_1\!:\!belongsTo(X,Y) \Rightarrow \mathcal{P}_1\!:\!Artifact(X))$	
$\forall X \forall Y(\mathcal{P}_1\!:\!belongsTo(X,Y) \Rightarrow \mathcal{P}_1\!:\!Movement(Y))$	

Fig. 3. Ontologies of $\mathcal{P}_1$ and $\mathcal{P}_2$

$\mathcal{P}_1$ Data	$\mathcal{P}_2$ Data
$\mathcal{P}_1$:$paints$(Picasso,Les-demoiselles-d-Avignon)	$\mathcal{P}_2$:$Painting$(Le-dejeuner-des-canotiers)
$\mathcal{P}_1$:$sculpts$(Picasso,La-femme-au-chapeau)	$\mathcal{P}_2$:$refersTo$(Les-demoiselles-d-Avignon,Cubism)
$\mathcal{P}_1$:$belongsTo$(Les-demoiselles-d-Avignon,Picasso-pink)	$\mathcal{P}_2$:$Sculpture$(The-statue-of-David)
$\mathcal{P}_1$:$belongsTo$(La-femme-au-chapeau,Modern-art)	$\mathcal{P}_2$:$Music$(Nutcracker)

Fig. 4. Data of $\mathcal{P}_1$ and $\mathcal{P}_2$

$\mathcal{P}_1$ mappings	$\mathcal{P}_2$ mappings
$\forall X \forall Y (\mathcal{P}_1{:}paints(X,Y) \Rightarrow \mathcal{P}_2{:}Painting(Y))$	$\forall X (\mathcal{P}_1{:}Artifact(X) \Rightarrow \mathcal{P}_2{:}Work(X))$
$\forall X \forall Y (\mathcal{P}_1{:}sculpts(X,Y) \Rightarrow \mathcal{P}_2{:}Sculpture(Y))$	$\forall X \forall Y (\mathcal{P}_1{:}belongsTo(X,Y) \Rightarrow \mathcal{P}_2{:}refersTo(X,Y))$

Fig. 5. Mappings of $\mathcal{P}_1$ and $\mathcal{P}_2$

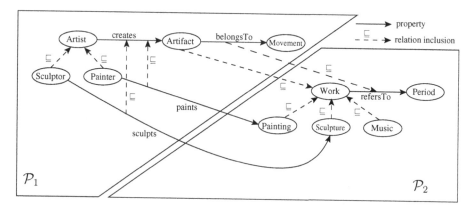

Fig. 6. Graphical representation of $schema(\mathcal{S})$

artistic period. It also stores that "The statue of David" is a sculpture and that "Nutcracker" is a music. The storage description of $\mathcal{P}_1$ and $\mathcal{P}_2$ is given in Figure 4.

In order to share data with $\mathcal{P}_2$, $\mathcal{P}_1$ has established two mappings to distinguish sculptor and painter creations from artist creations. This is done by the range typing of $\mathcal{P}_1$:$sculpts$ and $\mathcal{P}_1$:$paints$ with respectively the classes of sculptures and paintings of $\mathcal{P}_2$. $\mathcal{P}_2$ has also established mappings with $\mathcal{P}_1$ in order to state that the class of artifacts of $\mathcal{P}_1$ is contained in its class of artistic works, and that the property $\mathcal{P}_1$:$belongsTo$ is contained in its property $\mathcal{P}_2$:$refersTo$. Their mappings are given in Figure 5. Those mappings indicate that the shared relations of $\mathcal{P}_1$ are $\mathcal{P}_1$:$Artifact$ and $\mathcal{P}_1$:$belongsTo$, while the shared relations of $\mathcal{P}_2$ are $\mathcal{P}_2$:$Painting$ and $\mathcal{P}_2$:$Sculpture$.

Following our graphical conventions, the above SOMERDFS schema is given in Figure 6.

3   Query Answering Through Query Rewriting

Query answering is the main inference in a PDMS. Finding all the answers of a user query is, in general, a critical issue [16]. It has been shown in [17] that when a query has a finite number of *maximal conjunctive rewritings*, then its answer set can be obtained as the union of the answer sets of its rewritings.

Definition 5 (Conjunctive rewriting). *Given a* SOMERDFS *PDMS S, a query R is a conjunctive rewriting of a query Q iff Q subsumes R w.r.t. S. R is a maximal conjunctive rewriting of Q if there does not exist another conjunctive rewriting R' of Q strictly subsuming R.*

Theorem 1 shows that query answering in a SOMERDFS PDMS can be done through query rewriting.

Theorem 1. *Query answering of a user query can be achieved by a rewrite and evaluate strategy. The rewriting complexity is polynomial w.r.t. the size of the schema of the* SOMERDFS *PDMS and exponential w.r.t. the number of atoms in the query. The evaluation complexity is polynomial w.r.t. the size of the data of the* SOMERDFS *PDMS.*

Proof. The schema of a SOMERDFS PDMS forms a knowledge base $\mathcal{R}$ of function-free Horn rules with single conditions (see the FOL axiomatization of core-RDFS in Figure 2). A simple backward chaining algorithm [18] with cycle detection applied to each atom of a user query Q ensures to find all the maximal conjunctive rewritings of each atom of Q with atmost n chaining steps, if n is the number of rules in the schema. The reason is that each rule in a schema can only be used at most once (assuming cycle detections) because they have a single condition. Therefore, there are at most n maximal conjunctive rewritings (each one being reduced to one atom) for each of the k atoms of the user query.

It follows from [19] that when views, queries and rewritings are conjunctive queries, the set of all the (maximal) rewritings using views of a query can be obtained from the conjunctions of the rewritings of each atom of the query. In order to apply that result to our setting, we just have to reformulate the rewriting problem that we consider into the rewriting problem using views considered in [19]. For doing so, for each atom $p(\bar{X})$ we create a view, named $p(\bar{X})$, the body of which is the conjunction of the different atoms that can be derived (e.g., by standard forward-chaining) from $p(\bar{X})$ using the set $\mathcal{R}$ of rule:

$$ p(\bar{X}) \equiv \bigwedge_{\{p(\bar{X})\} \cup \mathcal{R} \vdash a(\bar{Y})} a(\bar{Y}). $$

Those views have no existential variable (for every $a(\bar{Y})$ such that $\{p(\bar{X})\} \cup \mathcal{R} \vdash a(\bar{Y})$, $\bar{Y} \subseteq \bar{X}$) because the FOL axiomatization of core-RDFS (see Figure 2) is made of safe rules only. Therefore, conjuncting views that are relevant to each atom of the query provides rewritings of the query. As shown in [20], it is not true in the general case where the conjunctions of views relevant to each atom of the query are just candidate rewritings for which subsumption with the query must be checked.

By construction, there are at most n views relevant for each atom of the query. Therefore, there are at most n^k maximal conjunctive rewritings of the user query, obtained by conjuncting rewritings of each atom of the query. Therefore, rewriting complexity in SOMERDFS is in $O(n^k)$. Note that in practice the value of n might be quite large while the one of k should be small.

Finally, evaluating a conjunctive query is in P w.r.t. data complexity [21]. Since a user query has a finite number of maximal conjunctive rewritings to evaluate, answering such a query is in P w.r.t. data complexity.   ☐

The proof of Theorem 1 provides a solution in order to deploy a SOMERDFS PDMS: one needs a peer-to-peer reasoner that performs backward chaining in distributed knowledge bases of FOL function-free Horn rules. To the best of our knowledge such a FOL peer-to-peer reasoner does not exist. However, there exists a propositional peer-to-peer reasoner: SOMEWHERE [5]. We will show that it is possible to encode FOL reasoning in SOMERDFS into propositional reasoning in SOMEWHERE.

Before presenting the corresponding reduction, we illustrate the rewrite and evaluate strategy for query answering in a SOMERDFS PDMS on the example of Section 2.8.

3.1   Illustrative Example (Continued)

Let us consider the user query $Q_1(X) \equiv P_2{:}Work(X)$ asked to the peer P_2. It is easy to see that its maximal rewritings are (e.g., using backward chaining on the Horn rules of $schema(S)$):

1. $R_1^1(X) \equiv P_2{:}Work(X)$
2. $R_2^1(X) \equiv P_2{:}Painting(X)$
3. $R_3^1(X) \equiv P_2{:}Sculpture(X)$
4. $R_4^1(X) \equiv P_2{:}Music(X)$
5. $R_5^1(X) \equiv \exists Y\ P_2{:}refersTo(X,Y)$
6. $R_6^1(X) \equiv P_1{:}Artifact(X)$
7. $R_7^1(X) \equiv \exists Y\ P_1{:}belongsTo(X,Y)$
8. $R_8^1(X) \equiv \exists Y\ P_1{:}creates(Y,X)$
9. $R_9^1(X) \equiv \exists Y\ P_1{:}paints(Y,X)$
10. $R_{10}^1(X) \equiv \exists Y\ P_1{:}sculpts(Y,X)$

The answer set of Q_1 is obtained by evaluating those rewritings.

$$Q_1(S) = \underbrace{\emptyset}_{R_1^1(S)} \cup \underbrace{\{\text{Le-dejeuner-des-canotiers}\}}_{R_2^1(S)} \cup \underbrace{\{\text{The-statue-of-David}\}}_{R_3^1(S)}$$

$$\cup \underbrace{\{\text{Nutcracker}\}}_{R_4^1(S)} \cup \underbrace{\{\text{Les-demoiselles-d-Avignon}\}}_{R_5^1(S)} \cup \underbrace{\emptyset}_{R_6^1(S)}$$

$$\cup \underbrace{\{\text{Les-demoiselles-d-Avignon,La-femme-au-chapeau}\}}_{R_7^1(S)} \cup \underbrace{\emptyset}_{R_8^1(S)}$$

$$\cup \underbrace{\{\text{Les-demoiselles-d-Avignon}\}}_{R_9^1(S)} \cup \underbrace{\{\text{La-femme-au-chapeau}\}}_{R_{10}^1(S)}.$$

Consider now the user query $Q_2(X,Y) \equiv P_2{:}Painting(X) \wedge P_2{:}refersTo(X,Y)$ asked to P_2. Its maximal rewritings are:

1. $R_1^2(X,Y) \equiv \mathcal{P}_2\text{:}Painting(X) \wedge \mathcal{P}_2\text{:}refersTo(X,Y)$
2. $R_2^2(X,Y) \equiv \mathcal{P}_2\text{:}Painting(X) \wedge \mathcal{P}_1\text{:}belongsTo(X,Y)$
3. $R_3^2(X,Y) \equiv \exists Z \; \mathcal{P}_1\text{:}paints(Z,X) \wedge \mathcal{P}_2\text{:}refersTo(X,Y)$
4. $R_4^2(X,Y) \equiv \exists Z \; \mathcal{P}_1\text{:}paints(Z,X) \wedge \mathcal{P}_1\text{:}belongsTo(X,Y)$

The answer set of Q_2 is obtained by evaluating those rewritings.

$$Q_2(\mathcal{S}) = \underbrace{\emptyset}_{R_1^2(\mathcal{S})} \cup \underbrace{\emptyset}_{R_2^2(\mathcal{S})} \cup \underbrace{\{(\text{Les-demoiselles-d-Avignon}, \text{Cubism})\}}_{R_3^2(\mathcal{S})}$$

$$\cup \underbrace{\{(\text{Les-demoiselles-d-Avignon}, \text{Picasso-pink})\}}_{R_4^2(\mathcal{S})}.$$

Note that the above rewritings suggest the need of optimization in order to be efficiently evaluated: some atoms appear in several rewritings and are thus evaluated several times. Standard caching techniques can be used for that purpose.

Q_1 and Q_2 highlight three kinds of rewritings.

- *Local rewritings* involve relations of the queried peer's vocabulary. For example, the rewriting R_4^1 shows that the data Nutcraker of $\mathcal{P}_2$, which is known as music, is an artistic work.
- *Distant rewritings* involve relations of a single distant peer's vocabulary. For example, the rewriting R_4^2 shows that Les demoiselles d'Avignon is a painting that refers to Cubism. It is worth noticing that Les demoiselles d'Avignon is already known from $\mathcal{P}_2$, but not as a painting.
- *Integration rewritings* involve relations of several peer's vocabularies. For example, the rewriting R_3^2 shows that Les demoiselles d'Avignon which is already known from $\mathcal{P}_2$ to refer to Cubism, refers also to the Pink period of Picasso.

3.2 Propositional Reduction of Query Rewriting in a SOMERDFS PDMS

In this section, we describe how to equivalently reduce query rewriting in a SOMERDFS PDMS to consequence finding over logical propositional theories in SOMEWHERE. To do this, we have to convert the distributed FOL knowledge base that corresponds to a SOMERDFS PDMS into a distributed propositional theory T that corresponds to a SOMEWHERE peer-to-peer inference system, and to show that we obtain the maximal conjunctive rewritings of a query $Q(\bar{X})$ from the proper prime implicates of $\neg Q$ w.r.t. T using the DECA algorithm of SOMEWHERE.

SOMEWHERE [5] is a peer-to-peer inference system (P2PIS), in which each peer theory is a set of propositional clauses built from a set of propositional variables. Any variable common to two connected peers can be stated as *shared*. In that case, both peers know that they share that variable. Any variable of a peer's vocabulary can also be stated as *target*. When a peer is solicited for computing consequences, the consequences it can send back are only those that contain target variables. From a logical point of view, the global theory of a SOMEWHERE P2PIS is the union of the propositional theories of its peers. From a reasoning point of view, each SOMEWHERE peer runs DECA [5] (DEcentralized Consequence finding Algorithm), which is a message-passing algorithm that computes the proper prime implicates of literals w.r.t. the global theory of the P2PIS. The point is that it does it in a fully decentralized manner, without knowing the whole global theory. DECA is sound, i.e., it computes only proper implicates of the input literal w.r.t. the global theory. DECA always terminates and notifies the user of its termination. We have exhibited in [5] a sufficient condition for DECA to be complete, i.e., to return *all* the *proper prime implicates* of the input literal (w.r.t. the global theory): for any two peers having a variable in common, there is a path of connected peers sharing that variable.

The following definition recalls the notion of proper prime implicate of a clause w.r.t. a propositional clausal theory.

Definition 6 (Proper prime implicate w.r.t. a theory). *Let T be a clausal theory and q be a clause. A clause m is said to be:*

- *a prime implicate of q w.r.t. T iff $T \cup \{q\} \models m$ and for any other clause m', if $T \cup \{q\} \models m'$ and $m' \models m$ then $m' \equiv m$.*
- *a proper prime implicate of q w.r.t. T iff it is a prime implicate of q w.r.t. T and $T \not\models m$.*

The propositional encoding of a SOMERDFS that we consider is given in Definition 7. It must translate appropriately the semantic connection between classes and properties. In particular, the typing of the properties must distinguish the typing of the domain from the typing of the range of a given property P. As we will see, this distinction is important for rebuilding the FOL rewritings from the propositional rewritings. In the FOL notation, the distinction relies on the place of the typing variable as argument of the property: in $\forall X \forall Y (P(X, Y) \Rightarrow C(X))$ the fact that the typing variable (i.e., X) appears as the first argument of P indicates that the *domain* of the property is typed by the class C, while in $\forall X \forall Y (P(X, Y) \Rightarrow C(Y))$ the fact that the typing variable (i.e., Y) appears as the second argument of P indicates that the *range* of the property is typed by the class C.

Therefore, for a given class C, we distinguish its two typing roles for properties by encoding it by two propositional variables C^{dom} and C^{range}. Thus, we encode the domain typing of a property P by a class C with the clausal form $\neg P \vee C^{dom}$ of the implication $P \Rightarrow C^{dom}$. Similarly, we encode the range typing of a property P by a class C with the clausal form $\neg P \vee C^{range}$ of the implication $P \Rightarrow C^{range}$.

Definition 7 (Propositional encoding of SOMERDFS). *We encode a SOMERDFS S into a SOMEWHERE $Prop(S)$ by encoding each SOMERDFS peer $\mathcal{P}$ in S into a SOMEWHERE peer $Prop(\mathcal{P})$ in $Prop(S)$:*

- *if $\forall X (C_1(X) \Rightarrow C_2(X))$ is in $\mathcal{P}$, $\neg C_1^{dom} \vee C_2^{dom}$ and $\neg C_1^{range} \vee C_2^{range}$ are in $Prop(\mathcal{P})$.*
- *if $\forall X, Y (P(X, Y) \Rightarrow C(X))$ is in $\mathcal{P}$, $\neg P^{prop} \vee C^{dom}$ is in $Prop(\mathcal{P})$.*
- *if $\forall X, Y (P(X, Y) \Rightarrow C(Y))$ is in $\mathcal{P}$, $\neg P^{prop} \vee C^{range}$ is in $Prop(\mathcal{P})$.*
- *if $\forall X, Y (P_1(X, Y) \Rightarrow P_2(X, Y))$ is in $\mathcal{P}$, $\neg P_1^{prop} \vee P_2^{prop}$ is in $Prop(\mathcal{P})$.*

It is important to notice that a dual encoding would have been possible, consisting in distinguishing the domain and range typing by encoding each property P by two propositional variables P^{dom} and P^{range}: a clause $\neg P^{dom} \vee C$ would encode the domain typing of a property P by a class C, while $\neg P^{range} \vee C$ would encode the range typing of a property P by a class C.

All the propositional variables in $Prop(\mathcal{P})$ are stated as *target*. A variable in $Prop(\mathcal{P})$ that corresponds to a relation shared with another peer $\mathcal{P}'$, is stated as *shared* with $Prop(\mathcal{P}')$.

As an illustration, Figure 7 represents the two peers of the SOMERDFS PDMS introduced in Section 2.8.

$\mathcal{P}_1$:
$\forall X(\mathcal{P}_1{:}Sculptor(X) \Rightarrow \mathcal{P}_1{:}Artist(X))$
$\forall X(\mathcal{P}_1{:}Painter(X) \Rightarrow \mathcal{P}_1{:}Artist(X))$
$\forall X \forall Y(\mathcal{P}_1{:}creates(X,Y) \Rightarrow \mathcal{P}_1{:}Artist(X))$
$\forall X \forall Y(\mathcal{P}_1{:}creates(X,Y) \Rightarrow \mathcal{P}_1{:}Artifact(Y))$
$\forall X \forall Y(\mathcal{P}_1{:}paints(X,Y) \Rightarrow \mathcal{P}_1{:}creates(X,Y))$
$\forall X \forall Y(\mathcal{P}_1{:}sculpts(X,Y) \Rightarrow \mathcal{P}_1{:}creates(X,Y))$
$\forall X \forall Y(\mathcal{P}_1{:}sculpts(X,Y) \Rightarrow \mathcal{P}_1{:}Sculptor(X))$
$\forall X \forall Y(\mathcal{P}_1{:}paints(X,Y) \Rightarrow \mathcal{P}_1{:}Painter(X))$
$\forall X \forall Y(\mathcal{P}_1{:}belongsTo(X,Y) \Rightarrow \mathcal{P}_1{:}Artifact(X))$
$\forall X \forall Y(\mathcal{P}_1{:}belongsTo(X,Y) \Rightarrow \mathcal{P}_1{:}Movement(Y))$
$\forall X \forall Y(\mathcal{P}_1{:}paints(X,Y) \Rightarrow \mathcal{P}_2{:}Painting(Y))$
$\forall X \forall Y(\mathcal{P}_1{:}sculpts(X,Y) \Rightarrow \mathcal{P}_2{:}Sculpture(Y))$
Shared
With $\mathcal{P}_2$: $\mathcal{P}_1{:}Artifact(X)$, $\mathcal{P}_1{:}belongsTo(X,Y)$

$\mathcal{P}_2$:
$\forall X(\mathcal{P}_2{:}Painting(X) \Rightarrow \mathcal{P}_2{:}Work(X))$
$\forall X(\mathcal{P}_2{:}Sculpture(X) \Rightarrow \mathcal{P}_2{:}Work(X))$
$\forall X(\mathcal{P}_2{:}Music(X) \Rightarrow \mathcal{P}_2{:}Work(X))$
$\forall X \forall Y(\mathcal{P}_2{:}refersTo(X,Y) \Rightarrow \mathcal{P}_2{:}Work(X))$
$\forall X \forall Y(\mathcal{P}_2{:}refersTo(X,Y) \Rightarrow \mathcal{P}_2{:}Period(Y))$
$\forall X(\mathcal{P}_1{:}Artifact(X) \Rightarrow \mathcal{P}_2{:}Work(X))$
$\forall X \forall Y(\mathcal{P}_1{:}belongsTo(X,Y) \Rightarrow \mathcal{P}_2{:}refersTo(X,Y))$
Shared
With $\mathcal{P}_1$: $\mathcal{P}_2{:}Painting(X)$, $\mathcal{P}_2{:}Sculpture(X)$

Fig. 7. The SOMERDFS PDMS of Section 2.8

Figure 8 corresponds to the encoding of this SOMERDFS PDMS into a SOME-WHERE P2PIS. The *Shared* section in the Figure 7 (resp. 8) makes explicit which local relations (resp. propositional variables) are known to be shared with others peers.

Proposition 1 states that the propositional encoding of a SOMERDFS PDMS leads to a SOMEWHERE P2PIS for which the DECA algorithm is complete.

Proposition 1 (Completeness of DECA for the propositional encoding of a SOMERDFS PDMS). *Let S be a SOMERDFS PDMS. Let $Prop(S)$ be the SOMEWHERE P2PIS resulting from the propositional encoding of S. DECA is complete for $Prop(S)$.*

Proof. By definition, in a SOMERDFS PDMS, a relation which appears in two peers comes from a mapping between those two peers and is shared between those two peers. In the propositional encoding, the only variables that can be common to two peer theories result from the encoding of a mapping. Therefore, in a SOMEWHERE P2PIS resulting from the encoding of a SOMERDFS PDMS, all the variables that are common to two peer theories are necessarily shared by those two peers, and the sufficient condition for the completeness of DECA is obviously satisfied.   □

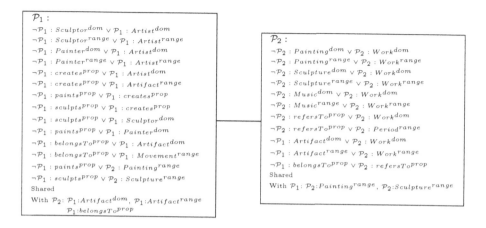

Fig. 8. Propositional encoding of the SoMeRDFS PDMS of Section 2.8

Proposition 2 establishes the connection between maximal conjunctive rewritings of queries made of a single atom in a SoMeRDFS PDMS and proper prime implicates of a literal in a SoMeWhere P2PIS. Note that Proposition 2 also suggests an optimization of the propositional encoding when query rewriting is used for query answering: the target variables should be only the ones resulting from relations for which facts are stored. Doing this, each conjunctive rewriting will be useful for query answering: it will provide at least one answer.

Proposition 2 (Propositional transfer). *Let S be a* SoMeRDFS *PDMS and let $Prop(S)$ be its propositional encoding into a* SoMeWhere *P2PIS.*

(i) $R(X) \equiv C'(X)$ *is a maximal conjunctive rewriting of a query $Q(X) \equiv C(X)$ w.r.t. S iff $\neg C'^{dom}$ is a proper prime implicate of $\neg C^{dom}$ w.r.t. $Prop(S)$*

(ii) $R(X) \equiv \exists Y P(X,Y)$ *is a maximal conjunctive rewriting of a query $Q(X) \equiv C(X)$ w.r.t. S iff $\neg P^{prop}$ is a proper prime implicate of $\neg C^{dom}$ w.r.t. $Prop(S)$.*

(iii) $R(X) \equiv \exists Y P(Y,X)$ *is a maximal conjunctive rewriting of a query $Q(X) \equiv C(X)$ w.r.t. S iff $\neg P^{prop}$ is a proper prime implicate of $\neg C^{range}$ w.r.t. $Prop(S)$.*

(iv) $R(X,Y) \equiv P'(X,Y)$ *is a maximal conjunctive rewriting of a query $Q(X,Y) \equiv P(X,Y)$ w.r.t. S iff $\neg P'^{prop}$ is a proper prime implicate of $\neg P^{prop}$ w.r.t. $Prop(S)$.*

Proof. We first exhibit some properties that will be used in the proof of the proposition. Let S be a SoMeRDFS PDMS and let $Prop(S)$ be its propositional encoding into a SoMeWhere P2PIS. Let C and P be respectively a class and a property of S, and C^{dom}, C^{range}, and P^{prop} be their corresponding variables in $Prop(S)$.

Let $I = (\Delta^I, .^I)$ be an interpretation of $\mathcal{S}$ and $(o, o') \in \Delta^I \times \Delta^I$. We build an interpretation $p_{o,o'}(I)$ of $Prop(\mathcal{S})$ as follows:

α_1. $(C^{dom})^{p_{o,o'}(I)} = true$ iff $o \in C^I$ and $(C^{range})^{p_{o,o'}(I)} = true$ iff $o' \in C^I$.

α_2. $(P^{prop})^{p_{o,o'}(I)} = true$ iff $(o, o') \in P^I$.

Let J be an interpretation of $Prop(\mathcal{S})$. We build $i(J) = (\Delta^I = \{dom, range\}, .^{i(J)})$ an interpretation of $\mathcal{S}$ as follows:

β_1. $dom \in C^{i(J)}$ iff $(C^{dom})^J = true$ and $range \in C^{i(J)}$ iff $(C^{range})^J = true$.

β_2. if $(P^{prop})^J = true$ then $R^{i(J)} = \{(dom, range)\}$ else $R^{i(J)} = \emptyset$.

Properties 1. and 2. follow from the definition of the above interpretations: For every interpretation I of $\mathcal{S}$ and $(o, o') \in \Delta^I \times \Delta^I$, for every interpretation J of $Prop(\mathcal{S})$:

1. I is a model of $\mathcal{S}$ iff $p_{o,o'}(I)$ is a model of $Prop(\mathcal{S})$.
2. $i(J)$ is a model of $\mathcal{S}$ iff J is a model of $Prop(\mathcal{S})$.

We now give the proof of the item (i) of the proposition. We do not provide the proofs of the items (ii), (iii) and (iv) because they are very similar to that of (i).

(i) ($\Leftarrow$) We have to prove that if $\neg C'^{dom}$ is a proper prime implicate of $\neg C^{dom}$ w.r.t. $Prop(\mathcal{S})$ then $R(X) \equiv C'(X)$ is a maximal conjunctive rewriting of a query $Q(X) \equiv C(X)$ w.r.t. $\mathcal{S}$.

Suppose that $\neg C'^{dom}$ is a proper prime implicate of $\neg C^{dom}$ w.r.t. $Prop(\mathcal{S})$. Let us first show that $R(X) \equiv C'(X)$ is a conjunctive rewriting of $Q(X) \equiv C(X)$ w.r.t. $\mathcal{S}$. If it is false, then there exists a model I of $\mathcal{S}$ and a constant b such that $b \in C'^I$ and $b \notin C^I$. Note that there always exists such a b since the core-RDFS data model does not allow building unsatisfiable logical sentences (w.r.t. $\mathcal{S}$). According to property 1., $p_{b,b}(I)$ is a model of $Prop(\mathcal{S})$. According to definition α_1 we have $(C'^{dom})^{p_{b,b}(I)} = true$ and $(C^{dom})^{p_{b,b}(I)} = false$, i.e., $(\neg C^{dom})^{p_{b,b}(I)} = true$ and $(\neg C'^{dom})^{p_{b,b}(I)} = false$. This contradicts the fact that $\neg C'^{dom}$ is an implicate of $\neg C^{dom}$ w.r.t. $Prop(\mathcal{S})$.

Let us show now that $R(X) \equiv C'(X)$ is a *maximal* conjunctive rewriting. If it is false, there exists a *maximal* conjunctive rewriting R' of Q w.r.t. $\mathcal{S}$ strictly subsuming R, i.e., there exists a model I of $\mathcal{S}$ and an element $o \in \Delta^I$ such that $o \in (R')^I$, $o \in Q^I$, and $o \notin R^I$. Theorem 1 states that all the maximal conjunctive rewritings of a user query can be obtained using a backward chaining algorithm with cycle detection. Because of the form of the core-RDFS rules in $schema(\mathcal{S})$ (Section 2), any maximal conjunctive rewriting of a query made of a single atom $Q(X) \equiv C(X)$ is either of the form $R'(X) \equiv A(X)$, or $R'(X) \equiv \exists Y B(X, Y)$, or $R'(X) \equiv \exists Y B(Y, X)$:

- $R'(X) \equiv A(X)$: According to property 1, $p_{o,o}(I)$ is a model of $Prop(\mathcal{S})$ and according to definition α_1 we have: $(A^{dom})^{p_{o,o}(I)} = true$, $(C^{dom})^{p_{o,o}(I)} = true$, and $(C'^{dom})^{p_{o,o}(I)} = false$, i.e., $(\neg A^{dom})^{p_{o,o}(I)} = false$, $(\neg C^{dom})^{p_{o,o}(I)} = false$, and $(\neg C'^{dom})^{p_{o,o}(I)} = true$. This contradicts the fact that $\neg C'^{dom}$ is a *prime* implicate of $\neg C^{dom}$ w.r.t. $Prop(\mathcal{S})$.

– $R'(X) \equiv \exists Y B(X, Y)$: Since $o \in R'$ then there exists $o' \in \Delta^I$ such that $(o, o') \in B^I$. According to property 1, $p_{o,o'}(I)$ is a model of $Prop(S)$ and according to definition α_1 and α_2 we have: $(B^{prop})^{p_{o,o'}(I)} = true$, $(C^{dom})^{p_{o,o'}(I)} = true$, and $(C'^{dom})^{p_{o,o'}(I)} = false$, i.e., $(\neg B^{prop})^{p_{o,o'}(I)} = false$, $(\neg C^{dom})^{p_{o,o'}(I)} = false$, $(\neg C'^{dom})^{p_{o,o'}(I)} = true$. This contradict the fact that $\neg C'^{dom}$ is a *prime* implicate of $\neg C^{dom}$ w.r.t. $Prop(S)$.

– $R'(X) \equiv \exists Y B(Y, X)$: This case is similar to the previous one.

(i) ($\Rightarrow$) We have to prove that if $R(X) \equiv C'(X)$ is a maximal conjunctive rewriting of a query $Q(X) \equiv C(X)$ w.r.t. S then $\neg C'^{dom}$ is a proper prime implicate of $\neg C^{dom}$ w.r.t. $Prop(S)$.

Suppose that $R(X) \equiv C'(X)$ is a maximal conjunctive rewriting of a query $Q(X) \equiv C(X)$ w.r.t. S.

Let us first show that $\neg C'^{dom}$ is an *implicate* of $\neg C^{dom}$ w.r.t. $Prop(S)$. Since $C'(X)$ is a conjunctive rewriting of $C(X)$, for every model I of S: $(C')^I \subseteq (C)^I$. If $\neg C'^{dom}$ is not an implicate of $\neg C^{dom}$ w.r.t. $Prop(S)$, then $\{\neg C^{dom}\} \cup Prop(S) \not\models \neg C'^{dom}$, i.e., $\{C'^{dom}\} \cup Prop(S) \not\models C^{dom}$, i.e., there exists a model J of $\{C'^{dom}\} \cup Prop(S)$ such that $(C^{dom})^J = false$ and $(C'^{dom})^J = true$. According to property 2., $i(J)$ is a model of S. According to definition β_1 we have $dom \notin (C)^{i(J)}$ and $dom \in (C')^{i(J)}$ thus $(C)^{i(J)} \not\subseteq (C')^{i(J)}$. This contradicts the fact that $R(X) \equiv C'(X)$ is a conjunctive rewriting of $Q(X) \equiv C(X)$ w.r.t. S.

Let us show now that $\neg C'^{dom}$ is a *proper* implicate of $\neg C^{dom}$ w.r.t. $Prop(S)$. Let I be a model of S such that $R^I \neq \emptyset$. Note that such a model always exists since the core-RDFS data model does not allow building unsatisfiable logical sentences (w.r.t. S). Let o be in C'^I. According to property 1, $p_{o,o}(I)$ is a model of $Prop(S)$ and according to definition α_1 we have $(C'^{dom})^{p_{o,o}(I)} = true$, i.e., $(\neg C'^{dom})^{p_{o,o}(I)} = false$. Therefore, there exists a model of $Prop(S)$ which is not a model of $\neg C'^{dom}$. That means that $\neg C'^{dom}$ is not an implicate of $Prop(S)$ alone.

Finally, let us show that $\neg C'^{dom}$ is a *prime* implicate of $\neg C^{dom}$ w.r.t. $Prop(S)$. Suppose that there exists a clause cl such that $Prop(S) \cup \{\neg C^{dom}\} \models cl$ and $cl \models \neg C'^{dom}$. Either cl is $\neg C'^{dom}$ since $\neg C'^{dom}$ is a literal and thus $\neg C'^{dom}$ is *prime*, or cl is the empty clause and thus $Prop(S) \cup \{\neg C^{dom}\}$ is unsatisfiable. Let us show that the latter case is not possible. Let I be a model of S such that $o \notin (C^{dom})^I$. It is always possible to build such a model: let $K = (\Delta^K, .^K)$ be a model of S such that $o \notin \Delta^K$, then $I = (\Delta^K \cup \{o\}, .^K)$ is a model of S such that $o \notin (C^{dom})^I$. According to the property 1, $p_{o,o}(I)$ is model of $Prop(S)$, and according to the definition α_1 we have: $(C^{dom})^{p_{o,o}(I)} = false$. Therefore, $p_{o,o}(I)$ is a model of $Prop(S) \cup \{\neg C^{dom}\}$ and thus $Prop(S) \cup \{\neg C^{dom}\}$ is always satisfiable. □

In the next section, we provide an algorithm built on top of DECA which computes *all* the maximal conjunctive rewritings of any user query.

4   Query Rewriting Algorithm of a SOMERDFS PDMS

The query rewriting algorithm of SOMERDFS, namely DECA^{RDFS}, is designed on top of DECA. On each SOMERDFS peer $\mathcal{P}$, DECA^{RDFS} acts as an interface between the user and DECA which works on $Prop(\mathcal{P})$.

The strategy of DECA^{RDFS} is to rewrite the user query's atoms independently with DECA, based on the result of Proposition 2, and then to combine their rewritings in order to generate some conjunctive rewritings of the user query w.r.t. a SOMERDFS PDMS. DECA^{RDFS} guarantees that all the maximal conjunctive rewritings of the user query w.r.t. a SOMERDFS PDMS are generated.

DECA^{RDFS} is presented in Algorithm 1. It uses the conjunctive distribution operator $\oslash$ on sets of FOL formulas: $S_1 \oslash \cdots \oslash S_n = \oslash_{i=1}^n S_i = \{F_1 \wedge \cdots \wedge F_n \mid F_1 \in S_1, \ldots, F_n \in S_n\}$. Note that if $S_i = \emptyset$, $i \in [1..n]$, then $\oslash_{i=1}^n S_i = \emptyset$.

Algorithm 1. DECA^{RDFS}

Require: A user query $Q(\bar{X}) \equiv \exists \bar{Y} \bigwedge_{i=1}^n r_i(\bar{X}_i, \bar{Y}_i)$ s.t. $\bar{X} = \bigcup_{i=1}^n X_i$ and $\bar{Y} = \bigcup_{i=1}^n Y_i$

Ensure: Output contains only conjunctive rewritings of Q w.r.t $\mathcal{S}$, including all the maximal conjunctive rewritings of Q w.r.t $\mathcal{S}$

```
 1: for i ∈ [1..n] do
 2:     ATOMREWRITINGSᵢ = ∅
 3:     if rᵢ(X̄ᵢ, Ȳᵢ) is of the form C(U) then
 4:         for imp ∈ DeCA(¬Cᵈᵒᵐ) do
 5:             if imp has the form ¬C′ᵈᵒᵐ then
 6:                 ATOMREWRITINGSᵢ = ATOMREWRITINGSᵢ ∪ {C′(U)}
 7:             else if imp has the form ¬P′ᵖʳᵒᵖ then
 8:                 ATOMREWRITINGSᵢ = ATOMREWRITINGSᵢ ∪ {∃ZP′(U,Z)} endif
 9:         end for
10:         for imp ∈ DeCA(¬Cʳᵃⁿᵍᵉ) do
11:             if imp has the form ¬P′ᵖʳᵒᵖ then
12:                 ATOMREWRITINGSᵢ = ATOMREWRITINGSᵢ ∪ {∃ZP′(Z,U)} endif
13:         end for
14:     else if rᵢ(X̄ᵢ, Ȳᵢ) is of the form P(U₁,U₂) then
15:         for imp ∈ DeCA(¬Pᵖʳᵒᵖ) do
16:             if imp has the form ¬P′ᵖʳᵒᵖ then
17:                 ATOMREWRITINGSᵢ = ATOMREWRITINGSᵢ ∪ {P′(U₁,U₂)}
18:         end for
19:     end if
20: end for
21: return ⊘ⁿᵢ₌₁ATOMREWRITINGSᵢ
```

4.1   Illustrative Example (Continued)

Let us consider the user query $Q_1(X) \equiv \mathcal{P}_2{:}Work(X)$ asked to $\mathcal{P}_2$ in the example of Section 2.8.

At Line 4 of $\text{DECA}^{\text{RDFS}}$, $\neg P_2{:}Work^{dom}$ is asked to DECA:

$\text{DECA}(\neg P_2{:}Work^{dom}) = \{\neg P_2{:}Work^{dom}, \neg P_2{:}Painting^{dom}, \neg P_2{:}Sculpture^{dom}, \neg P_2{:}Music^{dom}, \neg P_2{:}refersTo^{prop}, \neg P_1{:}Artifact^{dom}, \neg P_1{:}belongsTo^{prop}\}.$

At Line 10 of $\text{DECA}^{\text{RDFS}}$, $\neg P_2{:}Work^{range}$ is asked to DECA:

$\text{DECA}(\neg P_2{:}Work^{range}) = \{\neg P_2{:}Work^{range}, \neg P_2{:}Painting^{range}, \neg P_2{:}Sculpture^{range}, \neg P_2{:}Music^{range}, \neg P_1{:}Artifact^{range}, \neg P_1{:}creates^{prop}, \neg P_1{:}paints^{prop}, \neg P_1{:}sculpts^{prop}\}.$

It follows that, at Line 21, $\oslash_{i=1}^1 \text{ATOMREWRITINGS}_i = \{P_2{:}Work(X), P_2{:}Painting(X), P_2{:}Sculpture(X), P_2{:}Music(X), \exists Z P_2{:}refersTo(X,Z), P_1{:}Artifact(X), \exists T P_1{:}belongsTo(X,T), \exists U P_1{:}creates(U,X), \exists V P_1{:}paints(V,X), \exists W P_1{:}sculpts(W,X)\}.$

Therefore, $\text{DECA}^{\text{RDFS}}$ returns the maximal conjunctive rewritings of Q_1 w.r.t. S exhibited in the example of Section 3.1.

Let us consider now the user query $Q_2(X,Y) \equiv P_2{:}Painting(X) \wedge P_2{:}refersTo(X,Y)$ asked to P_2 in the example of Section 2.8.

In the first iteration of $\text{DECA}^{\text{RDFS}}$, $\neg P_2{:}Painting^{dom}$ is asked to DECA at Line 4 and $\neg P_2{:}Painting^{range}$ is asked to DECA at Line 10 with the following results:

$\text{DECA}(\neg P_2{:}Painting^{dom}) = \{\neg P_2{:}Painting^{dom}\},$
$\text{DECA}(\neg P_2{:}Painting^{range}) = \{\neg P_2{:}Painting^{range}, \neg P_1{:}paints^{prop}\}.$

In the second iteration of $\text{DECA}^{\text{RDFS}}$, $\neg P_2{:}refersTo^{prop}$ is asked to DECA at Line 15 with the following results:

$\text{DECA}(\neg P_2{:}refersTo^{prop}) = \{\neg P_2{:}refersTo^{prop}, \neg P_1{:}belongsTo^{prop}\}.$

It follows that, at Line 21,

$\oslash_{i=1}^2 \text{ATOMREWRITINGS}_i = \{\ P_2{:}Painting(X) \wedge P_2{:}refersTo(X,Y), P_2{:}Painting(X) \wedge P_1{:}belongsTo(X,Y), \exists Z\, P_1{:}paints(Z,X) \wedge P_2{:}refersTo(X,Y), \exists Z\, P_1{:}paints(Z,X) \wedge P_1{:}belongsTo(X,Y)\}.$

Therefore, $\text{DECA}^{\text{RDFS}}$ returns the maximal conjunctive rewritings of Q_2 w.r.t. S exhibited in the example of Section 3.1.

4.2   Properties of $\text{DECA}^{\text{RDFS}}$

The main properties of $\text{DECA}^{\text{RDFS}}$ are stated by the two following theorems.

Theorem 2 (Soundness of $\text{DECA}^{\text{RDFS}}$). *Let S be a SomeRDFS PDMS and let P be one of its peers. Any user query Q asked to P will produce a set $\text{DECA}^{\text{RDFS}}(Q)$ of queries containing only conjunctive rewritings of Q w.r.t. S.*

Proof. Theorem 1 in [5] states the soundness of DECA. Therefore, according to Proposition 2 in Section 3, ATOMREWRITINGS$_i$ ($i \in [1..n]$) at Line 21 contains only conjunctive rewritings of the ith atom of the user query Q.

The soundness of the output of DECA^{RDFS} at Line 21 results from the fact that, as we have shown in the proof of Theorem 1, we are in a setting where it has been proved [19] that conjuncting conjunctive rewritings of each atom of the query provides conjunctive rewritings of the query.   □

Theorem 3 (Completeness of DECA^{RDFS}). *Let $\mathcal{S}$ be a SOMERDFS PDMS and let $\mathcal{P}$ be one of its peers. Any user query Q asked to $\mathcal{P}$ will produce a set DECA$^{RDFS}(Q)$ of queries containing all the maximal conjunctive rewritings of Q w.r.t. $\mathcal{S}$.*

Proof. Theorem 2 in [5] states a sufficient condition for the completeness of DECA. Proposition 1 in Section 3 ensures that this condition is satisfied in $Prop(\mathcal{S})$. Therefore, the use of DECA at Line 4, Line 10, and Line 15 produces all the proper prime implicates of the given literals w.r.t. $Prop(\mathcal{S})$.

According to Proposition 2 in Section 3, ATOMREWRITINGS$_i$ ($i \in [1..n]$) at Line 21 contains *all* the maximal conjunctive rewritings of the ith atom of the user query Q.

The completeness of the output of DECA^{RDFS} at Line 21 results from the fact that, as we have shown in the proof of Theorem 1, we are in a setting where it has been proved [19] that conjuncting all the maximal conjunctive rewritings of each atom of the query provides all the maximal conjunctive rewritings of the query.   □

Theorem 4 (Termination of DECA^{RDFS}). *Let $\mathcal{S}$ be a SOMERDFS PDMS and let $\mathcal{P}$ be one of its peers. Any user query Q asked to $\mathcal{P}$ will produce a computation that always terminates.*

Proof. Theorem 1 in [5] states that DECA always terminates after having produced a *finite* set of proper prime implicates of a given literal w.r.t. $Prop(\mathcal{S})$. Therefore, it is obvious that DECA^{RDFS} always terminates.   □

Other interesting properties are inherited from DECA's properties: *anytime computation* and *termination notification*. Note that the latter property is crucial for an anytime algorithm.

Theorem 5 (Anytime computation of DECA^{RDFS}). *Let $\mathcal{S}$ be a SOMERDFS PDMS and let $\mathcal{P}$ be one of its peers. Any user query Q asked to $\mathcal{P}$ will return a set DECA$^{RDFS}(Q)$ of query rewritings as a stream.*

Proof. It is obvious that the n iterations at Line 1 are independent. Therefore, they can be parallelized.

Within an iteration, if there are several calls to DECA, those calls and the computations that follows are independent: they only *add* results in the same variable ATOMREWRITING$_i$. Therefore, those calls can be parallelized. Moreover, since DECA performs an anytime computation, the feeding of the

ATOMREWRITING$_i$ can be made anytime: each time a result is produced by
DECA (at Line 4, Line 10, and Line 15), that result is processed (within the for
loops at Line 4, Line 10, and Line 15).

It follows that the computation at Line 21 can also be made anytime: each time
an ATOMREWRITING$_k$ $(k \in [1..n])$ is fed with a formula F,
$\oslash_{i=1}^{k-1}$ATOMREWRITINGS$_i \oslash \{F\} \oslash \oslash_{i=k+1}^{n}$ATOMREWRITINGS$_i$ is returned in the
output stream.   □

Theorem 6 (Termination notification of DECA^{RDFS}). *Let* S *be a*
SOMERDFS *PDMS and let* P *be one of its peers. Any user query asked to*
P *will produce a computation, the end of which will be notified to the user.*

Proof. Theorem 3 in [5] states that DECA, which is anytime, notifies of its termination. Therefore, it is obvious that as soon as all the *finite number* of calls to
DECA have notified of there termination and the ATOMREWRITINGS$_i$ $(i \in [1..n])$
have been properly fed according to the results of these calls, DECA^{RDFS} can notifies the user of its termination after having returned $\oslash_{i=1}^{n}$ATOMREWRITINGS$_i$
at Line 21.   □

4.3 Scalability of DECA^{RDFS}

The scalability of DECA^{RDFS} is directly related to the scalability of DECA.
We can infer that DECA^{RDFS} has good scalability properties from the DECA
scalability experiments that are reported in [7]. Those experiments have been
performed on networks of 1000 peers deployed on a cluster of 75 heterogeneous
computers. The networks that have been considered have a topology of "small
world" [22] like in social networks: there are clusters of very connected peers
and a few connections between peers of different clusters. Each peer theory is
randomly generated as 70 clauses of length 2 from 70 variables, 40 of which
are ramdomly chosen as target variables. A peer is connected to 10 other peers
with which it shares 2 variables (randomly chosen). These connections take into
account the "small world" topology. From a peer point of view, these connections are done by adding in its theory 20 new clauses modeling the mappings
with its neighbours. Among the experiments performed on SOMEWHERE P2PISs
[7], the ones that are the most representative of the propositional encodings of
SOMERDFS PDMSs correspond to the *very easy* case for DECA in which all
the mappings correspond to clauses of length 2. It is due to the simplicity of the
RDFS model (no class constructor and no negation). In that case, it has been
experimentally shown that all the proper prime implicates of a given literal are
computed in 0.07 second in mean (over more than 300 different input literals).

This lets envision a good scalability of DECA^{RDFS}, since for any user query,
atoms are independently rewritten in parallel. Thus, the expected time to add
to the above 0.07 second in mean is the time needed to combine the rewritings
of the user query atoms (Line 21 in Algorithm 1).

5   Related Work

We have already presented in the introduction some PDMSs that have been developped for the Semantic Web: Edutella [2], RDFPeers [3], GridVine [4] or SomeOWL [5]. Like a SomeRDFS PDMS, a GridVine PDMS is based on RDFS and considers mappings between peer ontologies. However, the mappings considered in a GridVine PDMS are restricted to equivalence of properties, while we allow in a SomeRDFS PDMS more expressive mappings that can be inclusion of classes, inclusion of properties, and domain and range typing of properties. In contrast with a GridVine PDMS, the topology of a SomeRDFS PDMS is not fixed and results from the existence of mappings between peers.

Several peer-to-peer data management systems for other data models than those of the Semantic Web have been proposed recently.

Piazza [16,23], in contrast with Edutella, does not consider that the data distributed over the different peers must be described relatively to some existing reference schemas. Each peer has its own data and schema and can mediate with some other peers by declaring *mappings* between its schema and the schemas of those peers. The topology of the network is not fixed (as in Edutella) but accounts for the existence of mappings between peers (as in SomeOWL and SomeRDFS PDMSs): two peers are logically connected if there exists a mapping between their two schemas. The underlying data model of the first version of Piazza [16] is relational and the mappings between relational peer schemas are inclusion or equivalence statements between conjunctive queries. Such a mapping formalism encompasses the *Local-as-View* and the *Global-as-View* [24] formalisms used in information integration systems based on single mediators. The price to pay is that query answering is undecidable except if some restrictions are imposed on the mappings or on the topology of the network [16]. The currently implemented version of Piazza [23] relies on a tree-based data model: the data is in XML and the mappings are equivalence and inclusion statements between XML queries. Query answering implementation is based on practical (but not complete) algorithms for XML query containment and rewriting. The scalability of Piazza so far does not go up to more than about 80 peers in the published experiments and relies on a wide range of optimizations (mappings composition [25], paths pruning [26]), made possible by the centralized storage of all the schemas and mappings in a global server.

The peer data management system considered in [27] is similar to that of [16] but proposes an alternative semantics based on epistemic logic. With that semantics it is shown that query answering is always decidable (even with cyclic mappings). Answers obtained according to this semantics correspond to a subset of those that would be obtained according to the standard FOL semantics. However, to the best of our knowledge, these results are not implemented.

The Kadop system [28] is an infastructure based on distributed hash tables for constructing and querying peer-to-peer warehouses of XML resources semantically enriched by taxonomies and mappings. The mappings that are considered are simple inclusion statement between atomic classes.

We will end this section by relating the $\text{DeCA}^{\text{RDFS}}$ rewriting algorithm that we have described in Section 4, with the rewriting algorithm $PerfectRef$ used in [12] for reformulating a query w.r.t. $DL\text{-}Lite$ Tboxes. The subtle step of $PerfectRef$ consists in rewriting each atom of the query by applying *positive inclusions*. The result of the application of the two positive inclusion statements expressing domain and range role typing corresponds exactly to respectively Line 8 and Line 12 of the $\text{DeCA}^{\text{RDFS}}$ algorithm (applied in the centralized case for making the comparison meaningful). The difference is that while inclusion statements are applied on first-order atoms in $PerfectRef$, we proceed in two steps: first the variables of the query are removed and we compute propositional rewritings, second we obtain the FOL rewritings by simply adding variables (possibly fresh existential variables) appropriately, depending on whether the propositional rewritings come from propositional atoms of the form C^{dom} or C^{range}. The equivalent of the application of the positive inclusions is done in the first step, which applies to propositional atoms. This is an advantage for scalability issues in the decentralized case.

6   Conclusion and Future Work

We have presented the SomeRDFS model of PDMSs based on RDFS. It is the first work on distributed RDFS handling semantic heterogeneity between peers through more complex mappings than equivalence statements. The mappings that we have considered are RDFS statements involving classes or properties of different peers. Our approach for query answering in this setting relies on two steps: query rewriting results in a union of conjunctive queries over possibly different peers ; the answers are then obtained by evaluating each of those conjunctive queries on the appropriate peers. This paper has focused on the first step which is crucial for scalablity issues since it is within this step that the different peers possibly relevant to the query are discovered. For the answering step, we know which peers have to be interrogated and with which queries. The optimization issues that are relevant to this evaluation step are out of the scope of this paper. Query answering by rewriting is a standard approach in information integration systems based on centralized mediators. It raises new problems in a decentralized setting, in particular scalabiliy and even decidability [29]. The fact that in our approach query rewritings can be obtained through a propositional encoding step guarantees decidability and scalability.

In fact, we have shown how to deploy SomeRDFS PDMSs on top of the SomeWhere infrastructure for which experiments [7] have shown good scalability properties. As a comparison, a simple GridVine PDMS of 60 peers have been deployed and experimented in [4]: peer ontologies are in core-RDFS, 15 ontologies are used (each of which is used by 4 peers), each peer has 2 mappings and stores only 1 fact. On such a PDMS, a user query, which is similar to our user query made of a single atom, is answered in more that 10 seconds. In contrast, experiments presented in [7] show that on a more complex network with bigger ontologies (1000 peers, 1000 ontologies, 10 mappings per peer), the rewritings produced by DECA for any user query made of a single atom are obtained in 0.07 second in mean. This lets envision that the whole query answering (rewriting and evaluation) could be made in less than 1 or 2 seconds. Such a hint must be confirmed by a large-scale experimental study that we plan to conduct in the near future.

We also plan to extend the current SOMERDFS model for handling more complex ontologies and more complex mappings. In particular, it seems doable to consider *DL-Lite* both for expressing local ontologies over RDF facts and for expressing mappings between ontologies. Since the negation is supported at the propositional level in SOMEWHERE the DECA algorithm can be used to check the satisfiability of the global schema. Then it should be straightforward to extend the two-step DECA^{RDFS} rewriting algorithm to handle the additional constructors of *DL-Lite$_R$*. As a consequence, by a slight extension of the approach presented in this paper we could obtain a fast deployment of PDMS based on distributed *DL-Lite* (in which the mappings are interpreted in first-order semantics).

References

1. Berners-Lee, T., Hendler, J., Lassila, O.: The semantic web. Scientific American **284**(5) (2001)
2. Nedjl, W., Wolf, B., Qu, C., Decker, S., Sintek, M., al.: EDUTELLA: a P2P networking infrastructure based on RDF. In: WWW. (2002)
3. Cai, M., Frank, M.: RDFPeers: a scalable distributed RDF repository based on a structured P2P network. In: WWW. (2004)
4. Aberer, K., Cudré-Mauroux, P., Hauswirth, M., Pelt, T.V.: GridVine: Building internet-scale semantic overlay networks. In: ISWC. (2004)
5. Adjiman, P., Chatalic, P., Goasdoué, F., Rousset, M.C., Simon, L.: Distributed reasoning in a P2P setting: Application to the semantic web. Journal of Artificial Intelligence Research (JAIR) (2006)
6. Stoica, I., Morris, R., Karger, D., Kaasshoek, M., Balakrishnan, H.: CHORD a scalable P2P lookup service for internet applications. In: ACM SIGCOMM. (2001)
7. Adjiman, P., Chatalic, P., Goasdoué, F., Rousset, M.C., Simon, L.: Scalability study of P2P consequence finding. In: IJCAI. (2005)
8. ter Horst, H.J.: Extending the RDFS entailment lemma. In: ISWC. (2004)
9. de Bruijn, J., Franconi, E., Tessaris, S.: Logical reconstruction of normative RDF. In: OWLED. (2005)
10. de Bruijn, J., Franconi, E., Tessaris, S.: Logical reconstruction of RDF and ontology languages. In: PPSWR. (2005)
11. Farrugia, J.: Model-theoretic semantics for the web. In: WWW. (2003)
12. Calvanese, D., Giacomo, G.D., Lembo, D., Lenzerini, M., Rosati, R.: DL-Lite: Tractable description logics for ontologies. In: AAAI. (2005)
13. Calvanese, D., Giacomo, G.D., Lembo, D., Lenzerini, M., Rosati, R.: Data complexity of query answering in description logics. In: KR. (2006)
14. Grosof, B.N., Horrocks, I., Volz, R., Decker, S.: Description Logic Programs: combining logic programs with description logic. In: WWW. (2003)
15. Haase, P., Broekstra, J., Eberhart, A., Volz, R.: A comparison of RDF query languages. In: ISWC. (2004)

16. Halevy, A., Ives, Z., Suciu, D., Tatarinov, I.: Schema mediation in peer data management systems. In: ICDE. (2003)
17. Goasdoué, F., Rousset, M.C.: Answering queries using views: a KRDB perspective for the semantic web. ACM Journal - Transactions on Internet Technology (TOIT) **4**(3) (2004)
18. Russell, S., Norvig, P.: Artificial Intelligence: A Modern Approach. 2nd edition edn. Prentice-Hall, Englewood Cliffs, NJ (2003)
19. Levy, A.Y., Mendelzon, A.O., Sagiv, Y., Srivastava, D.: Answering queries using views. In: PODS. (1995)
20. Pottinger, R., Halevy, A.Y.: MiniCon: A scalable algorithm for answering queries using views. In: VLDB Journal 10(2-3). (2001)
21. Abiteboul, S., Hull, R., Vianu, V.: Foundations of Databases. Addison-Wesley (1995)
22. Watts, D.J., Strogatz, S.H.: Models of the small world. Nature **393** (1998)
23. Halevy, A., Ives, Z., Tatarinov, I., Mork, P.: Piazza: data management infrastructure for semantic web applications. In: WWW. (2003)
24. Halevy, A.Y. In: Logic-based techniques in data integration. Kluwer Academic Publishers (2000)
25. Madhavan, J., Halevy, A.: Composing mappings among data sources. In: VLDB. (2003)
26. Tatarinov, I., Halevy, A.: Efficient query reformulation in peer data management systems. In: SIGMOD. (2004)
27. Calvanese, D., Giacomo, G.D., Lenzerini, M., Rosati, R.: Logical fondation of P2P data integration. In: PODS. (2004)
28. Abiteboul, S., Manolescu, I., Preda, N.: Constructing and querying P2P warehouses of XML resources. In: SWDB. (2004)
29. Tatarinov, I., Ives, Z., Madhavan, J., Halevy, A., Suciu, D., Dalvi, N., Dong, X., Kadiyska, Y., Miklau, G., Mork, P.: The Piazza peer data management project. In: SIGMOD Record. Volume 32. (2003)

A Tool for Evaluating Ontology Alignment Strategies

Patrick Lambrix and He Tan

Department of Computer and Information Science
Linköpings universitet, Sweden
{patla,hetan}@ida.liu.se

Abstract. Ontologies are an important technology for the Semantic Web. In different areas ontologies have already been developed and many of these ontologies contain overlapping information. Often we would therefore want to be able to use multiple ontologies. To obtain good results, we need to find the relationships between terms in the different ontologies, i.e. we need to align them. Currently, there exist a number of systems that support users in aligning ontologies, but not many comparative evaluations have been performed and there exists little support to perform such evaluations. However, the study of the properties, the evaluation and comparison of the alignment strategies and their combinations, would give us valuable insight in how the strategies could be used in the best way. In this paper we propose the KitAMO framework for comparative evaluation of ontology alignment strategies and their combinations and present our current implementation. We evaluate the implementation with respect to performance. We also illustrate how the system can be used to evaluate and compare alignment strategies and their combinations in terms of performance and quality of the proposed alignments. Further, we show how the results can be analyzed to obtain deeper insights into the properties of the strategies.

Keywords: ontologies, alignment, evaluation.

1 Introduction

Intuitively, ontologies (e.g. [22,14]) can be seen as defining the basic terms and relations of a domain of interest, as well as the rules for combining these terms and relations. They are considered to be an important technology for the Semantic Web. Ontologies are used for communication between people and organizations by providing a common terminology over a domain. They provide the basis for interoperability between systems. They can be used for making the content in information sources explicit and serve as an index to a repository of information. Further, they can be used as a basis for integration of information sources and as a query model for information sources. They also support clearly separating domain knowledge from application-based knowledge as well as validation of data sources. The benefits of using ontologies include reuse, sharing and portability

S. Spaccapietra et al. (Eds.): Journal on Data Semantics VIII, LNCS 4380, pp. 182–202, 2007.

of knowledge across platforms, and improved maintainability, documentation, maintenance, and reliability. Overall, ontologies lead to a better understanding of a field and to more effective and efficient handling of information in that field. In the field of bioinformatics, for instance, the work on ontologies is recognized as essential in some of the grand challenges of genomics research [4] and there is much international research cooperation for the development of ontologies (e.g. the Gene Ontology (GO) [13] and Open Biomedical Ontologies (OBO) [33] efforts) and the use of ontologies for the Semantic Web (e.g. the EU Network of Excellence REWERSE [36,37]).

Many ontologies have already been developed and many of these ontologies contain overlapping information. Often we would therefore want to be able to use multiple ontologies. For instance, companies may want to use community standard ontologies and use them together with company-specific ontologies. Applications may need to use ontologies from different areas or from different views on one area. Ontology builders may want to use already existing ontologies as the basis for the creation of new ontologies by extending the existing ontologies or by combining knowledge from different smaller ontologies. In each of these cases it is important to know the relationships between the terms in the different ontologies. We say that we align two ontologies when we define the relationships between terms in the different ontologies. We merge two ontologies when we, based on the alignment relations between the ontologies, create a new ontology containing the knowledge included in the source ontologies.

Ontology alignment and merging is recognized as an important step in ontology engineering that needs more extensive research (e.g. [34]). Currently, there exist a number of systems that support users in aligning or merging ontologies in the same domain. These systems use different techniques, but it is not clear how well these techniques perform for different types of ontologies. Also, it is not clear whether and how different techniques could be combined to provide better alignments. The study of the properties, the evaluation and comparison of the alignment strategies and their combinations, would give us valuable insight in how the strategies could be used in the best way. It would also lead to recommendations on how to improve the alignment techniques. However, relatively few comparative evaluations on ontology merging and alignment have been performed [23,24,25,26,34,10,17] and no advanced tools for supporting these kinds of evaluations exist yet [20]. To be able to study the properties of the alignment techniques and their combinations and to compare them, we need tools that allow us to evaluate them in different settings. Such tools should allow us to apply the techniques and different combinations of techniques to different types of ontologies. The tools should also support evaluation and comparison of the techniques and their combinations in terms of e.g. performance and quality of the alignment. Further, we need support to analyze the evaluation results in different ways.

In this paper we propose a tool for evaluating ontology alignment strategies and their combinations. The tool covers the non-interactive part of the general framework for aligning ontologies as described in [25]. In section 3 we first

describe the KitAMO[1] framework for evaluating ontology alignment strategies
and then describe the current implementation. In section 4 the implementation
is evaluated with respect to performance. We also show how the tool can be
used to evaluate and compare strategies and their combinations in terms of performance and quality of the proposed alignment relationships. Further, we show
how the results can be analyzed to examine the advantages and disadvantages
of the strategies in more details. Related work is discussed in section 5 and the
paper concludes in section 6. In the next section we provide some background on
(biomedical) ontologies, ontology alignment systems and evaluations of ontology
alignment strategies.

2   Background

2.1   Ontologies

Ontologies differ regarding the kind of information they can represent. From a
knowledge representation point of view ontologies can have the following components (e.g. [22,38]). Concepts represent sets or classes of entities in a domain.
Instances represent the actual entities. They are, however, often not represented
in ontologies. Further, there are many types of relations. Finally, axioms represent facts that are always true in the topic area of the ontology. These can be
such things as domain restrictions, cardinality restrictions or disjointness restrictions. Depending on which of the components are represented and the kind of
information that can be represented, we can distinguish between different kinds
of ontologies such as controlled vocabularies, taxonomies, thesauri, data models,
frame-based ontologies and knowledge-based ontologies. These different types of
ontologies can be represented in a spectrum of representation formalisms ranging from very informal to strictly formal. For instance, some of the most expressive representation formalisms in use for ontologies are description logic-based
languages such as DAML+OIL and OWL.

2.2   Biomedical Ontologies

In this paper we have chosen to use test cases based on biomedical ontologies
(e.g. [22]). There are several reasons for this. Research in biomedical ontologies
is recognized as essential in some of the grand challenges of genomics research
[4]. The field has also matured enough to develop standardization efforts. An
example of this is the organization of the first conference on Standards and Ontologies for Functional Genomics (SOFG) in 2002 and the development of the
SOFG resource on ontologies. Further, there exist ontologies that have reached
the status of de facto standard and are being used extensively for annotation
of databases. Also, OBO was started as an umbrella web address for ontologies
for use within the genomics and proteomics domains. Many biomedical ontologies are already available via OBO. There are also many overlapping ontologies
available in the field.

---

[1] Toolkit for Aligning and Merging Ontologies.

The ontologies that we use in this paper are GO ontologies, Signal-Ontology (SigO) [43], Medical Subject Headings (MeSH) [28] and the Adult Mouse Anatomical Dictionary (MA) [16]. The GO Consortium is a joint project which goal is to produce a structured, precisely defined, common and dynamic controlled vocabulary that describes the roles of genes and proteins in all organisms. Currently, there are three independent ontologies publicly available over the Internet: biological process, molecular function and cellular component. The GO ontologies are a de facto standard and many different bio-databases are today annotated with GO terms. The terms in GO are arranged as nodes in a directed acyclic graph, where multiple inheritance is allowed. The purpose of the SigO project is to extract common features of cell signaling in the model organisms, try to understand what cell signaling is and how cell signaling systems can be modeled. SigO is based on the knowledge of the Cell Signaling Networks data source [41] and treats complex knowledge of living cells such as pathways, networks and causal relationships among molecules. The ontology consists of a flow diagram of signal transduction and a conceptual hierarchy of biochemical attributes of signaling molecules. MeSH is a controlled vocabulary produced by the American National Library of Medicine and used for indexing, cataloging, and searching for biomedical and health-related information and documents. It consists of sets of terms naming descriptors in a hierarchical structure. These descriptors are organized in 15 categories, such as the category for anatomic terms, which is the category we use. The purpose of MA is to provide an ontology for annotating and integrating different types of data pertinent to anatomy. It is based on the Mouse Embryo Anatomy Nomenclature Database [2] and will be integrated with the Anatomical Dictionary for Mouse Development to generate an anatomy ontology covering the entire lifespan of the laboratory mouse. The ontology contains more than 2400 anatomical terms. They are structured as directed acyclic graphs across *is-a* and *part-of* relationships. The hierarchy of the ontology is organized in both spatial and functional ways.

2.3   Ontology Alignment Systems

There exist a number of ontology alignment systems that support users in finding inter-ontology relationships. Some of these systems are also ontology merge systems. Many ontology alignment systems can be described as instantiations of the general framework defined in [25,26] (figure 1).

In our framework an alignment system receives as input two source ontologies. The system can be seen as being composed of two major parts. The first part (*I* in figure 1) computes alignment suggestions. The second part (*II*) interacts with the user to decide on the final alignments.

An alignment system can include several matchers. These matchers calculate similarities between the terms from the different source ontologies. The matchers can implement strategies based on linguistic matching, structure-based strategies, constraint-based approaches, instance-based strategies, strategies that use auxiliary information or a combination of these. Strategies based on linguistic

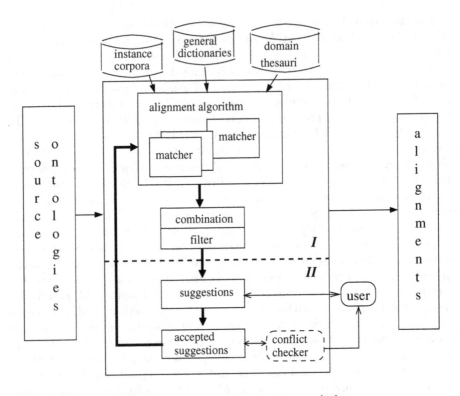

Fig. 1. A general alignment strategy [25]

matching make use of textual descriptions of the concepts and relations such as names, synonyms and definitions. The similarity measure between concepts is based on comparisons of the textual descriptions. Structure-based strategies use the structure of the ontologies to provide suggestions. For instance, previously accepted alignments can be used to influence the similarity values between the sub- and super-concepts of already aligned concepts. Other approaches use paths between already aligned concepts to generate new alignment suggestions. In the constraint-based approaches the axioms are used to provide suggestions. For instance, knowing that the range and domain of two relations are the same, may be an indication that there is a relationship between the relations. On their own these approaches may not be sufficient to provide high quality suggestions, but they may complement other approaches to reduce the number of irrelevant suggestions. In some cases instances are available directly or can be obtained. When instances are available, they may be used in defining similarities between concepts. Further, dictionaries and thesauri representing general or domain knowledge, or intermediate ontologies may be used to enhance the alignment process. Table 1 gives an overview of the used strategies per alignment system. For more information we refer to [26].

Table 1. Strategies used by alignment systems [26]

	linguistic	structure	constraints	instances	auxiliary
ArtGen [30]	name	parents, children		domain-specific documents	WordNet
ASCO [27]	name, label, description	parents, children, siblings, path from root			WordNet
Chimaera [29]	name	parents, children			
FCA-Merge [39]	name			domain-specific documents	
FOAM [12,6]	name, label	parents, children	equivalence		
GLUE [5]	name	neighborhood		instances	
HCONE [21]	name	parents, children			WordNet
IF-Map [19]				instances	a reference ontology
iMapper [40]		leaf, non-leaf, children, related node	domain, range	instances	WordNet
OntoMapper [35]	name	parents, children		documents	
(Anchor-) PROMPT [32]	name	direct graphs			
SAMBO [24,25,26]	name, synonym	is-a and part-of, descendants and ancestors		domain-specific documents	WordNet, UMLS
S-Match [15]	label	path from root	semantic relations codified in labels		WordNet

Alignment suggestions are then determined by combining and filtering the results generated by one or more matchers. Although most systems combine different approaches, not much research is done on the applicability and performance of these combinations. In the current systems similarity values are often combined using a weighted sum. In most systems the filtering consists of retaining the pairs of terms with a similarity value above a certain threshold as alignment suggestions. Recently, some more advanced filtering methods are proposed, such as in [3] where the structure of the ontologies is used to filter out alignment suggestions. By using different matchers and combining them and filtering in different ways we obtain different alignment strategies.

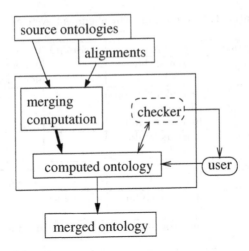

Fig. 2. A general merging algorithm [25]

The interactive component of the alignment system presents the suggestions to the user who accepts or rejects them. The acceptance and rejection of a suggestion may influence further suggestions. Also, some matchers (e.g. some structural matchers as in [32,24]) require as input already accepted suggestions. Further, a conflict checker is used to avoid conflicts introduced by the alignment relationships. The output of the alignment algorithm is a set of alignment relationships between terms from the source ontologies.

Figure 2 shows a simple merging algorithm. A new ontology is computed from the source ontologies and their identified alignment. The checker is used to avoid conflicts as well as to detect unsatisfiable concepts and, if so desired by the user, to remove redundancy.

2.4   Evaluation of Ontology Alignment Strategies

To date comparative evaluations of ontology alignment and merge systems have been performed by some groups ([34], [23,24,25,26] and the EON and I3CON contests). The EU OntoWeb project [34] evaluated the systems PROMPT [31] based on Protégé (with extension Anchor-PROMPT [32]), Chimaera [29] (described, not evaluated), FCA-Merge [39] and ODEMerge. This evaluation focused on such things as functionality, interoperability and visualization, but did not include tests on the quality of the alignment. In [23,24,26] PROMPT, Chimaera, FOAM and an early version of SAMBO were evaluated in terms of the quality of the alignment as well as the time it takes to align ontologies with these tools. Different alignment algorithms and their combinations were evaluated in [25,26]. The test cases were biomedical ontologies and ontologies about academia.

In 2004, two different experiments for the evaluation of the alignment tools were launched: the ontology alignment contest held by the International Workshop on the Evaluation of Ontology-based Tools (EON) [10] and the evaluation of ontology alignment tools organized by the Information Interpretation and Integration Conference (I3CON) [17]. Their main goals were to show how it is possible to evaluate ontology alignment tools and provide a framework for the evaluation of the alignment tools. In 2005 EON and I3CON organized a unique evaluation campaign. Its outcome is presented in [9]. In this experiment there were 7 participants. The participants were provided pairs of ontologies (OWL) and their expected results (RDF/XML). The participants submitted to the organizers their best alignment results which were generated under the same set of parameters. The alignment algorithms were to be performed without intervention. The test cases were from three topics, including bibliographic ontologies, ontologies constructed from Google, Yahoo and Looksmart web directories, and anatomy models FMA and OpenGalen. Not all participants finished all these tests. The organizers evaluated the results submitted by the participants and compared them. The evaluation measures were precision and recall.

3 KitAMO

In this section we present the KitAMO framework for evaluating ontology alignment strategies and present the current implementation. KitAMO supports the study, evaluation and comparison of alignment strategies and their combinations based on their performance and the quality of their alignments on test cases. This corresponds to the evaluation of the non-interactive alignment components (part *I* in figure 1) in an ontology alignment system. KitAMO also provides support for the analysis of the evaluation results.

3.1 Framework

Figure 3 illustrates the KitAMO framework for comparative evaluation of the different alignment components. KitAMO receives as input different alignment components that we want to evaluate, e.g. various matchers, filters and combination algorithms. KitAMO contains a database of evaluation cases which is built in advance. Each case consists of two ontologies and their expected alignments produced by experts on the topic area of the ontologies. The alignment components are evaluated using these cases.

The evaluation tool in the framework provides the wrapper which allows the alignment components to work on the ontologies in the database of evaluation cases, and provides the interface where the user can decide, e.g. which evaluation cases are used, and how these alignment components cooperate. The evaluation tool also has the responsibility to save the similarity values generated by the alignment components to the similarity database, and retrieves these similarity values from the database when required by the analysis tool.

The analysis tool receives as input data from the database of evaluation cases, similarity values retrieved by the evaluation tool from the similarity database, and possibly previously generated data from the analysis database. The analysis tool allows a user to analyze different properties of the evaluated alignment components and their combinations. For instance, it is possible to analyze such things

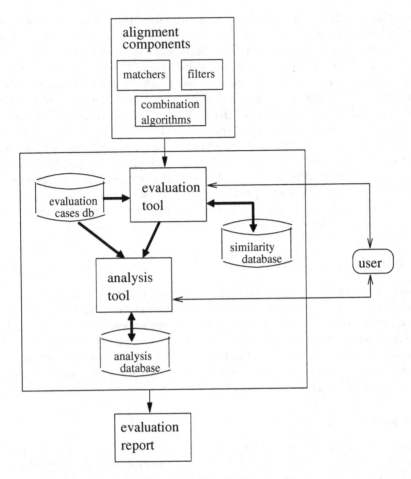

Fig. 3. The KitAMO framework

as the similarity values between terms from different matchers, the performance of the matchers, and the quality of the alignment suggestions generated by different matchers and their combinations with different filters. Through the analysis tool the user can also save the evaluation results into the analysis database and produce an evaluation report.

3.2 Implementation

In the current implementation of KitAMO we have focused on the evaluation of matchers. Instead of allowing different combination and filtering strategies as input, currently we implemented the most used strategies in KitAMO, i.e. a weighted sum as combination strategy and filtering based on a threshold value.

The matchers are added to KitAMO as plug-ins. Each matcher needs to implement the plug-in interface where similarity values between terms in ontologies are computed. When new matchers are added, the system is restarted in order to pick up the new plug-ins, and to take the change in configuration into account.

The current database of evaluation cases consists of five test cases based on two groups of biomedical ontologies. These cases were previously used in the evaluations in [25,26,42]. For the first two cases we use a part of a GO ontology together with a part of SigO. The first case, *behavior* (B), contains 57 terms from GO and 10 terms from SigO. The second case, *immune defense* (ID), contains 73 terms from GO and 15 terms from SigO. We used more terms from GO than from SigO because the granularity of GO is higher than the granularity of SigO for these topics. The other cases are based on MeSH (anatomy category) and MA. The three cases used in our test are: *nose* (containing 15 terms from MeSH and 18 terms from MA), *ear* (containing 39 terms from MeSH and 77 terms from MA), and *eye* (containing 45 terms from MeSH and 112 terms from MA). We translated the ontologies from the GO flat file format to OWL retaining identifiers, names, synonyms, definitions and is-a and part-of relationships. The alignments for these test cases were provided to us by biologists. In this implementation of the database we only considered equivalence and is-a relations between terms as alignment relationships. For each case we also stored the expected suggestions and the inferred suggestions. The expected suggestions is the minimal set of alignment suggestions that matchers are expected to generate for a perfect recall. This set does not include the inferred suggestions. Inferred suggestions can be inferred by a merging algorithm. An example of an inferred suggestion is that incus is-a ear ossicle. In this case we know that auditory bone (MA) is equivalent to ear ossicle (MeSH), and incus is-a auditory bone in MA. Then the system should derive that incus is-a ear ossicle.

The user starts the evaluation process by choosing an evaluation case. Then the user decides which matchers should be used in the evaluation from the list of matcher plug-ins configured in KitAMO. For instance, figure 4 shows that we have 4 matcher plug-ins (UMLSKSearch, TermWN, TermBasic and BayesLearning) and that we decided to perform the evaluations on the first two matchers. The selected matchers calculate similarity values between the terms in the chosen evaluation case, and the results are written to the similarity database. For the combination each matcher can be assigned a weight (weight in figure 5). The similarity values generated by the combination, i.e. the weighted sum, can also be saved to the similarity database by the user. For the filter the user can assign threshold values for individual matchers and the combination (threshold in figure 5).

KitAMO shows the result of an evaluation for a group of weights and thresholds in the form of a table as illustrated in figure 6. In the example we see that the number of expected suggestions (ES) is 27 for the evaluation case. UMLSKSearch found 23 correct alignments, 2 wrong suggestions and 1 inferred suggestion for the threshold 0.6. For the combination with weight 1.0 for UMLSKSearch and weight 1.2 for TermWN we found 24 correct suggestions, 2 wrong suggestions and no inferred suggestions for threshold 0.5. The user can save this data to the analysis database and at any time the user can look at previously saved data

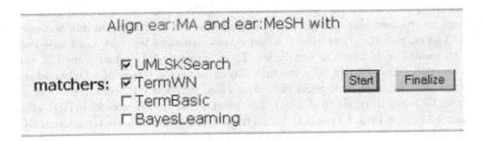

Fig. 4. The list of matcher plug-ins

	weight	threshold
UMLSKSearch	1.0	0.6
TermWN	1.2	0.6
Comb. Threshold		0.5

| Analyse | Save Comb. | ReStart |

Fig. 5. The weights and thresholds assignment

	ES	Th	C	W	I
UMLSKSearch		0.6	23	2	1
TermWN	27	0.6	26	19	2
Comb(1.0,1.2)		0.5	24	2	0

☐ Show Similarity Values   ⏱ Matcher Performance

☐ Show Analysis Results   Save Analysis

Fig. 6. The analysis result

(figure 7). The table with previously saved data can be sorted according to each column. The user can also look at the actual similarity values between the pairs of terms in the ontologies of the evaluation case. For instance, figure 8 shows a table with the terms in the ontologies together with the similarity values generated by the analyzed matchers and combinations. It also shows whether the pair is a correct alignment, an inferred suggestion or a wrong suggestion. The table can be sorted according to each column. Further, the user can look at the time

matcher	Th	C	W	I
(1.0UM,1.0TW)	0.50	23	2	0
(1.0UM,1.2TW)	0.50	24	2	0
TermWN	0.40	26	110	19
TermWN	0.50	26	65	8
TermWN	0.60	26	19	2
UMLSKSearch	0.40	23	2	1
UMLSKSearch	0.50	23	2	1
UMLSKSearch	0.60	23	2	1

Fig. 7. The previously saved analysis results

MA	MeSH	UMLSKSearch	TermWN	(1.0UM,1.2TW)	Sug
basilar membrane	basilar membrane	1.0000	1.0000	1.0000	C
tectorial membrane	tectorial membrane	1.0000	1.0000	1.0000	C
stapedius	stapedius	1.0000	1.0000	1.0000	C
scala tympani	scala tympani	1.0000	1.0000	1.0000	C
vestibular aqueduct	vestibular aqueduct	1.0000	1.0000	1.0000	C
utricle	saccule and utricle	1.0000	1.0000	1.0000	W
tensor tympani	tensor tympani	1.0000	1.0000	1.0000	C
middle ear	middle ear	1.0000	1.0000	1.0000	C
ear	ear	1.0000	1.0000	1.0000	C
spiral organ	organ of corti	1.0000	1.0000	1.0000	C
tympanic membrane	tympanic membrane	1.0000	1.0000	1.0000	C
auditory bone	ear ossicle	1.0000	1.0000	1.0000	C
cochlea	cochlea	1.0000	1.0000	1.0000	C
saccule	saccule and utricle	1.0000	1.0000	1.0000	W
incus	incus	1.0000	1.0000	1.0000	C

Fig. 8. The similarity table

matchers	Performance (s)
TermWN	41.156
UMLSKSearch	137.798

Fig. 9. The performance table

needed by the matchers for the computation of similarity values as illustrated in figure 9.

The user can always restart the evaluation process with a different group of matchers or with different combinations and thresholds. Finally, the user can export the similarity and analysis data to Excel files.

KitAMO is implemented in Java. It relies on the Jena ontology API [18] for parsing OWL files. MySQL is used for the databases in KitAMO.

4   Evaluation and Discussion

In this section we evaluate the performance of the system using our test cases. This gives us an indication of the extra amount of time that KitAMO needs to process the alignment evaluations. This extra amount of time should be compared to the time it takes to manually analyze the similarity results generated by different matchers. We also give an example use of the system.

4.1   Performance of the System

We have run KitAMO using our test cases on a PC with 128Mb memory and an AMD Athlon 64 processor. We divide the time needed for an evaluation task into four parts. The first part includes the time for loading the ontologies and for generating the final evaluation reports as output (I/O in table 2). The second part is the time needed by each matcher to calculate the similarity values (table 3). This is an inherent property of the matchers and is outside KitAMO's control. However, we note that KitAMO actually measures this time as part of an evaluation (e.g. figure 9). The third part is the time necessary to set up the evaluation (Setup in table 2). This includes the creation and initial set-up of the similarity database, the insertion of the similarity values into the database, and the creation of the analysis database. The fourth part is the time needed by the analysis tool for one evaluation given the selected matchers, weights and threshold (Analysis in table 2). The first, second and third parts are done only once per evaluation. The fourth part is repeated for each new analysis.

Table 2. Time for evaluation (in seconds)

Case	I/O	Setup	Analysis
B	2.4	2.4	0.3
ID	2.6	4.4	0.3
nose	2.9	1.7	0.4
ear	3.0	8.3	0.7
eye	3.4	14.5	1.1

Table 3. Average time for computation of similarity values based on 5 runs (in seconds)

Case	TermBasic	TermWN	UMLSKSearch	BayesLearning
B	0.7	11.0	33.6	50.9
ID	3.0	37.0	37.6	90.6
nose	0.6	7.3	44.1	24.5
ear	3.8	37.9	105.8	114.2
eye	8.0	60.4	132.2	173.1

As expected, the larger the ontologies, the more time the evaluation takes. With respect to the parts under KitAMO's control, the initial set-up takes the most time. Also this is expected as a number of databases needs to be created. However, the part that usually takes the most time is outside KitAMO's control, i.e. the calculation of the similarity values by the matchers. Both the initial set-up and the running of the matchers is performed only once. The actual analysis is fast and can be repeated to create new analysis results.

In the past we have run analysis experiments on the implemented test cases using the matchers in SAMBO (e.g. [25,26,42]). The time needed by each matcher to calculate the similarity values was similar to the time it takes in KitAMO. The analysis process was done manually and partly using Excel. This process needed to be repeated for each new analysis. While KitAMO generates the analysis results in seconds, this process was previously time-consuming and error-prone.

4.2   Example Use

In this part we show how we can use KitAMO for evaluating matchers and analyzing the results. We use the ear case to evaluate two matcher plug-ins TermWN and UMLSKSearch. The experiments are similar to the ones in [26].

TermWN [26] is a terminological matcher combined with the general thesaurus WordNet. The terminological matcher is a combination matcher based on the textual descriptions (names and synonyms) of concepts and relations. In the current implementation, the matcher combines two approximate string matching algorithms (n-gram and edit distance) and a linguistic algorithm. A n-gram is a set of n consecutive characters extracted from a string. Similar strings will have a high proportion of n-grams in common. Edit distance is defined as the number of deletions, insertions, or substitutions required to transform one string into the other. The greater the edit distance, the more different the strings are. The linguistic algorithm computes the similarity of the terms by comparing the lists of words of which the terms are composed. Similar terms have a high proportion of words in common in the lists. A Porter stemming algorithm is employed to each word. Further, the similarity measure is enhanced by looking up the hypernym relationships of the pairs of words in the terms in WordNet [45].

UMLSKSearch [26] uses domain knowledge. We utilize the Metathesaurus in the Unified Medical Language System (UMLS) [44] which contains more than 100 biomedical and health-related vocabularies. The Metathesaurus is organized using concepts. The concepts may have synonyms which are the terms in the different vocabularies in the Metathesaurus that have the same intended meaning. The similarity of two terms in the source ontologies is determined by their relationship in UMLS. In our experiments we use the UMLS Knowledge Source Server to query the Metathesaurus with source ontology terms. As a result we obtain concepts that have the source ontology term as their synonym. We assign a similarity value of 1 for exact matches of query results for the two terms, 0.6 if the source ontology terms are synonyms of the same concept and 0 otherwise.

We decide to experiment with thresholds 0.4, 0.5, 0.6, 0.7 and 0.8 for the two individual matchers, and different weights for the combination for the

matcher	Th	C	W	I
(1.0UM,1.0TW)	0.50	23	2	0
(1.0UM,1.2TW)	0.50	24	2	0
(1.0UM,1.4TW)	0.50	25	2	0
(1.0UM,1.6TW)	0.50	26	3	0
(1.0UM,1.8TW)	0.50	26	3	0
(1.0UM,2.0TW)	0.50	26	3	0
(1.0UM,3.0TW)	0.50	26	13	2
(1.0UM,5.0TW)	0.50	26	19	2
(1.2UM,2.0TW)	0.50	26	3	0
(1.2UM,3.0TW)	0.50	26	8	0
(1.2UM,5.0TW)	0.50	26	17	2
(1.4UM,2.0TW)	0.50	26	2	0
(1.4UM,3.0TW)	0.50	26	3	0
(1.4UM,5.0TW)	0.50	26	14	2
TermWN	0.40	26	110	19
TermWN	0.50	26	65	8
TermWN	0.60	26	19	2
TermWN	0.70	26	8	0
TermWN	0.80	25	3	0
UMLSKSearch	0.40	23	2	1
UMLSKSearch	0.50	23	2	1
UMLSKSearch	0.60	23	2	1
UMLSKSearch	0.70	22	2	0
UMLSKSearch	0.80	22	2	0

Fig. 10. The analysis results for the ear case

threshold 0.5. The analysis results are shown in figure 10. We have sorted the results according to the matchers and their thresholds. This allows us to analyze the influence of the thresholds for the matchers. For TermWN we see that the quality of the results differs significantly for the different thresholds. Although the number of correct suggestions is almost the same (25 or 26), the number of wrong suggestions goes from 3 to 8, 19, 65 and 110 when the threshold decreases. Also the number of inferred suggestions increases when the threshold decreases. This would suggest to use a high threshold for TermWN for this case. For UMLSKSearch the quality of results stays similar when the threshold changes.

For the combination the threshold is the same, but we have varied the weights for the matchers in the combination. In addition to comparing the different combinations to each other (e.g. the combinations with weights (1,1.4) and (1,1.6) give good results), we can also compare the combinations with the individual matchers. We note, for instance, that TermWN finds the correct suggestions that the combinations find. However, the combination finds fewer wrong suggestions. In the combination UMLSKSearch can be seen as the contributing factor to filter out the wrong and inferred suggestions. This is reasonable since the similarity values from UMLSKSearch can only be 1, 0.6 and 0. It also suggests that the available domain knowledge in UMLS has good quality.

We can also sort the table with respect to the threshold. This allows us to compare the influence of the threshold between the different matchers. We can also sort the table with respect to the number of correct suggestions. In the best case this gives us the best alignment situation. Otherwise, when there are also many wrong suggestions, it may give a good starting point for combining with other algorithms (as TermWN in the example) or for applying a more advanced filtering technique as in [3].

To examine the matchers in more detail we can use the similarity table as in figure 8. By sorting the table with respect to TermWN and looking at the pairs with similarity values above a certain threshold we can analyze the properties of TermWN. For instance, we observe that TermWN finds suggestions where the names of terms are slightly different, e.g. (stapes, stape). As the test ontologies contain a large number of synonyms, also suggestions where the names of terms are completely different can be found, e.g. (inner ear, labyrinth), where inner ear has labyrinth as synonym. By using WordNet, TermWN finds suggestions such as (perilymphatic channel, cochlear aqueduct) where cochlear aqueduct has perilymphatic duct as synonym, and duct is a synonym of channel in WordNet. On the other hand, since endothelium is a kind of epithelium in WordNet, TermWN generates a wrong suggestion (corneal endothelium, corneal epithelium). Sorting the table with respect to UMLSKSearch we can analyze the properties of that matcher. As the similarity values assigned by UMLSKSearch can only be 1, 0.6 and 0, we obtain good results for the threshold 0.6. (This was already clear from the table in figure 10.) The matcher finds suggestions of which the terms have completely different names and synonyms, or have no synonyms at all, e.g. (external acoustic meatus, ear canal). The matcher works for some terms with slightly different names, e.g. (optic disc, optic disk), which are mapped to the concept optic disc in UMLS, but does not work for others, e.g. (stapes, stape), which are mapped to different concepts in UMLS.

The number of expected suggestions for the ear case is 27 (see figure 6). To find out the expected suggestion that is not found by any of the matchers we can check the similarity table as in figure 8. By sorting the similarity table according to the similarity values of a matcher, and looking at the values below the thresholds we will easily find that the only pair marked with 'C' in the 'Sug' column is (auricle, ear cartilage). This pair receives a very low similarity value from TermWN as the strings are very different and also the synonyms in WordNet are very different. We can also see that the terms are not synonyms in UMLS.

The similarity table can also be sorted with respect to the terms in the first ontology or the terms in the second ontology. This allows for checking for a term in one ontology which term in the other ontology is closest related according to the different matchers.

An advantage of using a system like KitAMO is that we can experiment with different (combinations of) strategies and different (combinations of) types of ontologies. For instance, the evaluation in our example may give an indication about what (combinations of) strategies may work well for aligning ontologies with similar properties as our test ontologies. However, when choosing a strategy other factors, such as time, may also play a role. For instance, KitAMO shows that UMLSKSearch is more time consuming than TermWN.

5   Related Work

The experiments for EON and I3CON used tools in the evaluations [11,1]. An API for ontology alignment for EON is described in [11,7]. In the API the interface *AlignmentProcess* provides the method *align* which needs to be implemented to perform the computation of the alignments. The alignment algorithms should not require user intervention. In the API there are several linguistic-based alignment algorithms implemented that compute similarity values between terms. The different components of ontologies, e.g. concepts, instances and relations can be aligned. The API also allows to choose a filter method out of a few predefined methods, such as threshold-based filtering or retaining the n % pairs with highest similarity values. The *evaluator* is the interface for the evaluation of two alignment results. In the API two evaluators are implemented. One computes the precision, recall, fallout and f-measure of an alignment result. The other produces a weighted symmetric difference between two alignments. The API supports source ontologies in OWL, and expected alignments which are represented in RDF/XML. The alignment results can be output as RDF, OWL, XSLT, SWRL and COWL files. The evaluation results are reported in a RDF/XML file.

OLA [8] is a GUI application implemented on top of the API. OLA supports ontologies represented in OWL-Lite. The ontologies can be visualized as graphs. After loading two ontologies, choosing an alignment algorithm, and specifying the parameters for alignment (e.g. a threshold), the system runs the alignment algorithm. After the computation the alignments and their similarity values can be presented in a table and output as an XML file. Further, OLA provides a tool for alignment comparison. After loading two alignments in the form of XML files which were the results of the alignment tool, the precision, recall, fallout and f-measure of the alignments are computed. The results are displayed and the user can compare them. The evaluation results can also be saved as an XML file.

Both the EON tools and KitAMO focus on the non-interactive part of the alignment framework. KitAMO provides an integrated system for comparative evaluation of alignment strategies and their combinations. In KitAMO after the computation of the similarity values, the evaluations can be performed for different alignment algorithms with different thresholds, and also for different combinations with different algorithms, weights and thresholds. The EON tools do not support the evaluation of the combination of different alignment algorithms. Also, to evaluate different alignment algorithms and different thresholds, batch programs in Java based on the API need to be implemented. OLA can also only compare two alignment results. While OLA presents the alignment results to the user, KitAMO presents the alignment results as well as the similarity values for all pairs of terms. KitAMO also allows to sort the table according to the different columns which gives the user the opportunity to analyze the properties of the alignmdet strategies. In OLA the tool for alignment comparison computes the precision, recall, fallout and f-measure of the alignments, while KitAMO presents the number of the correct, wrong and inferred suggestions to the user in a table. The measures presented by OLA can be easily computed and we intend to add these to the interface. KitAMO also allows to store the evaluation results from different matchers and combinations, and with different thresholds. This allows for a deeper comparison of the strategies. Further, KitAMO computes the performance of the strategies.

6   Conclusions

In this paper we proposed the KitAMO framework for comparative evaluation of the non-interactive alignment components, including alignment algorithms, combination algorithms and filters. We presented our current implementation of the framework. In this implementation we focused on the evaluation of different alignment algorithms and implemented the most used combination and filter methods. We evaluated the implementation with respect to performance. We also showed how the system can be used to evaluate and compare alignment algorithms and their combinations in terms of performance and quality of the proposed alignments and how these results lead to deeper insights into the properties of the strategies.

In the future we will test the scalability of KitAMO. We will also further develop different aspects of KitAMO. First, we will provide support for the evaluation of combination and filter methods. We will also use the framework as a basis for implementing and testing new alignment components. For the evaluation cases ontologies from different topic areas and with different representational complexity should be included. The current test cases are small pieces from larger ontologies. Although the expected alignments for large 'real life' ontologies are hard to obtain, they are necessary for better evaluations. Further, we will add different ways of visualizing the alignment and evaluation results.

Acknowledgments

We acknowledge the financial support of the Swedish Research Council (Vetenskapsrådet), the Center for Industrial Information Technology (CENIIT), the Swedish national graduate school in computer science (CUGS), and the EU Network of Excellence REWERSE (Sixth Framework Programme project 506779).

References

1. Ashpole B (2004) Ontology translation protocol (ontrapro). *Proceedings of the Performance Metrics for Intelligent Systems Workshop.*
2. Bard JL, Kaufman MH, Dubreuil C, Brune RM, Burger A, Baldock RA, Davidson DR (1998) An internet-accessible database of mouse developmental anatomy based on a systematic nomenclature. *Mechanisms of Development*, 74:111-120.
3. Chen B, Tan H, Lambrix P (2006) Structure-based filtering for ontology alignment. *Proceedings of the IEEE WETICE Workshop on Semantic Technologies in Collaborative Applications.*
4. Collins F, Green E, Guttmacher A, Guyer M (2003) A vision for the future of genomics research. *Nature*, 422:835-847.
5. Doan A, Madhavan J, Domingos P, Halevy A (2003) Ontology matching: A machine learning approach. Staab, Studer (eds) *Handbook on Ontologies in Information Systems*, pp 397-416, Springer.
6. Ehrig M, Haase P, Stojanovic N, Hefke M (2005) Similarity for Ontologies - A Comprehensive Framework. *Proceedings of the 13th European Conference on Information Systems.*
7. Euzenat J (2005) An API for Ontology alignment (version 1.3).
8. Euzenat J, Loup D, Touzani D, Valtchev D (2004) Ontology Alignment with OLA. *Proceedings of the 3rd International Workshop on Evaluation of Ontology-based Tools.*
9. Euzenat J, Stuckenschmidt H, Yatskevich M (2005) Introduction to the Ontology Alignment Evaluation 2005. *Proceedings of the K-CAP 2005 Workshop on Integrating Ontologies.*
10. Euzenat J (2004) Introduction to the EON ontology alignment context. *Proceedings of the 3rd International Workshop on the Evaluation of Ontology-based Tools.*
11. Euzenat J (2004) An API for ontology alignment. *Proceedings of the 3rd International Semantic Web Conference*, pp 698-712.
12. FOAM. http://www.aifb.uni-karlsruhe.de/WBS/meh/foam/
13. The Gene Ontology Consortium (2000) Gene Ontology: tool for the unification of biology. *Nature Genetics*, 25(1):25-29. http://www.geneontology.org/.
14. Gómez-Pérez A (1999) Ontological Engineering: A state of the Art. *Expert Update*, 2(3):33-43.
15. Giunchiglia F, Shvaiko P, Yatskevich M (2004) S-Match: an algorithm and an implementation of semantic matching. *Proceedings of the European Semantic Web Symposium*, LNCS 3053, pp 61-75.
16. Hayamizu TF, Mangan M, Corradi JP, Kadin JA, Ringwald M (2005) The Adult Mouse Anatomical Dictionary: a tool for annotating and integrating data. *Genome Biology*, 6(3):R29
17. I3CON (2004) http://www.atl.lmco.com/projects/ontology/i3con.html
18. Jena - A Semantic Web Framework for Java. http://jena.sourceforge.net/
19. Kalfoglou Y, Schorlemmer M (2003) IF-Map: an ontology mapping method based on information flow theory. *Journal on Data Semantics*, 1:98-127.
20. KnowledgeWeb Consortium (2004) Deliverable 2.2.4 (Specification of a methodology, general criteria, and benchmark suites for benchmarking ontology tools). http://knowledgeweb.semanticweb.org/
21. Kotis K, Vouros GA (2004) The HCONE Approach to Ontology Merging. *Proceedings of the European Semantic Web Symposium*, LNCS 3053, pp 137-151.

22. Lambrix P (2004) Ontologies in Bioinformatics and Systems Biology. Chapter 8 in Dubitzky W, Azuaje F (eds) *Artificial Intelligence Methods and Tools for Systems Biology*, pp 129-146, Springer.
23. Lambrix P, Edberg A (2003) Evaluation of ontology merging tools in bioinformatics. *Proceedings of the Pacific Symposium on Biocomputing*, 8:589-600.
24. Lambrix P, Tan H (2005) Merging DAML+OIL Ontologies. Barzdins, Caplinskas (eds) *Databases and Information Systems*, pp 249-258, IOS Press.
25. Lambrix P, Tan H (2005) A Framework for Aligning Ontologies. *Proceedings of the 3rd Workshop on Principles and Practice of Semantic Web Reasoning*, LNCS 3703, pp 17-31.
26. Lambrix P, Tan H (2006) SAMBO - A System for Aligning and Merging Biomedical Ontologies. *Journal of Web Semantics, special issue on Semantic Web for the Life Sciences*.
27. Le BT, Dieng-Kuntz R, Gandon F (2004) On ontology matching problem (for building a corporate semantic web in a multi-communities organization). *Proceedings of 6th International Conference on Enterprise Information Systems*.
28. Medical Subject Headings. http://www.nlm.nih.gov/mesh/
29. McGuinness D, Fikes R, Rice J, Wilder S (2000) An Environment for Merging and Testing Large Ontologies. *Proceedings of the Seventh International Conference on Principles of Knowledge Representation and Reasoning*, pp 483-493.
30. Mitra P, Wiederhold G (2002) Resolving terminological heterogeneity in ontologies. *Proceedings of the ECAI Workshop on Ontologies and Semantic Interoperability*.
31. Noy NF, Musen M (2000) PROMPT: Algorithm and Tool for Automated Ontology Merging and Alignment. *Proceedings of Seventeenth National Conference on Artificial Intelligence*, pp 450-455.
32. Noy NF, Musen M (2001) Anchor-PROMPT: Using Non-Local Context for Semantic Matching. *Proceedings of the IJCAI Workshop on Ontologies and Information Sharing*, pp 63-70.
33. OBO - Open Biomedical Ontologies. http://obo.sourceforge.net/
34. OntoWeb Consortium (2002) Deliverables 1.3 (A survey on ontology tools) and 1.4 (A survey on methodologies for developing, maintaining, evaluating and reengineering ontologies). http://www.ontoweb.org
35. Prasad S, Peng Y, Finin T (2002) Using Explicit Information To Map Between Two Ontologies, *Proceedings of the AAMAS Workshop on Ontologies in Agent Systems*.
36. REWERSE. Backofen R, Badea M, Burger A, Fages F, Lambrix P, Nutt W, Schroeder M, Soliman S, Will S (2004) State-of-the-art in Bioinformatics. REWERSE Deliverable A2-D1.
37. REWERSE. Backofen R, Badea M, Barahona P, Burger A, Dawelbait G, Doms A, Fages F, Hotaran A, Jakoniene V, Krippahl L, Lambrix P, McLeod K, Möller S, Nutt W, Olsson B, Schroeder M, Soliman S, Tan H, Tilivea D, Will S (2005) Usage of bioinformatics tools and identification of information sources. REWERSE Deliverable A2-D2.
38. Stevens R, Goble C, Bechhofer S (2000) Ontology-based knowledge representation for bioinformatics. *Briefings in Bioinformatics*, 1(4):398-414.
39. Stumme G, Mädche A (2001) FCA-Merge: Bottom-up merging of ontologies. *Proceedings of the 17th International Joint Conference on Artificial Intelligence*, pp 225-230.
40. Su XM, Hakkarainen S, Brasethvik T (2004) Semantic enrichment for improving systems interoperability. *Proceedings of the ACM Symposium on Applied Computing*, pp 1634-1641.

41. Takai-Igarashi T, Nadaoka Y, Kaminuma T (1998) A Database for Cell Signaling Networks. *Journal of Computational Biology*, 5(4):747-754.

42. Tan H, Jakonienė V, Lambrix P, Aberg J, Shahmehri S (2006) Alignment of biomedical ontologies using life science literature, *Proceedings of the International Workshop on Knowledge Discovery in Life Science Literature*, LNBI 3886, pp 1-17.

43. Takai-Igarashi T and Takagi T (2000), SIGNAL-ONTOLOGY: Ontology for Cell Signalling. *Genome Informatics*, 11:440-441.

44. UMLS. http://www.nlm.nih.gov/research/umls/about_umls.html

45. WordNet. http://wordnet.princeton.edu/

Processing Sequential Patterns
in Relational Databases

Xuequn Shang[1,*] and Kai-Uwe Sattler[2]

[1] School of Computer Science, Northwestern Polytechnical University
710072, Shaanxi, China
shang@nwpu.edu.cn
[2] Department of Computer Science and Automation,
Technical University of Ilmenau, Germany
kus@tu-ilmenau.de

Abstract. Integrating data mining techniques into database systems has gained popularity and its significance is well recognized. However, the performance of SQL based data mining is known to fall behind specialized implementations. Reasons for this are among others the prohibitive nature of the cost associated with extracting knowledge as well as the lack of suitable declarative query language support. Recent studies have found that for association rule mining and sequential pattern mining with carefully tuned SQL formulations it is possible to achieve performance comparable to systems that cache the data in files outside the DBMS. However, most of the previous pattern mining methods follow the method of *Apriori*, which still encounters problems when a sequential database is large and/or when sequential patterns to be mined are numerous and long.

In this paper, we present a novel SQL based approach that we recently proposed, called *Prospad* (PROjection Sequential PAttern Discovery). *Prospad* fundamentally differs from an Apriori-like candidate set generation-and-test approach. This approach is a pattern growth-based approach without candidate generation. It grows longer patterns from shorter ones by successively projecting the sequential table into subsequential tables. Since a projected table for a sequential pattern i contains all and only necessary information for mining the sequential patterns that can grow from i, the size of the projected table usually reduces quickly as mining proceeds to longer patterns. Moreover, a depth first approach is used to facilitate the projecting process in order to avoid creating and dropping costs of temporary tables.

1 Introduction

One of the most important data mining issues is the discovery of sequential patterns, which involves finding frequent subsequences as patterns in a sequence

---

* This work was performed while Xuequn Shang was with the Department of Computer Science, University of Magdeburg, Germany.

S. Spaccapietra et al. (Eds.): Journal on Data Semantics VIII, LNCS 4380, pp. 203–217, 2007.
© Springer-Verlag Berlin Heidelberg 2007

database. Application areas for this issue include analysis of customer purchase behavior, web access pattern, disease treatments, DNA sequences, and so on. For example, considering the sequences of customer purchases, the discovered patterns are the sequences of commodities most frequently bought by the customers. An example could be that 78% of people who buy a computer and then a printer also buy a digital camera within a month. These patterns can be used for shelf placement and promotions, etc.

The sequential pattern mining problem was first introduced by Agrawal and Srikant [AS95] and further generalized in [SA96]. Most of the algorithms used today typically employ sophisticated in-memory data structures, where the data is stored into and retrieved from flat files. However, because the mined datasets are often stored in relational format and relational databases are one of the biggest resources of mining objects, the integration of data mining with relational database systems is an emergent trend in database research and development area [Cha98]. There are several potential advantages of an SQL implementation. First of all, SQL-based mining approaches promise scalability wrt. the size of the datasets. In contrast, in-memory-based approaches can only handle datasets which fit into the memory efficiently. For larger datasets they have to limit the dataset (e.g. by sampling [Toi96]) or will get a significant performance loss due to memory paging. Furthermore, SQL-aware mining systems can exploit the powerful mechanisms for accessing, filtering, and indexing data, as well as SQL parallelization the database systems provide. In addition, they have the ability to support ad-hoc mining, i.e. allowing to mine arbitrary query results from multiple abstract layers of database systems or data warehouses.

From the performance perspective, data mining algorithms that are implemented with the help of SQL are usually considered inferior to algorithms that process data outside the database systems. One of the important reasons is that offline algorithms employ sophisticated in-memory data structures and try to reduce the scan of data as much as possible, while SQL-based algorithms either require several scans over the data or require many and complex joins between the input tables. This fact motivated us to develop a new SQL-based algorithm which avoids making multiple passes over the large original input table and complex joins between the tables.

The remainder of this paper is organized as follows. In section 2, we briefly discuss sequential pattern mining algorithms and implementations employing SQL queries. The *Prospad* algorithm is explained in section 3. Section 4 presents several experiments that assess the performance of the algorithms based on synthetic datasets. We conclude the paper in section 5 and give a brief outlook on future work.

2   Sequential Pattern Mining with SQL

2.1   Problem Statement

Given a database of sequences, where each sequence is a list of transactions ordered by the transaction time and each transaction contains a set of items.

The sequential pattern mining problem can be formally defined as follows. Let $I = \{i_1, i_2, \ldots, i_m\}$ be a set of items. An itemset is a subset of items. A sequence $s = \langle s_1, s_2, \ldots, s_n \rangle$ is an ordered list of itemsets, where $s_i \subseteq I$, $i \in \{1, \ldots, n\}$. The number of itemsets in a sequence is called the length l of the sequence.

A sequence $s_a = \langle a_1, a_2, \ldots, a_n \rangle$ is a subsequence of another sequence $s_b = \langle b_1, b_2, \ldots, b_m \rangle$ if there exist integers $1 \leq i_1 < i_2 < \ldots < i_n \leq m$ such that $a_1 \subseteq b_{i1}, a_2 \subseteq b_{i2}, \ldots, a_n \subseteq b_{in}$.

A sequence database D is a set of tuples $(cid, tid, itemset)$, where cid is a customer or sequence id, tid is a transaction id based on the transaction time, $itemset$ is a set of items. A sequence consists of all the transactions of a customer, where each transaction corresponds to a list of items, and a list of transactions corresponds to a sequence.

The *support* of a sequence s in a sequence database D, denoted as $supp_D(s)$, is the number of sequences in the database containing s in the same sense as defined in [SA96]: a sequence s_b *contains* another sequence s_a if s_a is a subsequence of s_b.

Given a support threshold min_supp, a sequence s is called a *frequent sequential pattern* in D if $supp_D(s) \geq min\_supp$. Given a sequence database and min_supp, the problem of mining sequential patterns is to discover all frequent sequential patterns with a user-specified minimum support min_supp in the database.

2.2   Algorithms for Mining Sequential Patterns

There are several algorithms for mining sequential patterns. These algorithms can be classified into two categories: *Apriori-based* [AS95, SA96, AFGY02] and *Pattern-growth* [PHMA+01, AO04] methods.

- *Apriori-based* approaches are based on an anti-monotone *Apriori* heuristic: if any length k pattern is not frequent in the database, its super-pattern of length $(k+1)$ can never be frequent. They start with the discovery of frequent 1-sequences and then generate the set of potential frequent $(k+1)$-sequences from the set of frequent k-sequences. This kind of algorithm, though reducing search space, may still suffer from the following three nontrivial, inherent costs:
  - It is costly to handle a huge number of candidate sets.
  - It is tedious to repeatedly scan the database.
  - It generates a combinatorially explosive number of candidates when mining large sequential patterns.
- *Pattern-growth* methods are a more recent approach to deal with the problems of mining sequential patterns. The key idea is to avoid repeatedly scanning the entire database and testing and generating large set of candidates, and to focus the search on a restricted portion of the initial database. *PrefixSpan* [PHMA+01] is the most promising of the *Pattern-growth* approaches. It recursively projects a sequence database into a set of smaller projected sequence databases and mines frequent patterns locally in each projected database. *PrefixSpan* achieves high efficiency, compared to *Apriori-based* approaches.

2.3 Sequential Pattern Mining Based on SQL

Recently, researchers have started to focus on issues to integrating mining with database systems. There have been language proposals to extend SQL to support mining operators. The Data Mining Query Language DMQL [HFW96] proposed a collection of such operators for classification rules, characteristics rules, association rules, etc. In [Woj99], Wojciechowski proposed an SQL-like language capable of expressing queries concerning all classes of patterns.

There are some SQL-based approaches proposed to mine sequential patterns in [TS98], for example k-way joins or subquery-based. Almost all proposed sequential pattern mining algorithms with SQL are based on *Apriori*, which consist of a sequence of steps proceeding in a bottom-up manner. The result of the k-th step is the set of frequent itemsets, denoted as F_k. The first step computes frequent 1-itemsets F_1. The candidate generation phase computes a set of potential frequent k-itemsets C_k from F_{k-1}. The support counting phase filters out those itemsets from C_k that appear more frequently in the given set of transactions than the minimum support and stores them in F_k.

Before data can be mined with SQL, it has to be made available as relational tables. The input sequence data is transformed into the first normal form table T with three column attributes: sequence identifier (cid), transaction identifier (tid) and item identifier ($item$). For a given cid, typically there are multiple rows in the sequence table corresponding to different items that belong to transactions in the data sequence. The output is a collection of frequent sequences. The schema of the frequent sequences table is ($item_1, eno_1, \ldots, item_k, eno_k, len$). The len attribute gives the length of the sequence. The eno attributes stores the element number of the corresponding items.

In [TS98], Thomas et al. addressed the problem of mining sequential patterns using SQL queries and developed SQL formulations. The statement for generating C_k from F_{k-1} in SQL-92, is shown in Figure 1.

A well known approach for support counting using SQL-92 presented in [TS98], is similar to k-Way joins for association rule mining [STA98]. In addition to the constraint of min_supp, [TS98] adds further constraints including $window$-$size$, max-gap, and min-gap.

[TS98] points out that it is possible to express complex sequential pattern mining computations in SQL. The approach, however, shares similar strengths

```
insert into Ck
    select    I1.item1, I1.eno1, ..., I1.itemk-1, I1.enok-1, I2.itemk-1,
              I1.enok-1 + I2.enok-1 - I2.enok-2
    from      Fk-1 I1, Fk-1 I2
    where     I1.item2 = I2.item1 and ...and
              I1.itemk-1 = I2.itemk-2 and
              I1.eno3 - I1.eno2 = I2.eno2 - I2.eno1 and ...and
              I1.enok-1 - I1.enok-2 = I2.enok-2 - I2.enok-3
```

Fig. 1. Candidate generation phase in SQL-92

and weaknesses as the *Apriori* method. Nearly all proposed approaches use the same statement for generating candidate k-itemsets and differ only in the statements used for support counting. [TS98] also uses object-relational extensions in SQL like UDFs, BLOBs, table functions, etc. to improve performance.

For frequent pattern mining, an SQL-based frequent pattern growth method called *Propad* [SS05] has been developed for efficient mining frequent patterns in relational database systems. The general idea of *Propad* is to successively transform the original transaction table into a set of frequent item-related projected tables, then to separately mine each one of the tables as soon as they are built. In this paper, we explore the spirit of *Propad* for mining sequence patterns.

3   Prospad: PROjection Sequential PAttern Discovery in SQL

In this section, we illustrate our novel SQL-based sequential pattern mining method called *Prospad* using an example. This method first recursively generates a set of frequent sequence-related projected tables and then mines locally frequent patterns in each projected table.

Let us give an example with four sequences in Figure 2(a) and support threshold 2. The input sequence data is transformed into the first normal form table

CID	TID	Sequence
1	1	a
1	2	a, b, c
1	3	a, c
1	4	d
1	5	c, f
2	1	a, d
2	2	c
2	3	b, c
2	4	a, e
3	1	e, f
3	2	a, b
3	3	d, f
3	4	c
3	5	b
4	1	e
4	2	g
4	3	a, f
4	4	c
4	5	b
4	6	c

(a) Sequence Database

CID	TID	Item
1	1	a
1	2	a
1	2	b
1	2	c
1	3	a
1	3	c
1	4	d
1	5	c
1	5	f
2	1	a
2	1	d
2	2	c
2	3	b
2	3	c
2	4	a
2	4	e
...	...	...
4	4	c
4	5	b
4	6	c

(b) T

Fig. 2. A sequence database and its relational format

CID	TID	Item
1	3	a
1	3	c
1	4	d
1	5	c
1	5	f
2	3	b
2	3	c
2	4	a
2	4	e
3	5	b
4	5	b
4	6	c

Fig. 3. An example projected table

T with three column attributes: sequence identifier (cid), transaction identifier (tid) and item identifier ($item$), as shown in Figure 2(b).

Before the new algorithm is presented, let us give some definitions as follows.

Definition 1. *Given a sequence pattern p and a frequent item i in the sequence database D, a sequence-extended pattern can be formed by adding the item i to its prefix sequence p, and an itemset-extended pattern can be formed by adding the item i to the last itemset of the prefix sequence p.*

For example, if we have a sequence pattern $\{(a),(c)\}$, and a frequent item b, then $\{(a),(c),(b)\}$ is a sequence-extended pattern and $\{a,(c,b)\}$ is an itemset-extended pattern.

Definition 2. *Given a sequence table T, a frequent sequence s-related projected table, denoted as PT_s, has three column attributes: sequence identifier (cid), transaction identifier (tid), item identifier (item), which collects all sequences containing s. Moreover, in the sequence containing s, only the subsequence prefixed with the **first occurrence** of s should be considered.*

Take frequent sequence c in T shown in Figure 2(b) for example. The sequences containing c are $\{1,2,3,4\}$. In the sequence 1, the first transaction containing c is 2. Prefixed by c are $(1, 3, a)$, $(1, 3, c)$, $(1, 4, d)$, $(1, 5, c)$, and $(1, 5, f)$. These sequences can be collected in the table PT_c. Similarly, the table PT_c also includes $(2, 3, b)$, $(2, 3, c)$, $(2, 4, a)$, $(2, 4, e)$, $(3, 5, b)$, $(4, 5, b)$, $(4, 6, c)$. The projected table PT_c is shown in Figure 3.

In order to avoid repetitiousness and to ensure each frequent item is projected to at most one projected table, we suppose items to be in in alphabetical order. The mining process can be regarded as a process of frequent sequence growth, which is facilitated by projecting sequence tables in a top-down fashion. The whole process works as follows:

- **Step 1.** At the first level we simply gather the count of each item. Items that satisfy the minimum support are inserted into the transformed transaction table TF that has the same schema as transaction table T. The complete set of frequent 1-items is $\{a : 4,\, b : 4,\, c : 4,\, d : 3,\, e : 3,\, f : 3\}$. They are included in the table TF as shown in Figure 4(a).

  The SQL statements used to create table TF are illustrated as follows. First, we count the support if items using an aggregation query and insert frequent items into table F. We use `select distinct` before the `group by` to ensure that only distinct data sequences are counted. Second, by joining the original table T and the table containing all frequent items we construct TF.

```
insert into F
    select    S.item, count(*)
    from      (select distinct item, cid from T) as S
    group by  item
    having    count(*) ≥ min_supp
```

```
insert into TF
    select    T.cid, T.tid, T.item
    from      T, F
    where     T.item = F.item
```

- **Step 2.** At the second level, for each frequent 1-item i in the table TF we construct its respective projected table PT_i. This is done by two phases. In the first phase we find all sequences in TF containing i, in which only the subsequence prefixed with the first occurrence of i should be collected. This can be expressed in SQL as follows. We use a temporary table $TEMP\_id$ to collect the first occurrence of i in each sequence containing i.

```
insert into TEMP_id
    select    cid, min(tid) as tid
    from      TF
    where     item = i
    group by  cid
```

```
insert into PT_i (
    select    t1.*
    from      TF t1, TEMP_id t2
    where     t1.cid = t2.cid and t1.tid > t2.tid
    union
    select    *
    from      TF
    where     (cid, tid) in (select cid, tid from TEMP_id) and item > i)
```

- **Step 3.** The next phase finds all items that could be an itemset-extended pattern in the PT_i. All the items that occur in the same transaction as i can itemset-extend the current pattern. And then we update all these items by appending $'-'$ to distinct an itemset-extended pattern from a sequence-extended pattern. The SQL statements can be expressed as follow:

```
insert into TEMP_item
    select    cid, tid, min(item) as item
    from      PT_i
    where     (cid, tid) in (select cid, tid from TEMP_id)
    group by cid, tid
```

```
update PT_i
set       item = item || '-'
where     (cid, tid, item) in (select cid, tid, item from TEMP_item)
```

- **Step 4.** Then we look for local frequent items. Frequent 1-items are regarded as the prefixes, frequent 2-patterns are gained by simply combining the prefixes and their local frequent itemsets. For instance, we get the frequent 1-items $\{a, b, c, d, e, f\}$, their respective projected tables PT_a, PT_b, PT_c, PT_d, PT_e, PT_f. Starting from item a, the a-related projected table is constructed as follows: we find all frequent patterns wrt. item a, which is the base item of the tested projected table. All items that are locally frequent with a, $\{a : 2, b : 4, b- : 2, c : 4, d : 2, f : 2\}$, are inserted into the table PT_a, as shown in Figure 4(a-e). Then, the frequent 2-itemsets associated with item a $\{\{a,a\}, \{a,b\}, \{(a,b)\}, \{a,c\}, \{a,d\}, \{a,f\}$ can be found.
- **Step 5.** At the next level, for each frequent item j in the projected table PT_i we recursively construct its projected table $PT_{i,j}$ and gain its local frequent items. A projected table is filtered if no frequencies can be derived. For instance, if no local frequent items in the $PT_{a,a}$, as shown in Figure 4(i) can be found, the processing for mining frequent sequential patterns associated with aa terminates.

Basically, the projecting process can be facilitated either by breadth first approach or by depth first approach. In a *breadth first approach*, we have two alternatives to represent projected transaction tables. The first one is: each frequent item has its corresponding projected transaction table and local frequent sequences table at level k. That means, n projected tables need to be generated if we have n frequent sequences at level k. It is obviously impractical because too many temporary tables have to be kept – especially for dense datasets and low support threshold. The second alternative is to use one projected transaction table is used at each level. Normally, this projected transaction table is too large to efficiently join in subsequent mining procedures, especially at level 2.

In order to avoid creating and dropping many temporary tables, we use a *depth first approach*. Let $\{i_1, i_2, \ldots, i_n\}$ be the frequent 1-sequence. We can first find the complete set of frequent sequences containing $\{i_1\}$. Conceptually, we construct $\{i_1\}$-projection table and then apply the techniques recursively. After that, we can find the complete set of frequent sequences containing $\{i_2\}$ but no item $\{i_1\}$. Similarly, we can find the complete set of frequent sequences.

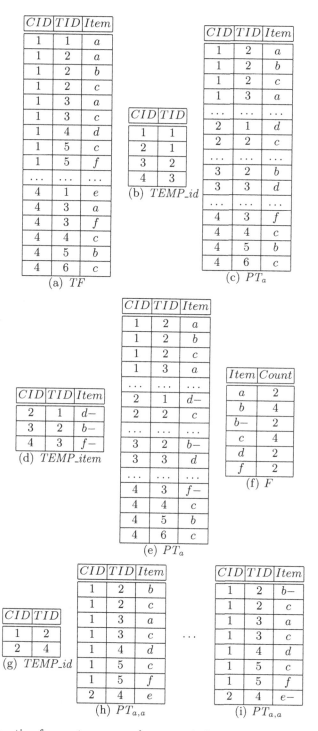

Fig. 4. Constructing frequent sequences by successively projecting transaction table T

To construct the projection table associated with item i we use temporary projection tables *TEMP_id*, *TEMP_item* to collect all frequent items (larger than i) in the transactions containing i. The frequent itemset table F is used to store local frequent items of each *TEMP_item*. In fact, these temporary tables are only required during the construction of the projection table *PT*. In that case, we create one *TEMP_id*, *TEMP_item* and one F during the whole mining procedure. These tables can bethey can be cleared for constructing the other *PT*s after one *PT* is constructed. Moreover, in the whole mining procedure, the *PT* tables of each frequent item are not constructed together. The mining process for each frequent item is independent of that for others. In that case, we only need one *PT* table at the each level. The number of *PT* tables is the same magnitude as the length of maximum frequent pattern.

Now we summarize the algorithm PROjection Sequential PAttern Discovery, abbreviated as *Prospad*, as listed in Figure 5.

Analysis: The mining process can be facilitated by projecting sequence tables in a top-down fashion. In our method, we are trying to find all frequent sequences with the respect to one frequent item, which is the base item of the tested projected table. All items that are locally frequent with i will participate in building the i-related projected table. Our method of *Prospad* has the following merits:

- It avoids repeated scannings of the original sequence table, only needs to scan the local projected transactions table to generate a descendant, transformed transaction (sequence) tables.
- It avoids complex joins between candidate sequence tables and transaction tables, replacing by simple joins between smaller projected tables and frequent sequences tables.
- It avoids creating and dropping cost of some temporary tables by using DFS instead of BFS.

4   Performance Evaluation

In order to evaluate the efficiency of *Prospad*, we have done extensive experiments on various kinds of datasets with different features. We have compared our approach implemented in Java and using SQL/JDBC for database access to a SQL-based implementation of *Apriori*. Furthermore, wee have chosen a loose-coupling approach *PS* based on PrefixSpan which is implemented in Java, too. *PS* accesses the input table in the DBMS using a JDBC interface and mines sequential patterns in memory.

4.1   Datasets

We use synthetic sequence data generation with the program described in Apriori algorithm paper [AS95] for experiments. The nomenclature of these datasets is of the form $CwwTxxSyyIzz$, where ww denotes the total number of sequences

---

Input: a sequence table T and
    a minimum support threshold ξ
Output: a frequent pattern table PAT

$pass\_num := 0;$
$prefix := null;$
/* **Step 1** */
get the transformed transaction table TF by removing
    infrequent (wrt. ξ) items from T;
/* **Step 2** */
insert the frequent 1-items into PAT;
create projection table PT;
foreach distinct frequent item i in TF **do**
    /* **Step 3** */
    $prefix := i;$
    call findFP($prefix, 1$);
done

procedure findFP($prefix, k$)
    if PT_k has frequent items **then**
        combine $prefix$ with frequent item sets and
            insert them into PAT;
        if PT_k is not be filtered **then**
            if $k + 1 > pass\_num$ **then**
                create table PT_{k+1};
                $pass\_num = k + 1;$
            else
                clear table PT_{k+1};
            endif
            /* **Step 4** */
            construct PT_{k+1} by projection;
            find local frequent items;
            foreach frequent item j in PT_{k+1} **do**
                /* **Step 5** */
                $prefix := prefix + j;$
                call findFP ($prefix, k + 1$);
            done
        endif
    endif

Fig. 5. Algorithm for Prospad

in K (1000's). xx denotes the average number of items in a transaction and yy denotes the average number of transactions in a sequence. On average, a frequent sequential pattern consists of four transactions, and each transaction is composed of zz items. We report experimental results on two datasets, they are respectively C10T8S8I8 and C200T2.5S10I1.25. As a real-world dataset we use Gazelle from KDDCUP-2000 provided by Blue Martini Software. Gazelle contains click-stream data where each session has several page views done by a customer over a short time. We treat product pages viewed in one session as an itemset and each page view as an event. Different sessions of a user are considered as a sequence. The dataset contains 29369 sequences, 35722 sessions, and 87546 page views. There are 1423 different products. Gazelle is a very sparse dataset but contains a few very long frequent sequences with low support threshold.

4.2 Performance Comparison

In this subsection, we present results comparing the performance and memory consumption of *Prospad* to a *k*-Way-join-based implementation and *PS*. Our experiments were performed on Version 8 of IBM DB2 EEE installed on Linux operation system with Pentium IV 2.0GHz processor. The performance measure was the execution time of the algorithm on the datasets with different support threshold.

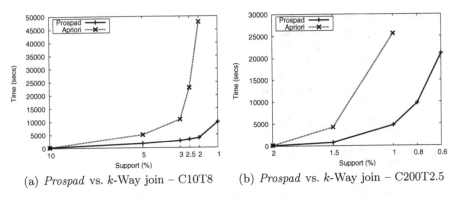

(a) *Prospad* vs. *k*-Way join – C10T8   (b) *Prospad* vs. *k*-Way join – C200T2.5

Fig. 6. Evaluation results: *Prospad* vs. *k*-Way join

Figure 6(a) and (b) show the total time taken by the two approaches on the two datasets respectively: *k*-way joins, *Prospad*. In Fig. 6(a) for the support of 1% and in Fig. 6(b) for the support of 0.8%, the running times of the *k*-way join based *Apriori* approach were so large that we had to abort the runs in many cases.

As the support is high, the frequent sequences are short and the number of sequences is not large. From the graph we can make the following observations: The advantages of *Prospad* over *Apriori* are not so impressive. *Prospad* is even slightly worse than *Apriori*. For example, the maximal length of frequent patterns is 1 and the number of frequent sequences is 89 when the datasets is C10T8S8I8 with the support threshold 10%, *Apriori* can finish the computation shorter than the time for *Prospad*. However, as the support threshold goes down, the gap is becoming wider: *Prospad* is much faster than *Apriori*. When the support is low, the number as well as the length of frequent sequences increase

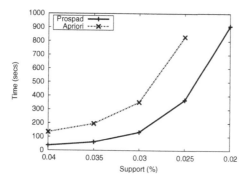

Fig. 7. *Prospad* vs. *k*-Way join – Gazelle

dramatically. Candidate sequences that *Apriori* must handle become extremely large, joining the candidate sequences with sequence tables becomes very expensive. In contrast, *Prospad* avoids candidates generation and test. That's why *Prospad* can get significant performance improvement.

Figure 7 shows the performance comparison among the two approaches for Gazelle data set. Gazelle is a very sparse dataset and has some long frequent sequences when the support threshold is set low (0.05%). We can see that *Prospad* is much more efficient than *Apriori*. The *Apriori* cannot stop running in an appropriate time when the support threshold is no greater than 0.02%.

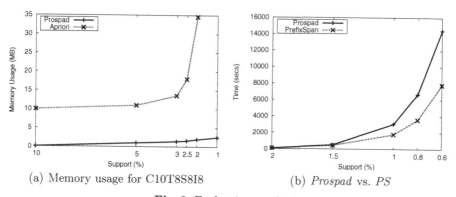

(a) Memory usage for C10T8S8I8   (b) *Prospad* vs. *PS*

Fig. 8. Evaluation results II

In terms of memory consumption, *Prospad* consumes less memory than *Apriori*, since it uses DFS that only keeps track of the prefix-lists for the extension of a given sequence, as well as it applies simple joins. Figure 8(a) shows that both algorithms spend more memory as the support is low, since the number as well as the length of frequent sequences is high.

Figure 8(b) shows that the algorithm *PS* outperforms the *Prospad* method for the C200T2.5S10I1.25 with low minimum support. As being an in-memory approach, however, the available memory is a limitation of input size.

5   Summary and Conclusion

In this paper, we propose an efficient SQL based algorithm to mine sequential patterns in relational database systems. Rather than *Apriori*-like methods it adopts the divide-and-conquer strategy and projects the sequence table into a set of frequent item-related projected tables. Experimental studies show that the *Prospad* algorithm can get higher performance than *k*-way joins based on *Apriori*-like approaches especially on large and dense datasets, but it has severe limitations in performance compared to in-memory *PrefixSpan* algorithms.

There remain lots of further investigations. We plan to do more experimentation on different datasets, including real datasets and to consolidate the experiences in mining all classes of patterns with SQL. Furthermore, we want to explore index techniques based on *Prospad* to make SQL-based approaches more efficient.

References

[AFGY02]   J. Ayres, J. Flannick, J. Gehrke, and T. Yiu. Sequential Pattern Mining using a Bitmap Representation. In *Proc. of the 8th Int. Conference on Knowledge Discovery and Data Mining (KDD-02)*, pages 429–435, New York, NY, USA, 2002. ACM Press.

[AO04]   C. Antunes and A. L. Oliveira. Sequential Pattern Mining Algorithms: Trade-offs between Speed and Memory. In *2nd Int. Workshop on Mining Graphs, Trees and Sequences*, Pisa, Italy, September 2004.

[AS95]   R. Agrawal and R. Srikant. Mining Sequential Patterns. In *Proc. of the 11th Int. Conference on Data Engineering (ICDE'95)*, pages 3–14, Taipei, Taiwan, 1995. IEEE Computer Society Press.

[Cha98]   S. Chaudhuri. Data Mining and Database Systems: Where is the Intersection? *Bulletin of the IEEE Computer Society Technical Committee on Data Engineering*, 21(1), March 1998.

[HFW96]   J. Han, Y. Fu, and W. Wang. DMQL: A Data Mining Query Language for Relational Database. In *Proc. of the 1996 SIGMOD Workshop on Research Issues on Data Mining and Knowledge Discovery*, Montreal, Canada, 1996.

[PHMA+01]   J. Pei, J. Han, B. Mortazavi-Asl, H. Pinto, Q. Chen, U. Dayal, and M. Hsu. PrefixSpan: Mining Sequential Patterns Efficiently by Prefix-Projected Pattern Growth. In *Proc. of the Int. Conf. on Data Engineering (ICDE'01)*, pages 215–224, Heidelberg, Germany, April 2001.

[SA96]   R. Srikant and R. Agrawal. Mining Sequential Patterns: Generalizations and Performance Improvements. In *Proc. of 5th Int. Conf. Extending Database Technology (EDBT'96)*, volume 1057, pages 3–17. Springer-Verlag, 1996.

[SS05]   X. Shang and K. Sattler. Depth-First Frequent Itemset Mining in Relational Databases. In *Proc. ACM Symposium on Applied Computing SAC 2005*, New Mexico, USA, 2005.

[STA98]   S. Sarawagi, S. Thomas, and R. Agrawal. Integrating Association Rule Mining with Relational Database Systems: Alternatives and Implications. In *Proc. of the Int. Conf. on Management of Data (SIGMOD'98)*, pages 345–354, Seattle, WA, June 1998. ACM Press.

[Toi96]   H. Toivonen. Sampling Large Databases for Association Rules. In *Proc. of Int. Conf. Very Large Data Bases (VLDB'96)*, pages 134–145, 1996.

[TS98]   S. Thomas and S. Sarawagi. Mining Generalized Association Rules and Sequential Patterns Using SQL Queries. In *Proc. of the 4th Int. Conference on Knowledge Discovery and Data Mining (KDD-98)*, pages 344–348, 1998.

[Woj99]   M. Wojciechowski. Mining Various Patterns in Sequential Data in an SQL-like Manner. In *Advances in Databases and Information Systems, 3rd East European Conference (ADBIS'99A) – Short Papers*, pages 131–138, 1999.

Author Index

Lecture Notes in Computer Science

For information about Vols. 1–4281

please contact your bookseller or Springer